MANY ROADS
TO JUSTICE

THE LAW-RELATED WORK OF
FORD FOUNDATION GRANTEES
AROUND THE WORLD

MANY ROADS TO JUSTICE

The Law-Related Work of Ford Foundation Grantees Around the World

Mary McClymont
Stephen Golub
Editors

THE FORD FOUNDATION

Library of Congress Cataloguing-in-Publication Data

Many roads to justice : the law-related work of Ford Foundation
  grantees around the world / Mary McClymont, Stephen
  Golub, editors.
    ISBN 0-916584-54-2
    1. Ford Foundation.   2. Public interest law.   3. Human
  rights.   I. McClymont, Mary (Mary E.)   II. Golub, Stephen
  1955–
  JZ5524.M36   2000
  323—dc21   99-088905

 572 February 2000

Printed and bound in the United States of America

CONTENTS

v

Part 2   Thematic Perspectives

PREFACE

Its role as an international funder exposes the Ford Foundation to activities that involve people from around the globe in many walks of life. From this vantage point, we are fortunate to witness a wide range of efforts to achieve justice and equity in vastly different settings. Continually, we are inspired by the remarkable creativity and diversity of these activities—the varied ways groups are able to devise new strategies and adapt old ones to meet their goals. But we are equally impressed with the striking congruencies, often unplanned, that turn up between grantee projects in places as different from each other as Peru and Poland.

In one field of work, these patterns of diversity and symmetry run deep. Across the world, a variety of groups, some with Ford funding, are pursuing many roads toward the same end: using the law as an instrument to advance human rights and social justice. While the ideal of justice is still a distant landmark, nongovernmental organizations have made real progress toward that goal. The evidence of such efforts is seen in the countless people whose lives have been changed—abused women in Bangladesh, racial minorities in Brazil, farmers in the Philippines, the homeless in Nigeria, and many others.

This book attempts to convey some of the challenges that those wielding the law for social change purposes have faced and the successes they have achieved. By intention, it is more a studied appreciation than a critical analysis of their efforts. We asked an international team of consultants to help us document and describe how various law-based strategies have worked in very different settings, to draw out connections between those efforts, and to highlight some of the insights that emerge from grantees' experiences in law-related work. We also asked them to help us learn more about the ways the Foundation has played a role in these efforts. Known as the Global Law Programs Learning Initiative (GLPLI), this effort is not definitive, but rather suggestive. Our goal is to contribute to more serious future reflection and, ultimately, more effective programs in this field.

We hope that the insights emerging from our review of the work of Ford and its grantees will help strengthen Foundation programming, suggest grantmaking directions for the consideration of other donors, and provide some strategic insights and ideas for all those involved in using the law to build a more equitable world.

Mary McClymont
Senior Director
Peace and Social Justice Program, The Ford Foundation

ACKNOWLEDGMENTS

The GLPLI project, and this book, reflect a collective effort. Many Ford Foundation grantee partners engaged in public interest law work generously shared their insights, experiences, and time, without which this book would simply not have been possible. Too numerous to list here, they are cited in the contributors' lists following the case studies, which are chapters in Part 1.

At the core of GLPLI was a thirteen-member team. The authors (listed elsewhere in this volume) not only bear primary responsibility for their individual papers; they also reviewed each other's drafts, posed questions, and formulated ideas that were considered by other members of the group. The collaborative process included meeting as a team and discussing virtually every facet of the project. Apart from the authors, the core team included several other individuals. Anthony Romero, the Foundation's director of the Human Rights and International Cooperation unit, offered critical perspectives and suggestions that enriched and advanced team discussions. Editorial advisors Tom Lansner and Sara Bullard skillfully shepherded this text from inception to production. Daria Caliguire diligently performed key research tasks. Monica Lynn's unfailing administrative support and editorial assistance were essential at all levels of the project.

GLPLI benefited as well from current Ford Foundation staff, who shared useful information and valuable ideas at various stages of the project. Those staff members, who undertake law-related programming in offices around the world, included Akwasi Aidoo, Fateh Azzam, Aaron Back, Alice Brown, Phyllis Chang, David Chiel, Larry Cox, Mallika Dutt, Joseph Gitari, Irena Grudzinska Gross, Gary Hawes, Taryn Higashi, Alan Jenkins, Mary McAuley, Helen Neuborne, Edward Telles, Augusto Varas, and Alex Wilde. Ford program assistants Lori Mann and Hisham Elkoustaf, and senior communications advisor Thea Lurie, also provided useful contributions. Miriam Aukerman gave helpful comments on the manuscript.

A number of former Ford Foundation staff helpfully recounted their experiences as well. They are cited in or listed after the individual case studies in Part 1. Thanks to William Carmichael, Shepard Forman, Lynn Huntley, and Franklin Thomas, who provided historical perspectives that benefited the entire project.

Several other people played important roles in making this book a reality. GLPLI profited from the knowledge of several external specialists, who were asked to critically review some or all of the papers. Their frank appraisals substantially helped sharpen and improve the final product. The outside experts included José Zalaquett, Professor of Law, University of Chile; Terrence George, Chief Program Officer, Consuelo Zobel Alger Foundation; and Rick Messick, Senior Public Sector Specialist and codirector of the World Bank's Thematic Group in Legal Institutions. Of course, any inaccuracies in the text are the responsibility of the Ford Foundation alone.

As vice president of the Foundation's Peace and Social Justice program, Bradford Smith provided thoughtful guidance during the GLPLI process. And the project would not have been possible without Ford Foundation President Susan Berresford's stimulus toward greater institutional learning, and her continuing commitment to public interest law work around the world.

Mary McClymont

Introduction:
A Guide to This Volume

STEPHEN GOLUB & MARY McCLYMONT

For more than forty years, the Ford Foundation has supported groups that use the law to secure human rights and improve the lives of people in vastly different settings around the world. Funding for law-related projects began in the 1950s in the United States and by the 1970s had been extended to parts of Latin America and South Africa. As we enter the year 2000, the Foundation is involved in sustained grantmaking for public interest law groups in over twenty-five countries through its New York headquarters and eleven of its overseas offices around the globe.

The activities of Ford grantees vary with the diverse contexts of their work. But, in large part, groups cited in this volume and others like them share a common goal: they use law as an instrument to promote the rights and advancement of disadvantaged populations and to further social justice. For simplicity's sake, grantee efforts are referred to in this volume as "public interest law" or "law-related work," although in the context of some countries these activities may go by other names: social action litigation, legal services, or developmental legal aid, for example.

The bulk of Foundation support for law-related work goes to nongovernmental organizations (including university-based bodies), although some funding goes to governmental or other institutions. Nongovernmental organizations (NGOs) build individuals' legal awareness and train paralegals to use the law individually and collectively. They offer legal aid and expand the opportunities of underrepresented people to use the justice system. Groups bring test case or "impact" litigation geared to change legal doctrine or public attitudes, and to benefit large populations. They undertake law-related research and advocacy to further legal reform efforts, pursue administrative change, and seek enforcement of laws. Community mobilization and media efforts often complement their work.

The Global Law Programs Learning Initiative

This volume comprises papers produced under the Ford Foundation's Global Law Programs Learning Initiative (GLPLI), an effort to derive and disseminate insights flowing from the law-related work of the Foundation and its grantees around the world. The impetus for GLPLI stems in part from an internal Foundation learning agenda that cuts across all of Ford's programs, aiming to help improve grantee efforts and Ford grantmaking. Of equal importance, as the field of public interest law has developed worldwide, so has the need for better understanding of the various strategies used in this work. In particular, the increased salience of this field has generated requests for more information about Ford's programming from other donors, NGOs, and the legal community at large. Until now, however, the Foundation has not carried out a wide-ranging review of this work.

In early 1998, the Foundation's Peace and Social Justice program, which provides most of the Foundation's law-oriented funding, brought together the authors of the chapters of this volume: an international team of legal scholars, activists, and social scientists. They were asked to undertake an eighteen-month documentation of the activities of Ford and its grantees in selected areas of the legal field. These GLPLI consultants were not requested to conduct an evaluation or objective scientific study, or to precisely measure the impact of law-related work. Rather, their task, working closely with Ford staff, was to collect and report on the experiences of one donor and its grantees in this area. The hope was to convey some of the challenges that grantees have faced around the world and provide a sense of how they have used particular legal strategies in very different settings. Ford also invited the consultants to help draw lessons about the Foundation's grantmaking approaches and consider where improvement was needed. This dual focus on grantees and the Foundation aimed to provide a resource for legal practitioners and advocates, for analysts and scholars, and for fellow donors.

Given the often experimental nature of many of these activities, there have been failures along with successes. The failures themselves yield important lessons, and some of them are noted in these papers. The focus in this volume, however, is primarily on successful models of law-related work, with the hope that some strategies might prove useful to broad and varied audiences. Virtually all of the groups discussed in the book are or have been Ford Foundation grantees. (Many also, of course, receive substantial support from other donors.)

GLPLI team members conducted interviews, document reviews, and on-site visits in a total of sixteen countries where grantees are at work: Argentina, Bangladesh, Chile, China, Colombia, the Czech Republic, Hungary, India, Namibia, Peru, the Philippines, Poland, Russia, Slovakia, South Africa, and the United States. The team relied primarily on reflections and analysis drawn from past and present grantees and Ford staff, supplemented by occasional observations from independent parties (such as journalists, social scientists, and development professionals) familiar with their efforts. Given the extensive backgrounds of team members in some of the countries and regions studied, the project inevitably also drew on their personal experience.

An attempt to summarize all of the law-related efforts funded by the Foundation, even just in the selected communities and regions profiled here, would require several volumes. This book instead offers the experiences and insights from a sampling of grantee activities that reflect a variety of geographic settings and strategic approaches.

Even within this limited scope, the task of offering a balanced portrait of public interest law work is daunting. Perspectives and priorities vary widely from one setting to another; the same terminology means different things in different places; and developments in the field rapidly change. They take a broad view, knowing that the stories they tell here will not answer all questions or meet all needs. The authors present their own perspectives on Ford and its grantees' efforts, informed primarily by those they interviewed. Unless otherwise noted, the activities and developments the chapters herein describe were current as of August 1999, when the project's research phase came to a close.

Ultimately, the GLPLI endeavor resulted in the set of papers contained in this volume—case studies and thematic perspectives. Together they describe and reflect on grantee strategies and activities, as well as on some of the Foundation's own funding approaches.

The **seven case studies,** Part 1, trace the stream of law-related programs the Foundation has supported in specific contexts, mostly through grants made out of Ford offices based in countries around the world: South Africa, South America's Andean Region and Southern Cone, the United States, Bangladesh, China, the Philippines, and Eastern Europe. (The Foundation has also supported significant law efforts in places not covered in the case studies, including Brazil, Mexico, India, Russia, and countries in the Middle East, and North, West, and East Africa.) These case studies were selected to demonstrate geographical diversity as well as differing histories and durations of Ford's law programs. South Africa, the United States, and the Andean Region/Southern Cone reflect long-standing activity, for example, whereas Foundation engagement with Bangladesh and Eastern Europe is considerably more recent.

The **five thematic perspectives,** Part 2, deal with selected aspects of law-related work, including strategies and approaches used by grantees in a range of national, regional, and international settings: university legal aid clinics, public interest litigation, nonlawyers as community legal resources, policy-related research, and NGO adaptations to major political transitions. To illustrate these themes, examples are drawn from activities of grantees that depict some of the breadth and diversity of Ford-supported projects. These examples do not by any means represent the full range of work in a particular thematic area, but are selected from dozens of comparable projects, with the majority from the countries where case studies were done.

Many Roads to Justice is just a first step in coming to understand the diverse ways that Ford grantees put law to work in the interest of human rights and social justice. This introduction now highlights key goals of Foundation-supported law work, and illuminates some significant aspects of Ford/grantee partnerships that guide the work. Brief descriptions of chapter contents follow.

Features of Foundation-Supported Public Interest Law Work

Goals

As the accounts in this volume make clear, law-based strategies serve as an important tool of Ford grantees for advancing human rights, equitable and sustainable development, civic participation, and government accountability. The most fundamental of these goals is the promotion and protection of human rights, often on behalf of disadvantaged groups. Law used in this way has challenged repressive governments, won systemic change for vulnerable populations, and protected individuals from human rights violations. Grantees are increasingly employing legal strategies to address social, cultural, and economic rights in addition to civil and political rights.

Human rights–related law efforts are, at bottom, about concrete improvements in people's lives, improvements that, even when incremental, can make a tremendous difference to that large slice of humanity that lives on the margins of economic and physical security. Advancing human rights and achieving concrete benefits for individuals and groups often include advocating for more equitable institutional processes and practices, so as not to leave the poor and vulnerable behind.

Law can also promote the goal of equitable and sustainable development, which aims to secure overall economic progress for a society, as well as political, social, and economic changes that build the capacities of disadvantaged populations, eliminate barriers to their participation in community and government decision-making, and improve their material and social circumstances. Such phenomena cannot be measured in strict economic terms. They reflect a broader, more holistic conception of development that extends beyond economic growth to embrace a healthy environment, equal status for women, and other dimensions of human well-being.

Viewed through this lens, law is a tool not only for the vital goals of bringing concrete benefits to marginalized groups, advancing their human rights, and promoting their development, but for raising their capacities to generate, participate in, and sustain social change on their own. Some change occurs on the formal level of laws, regulations, and policies, but takes on added value when it flows from the contributions of affected groups previously excluded from involvement in such decisionmaking. The value is in the substance of the resulting laws, of course, but also in the process of civic participation. For example, women who combat societal and cultural notions of inferiority can utilize laws—international and domestic—to assert their equality. Communities that feel powerless to stop livelihood-destroying environmental damage can take first steps toward combating it by learning that it is illegal, and organizing around this knowledge.

Increasing government accountability is another goal of grantee law-related work. Foundation-supported research, litigation, and legal aid efforts have sought to hold government officials accountable. In some instances, NGOs can help build these individuals' skills or broaden their perspectives so they may be more effective in responding to community needs. In others, however, NGOs challenge government personnel who may be either indifferent or resistant to doing their jobs. This has involved lawsuits and formal grievances to higher officials, as well as resort to more informal, political channels. In addition, paralegals and other nonlawyers utilize the law on a community level to press government to be more responsive.

In their efforts to reach these goals, activists and practitioners face significant and varied obstacles. One difficulty faced by almost all such groups, however, is the problem of legal implementation: getting laws on the books enforced on the ground. This challenge cuts across most societies and issues. In such fields as human rights, gender equity, and the environment, even the best laws (and sometimes especially the best laws) all too typically go unenforced in the absence of pressure from NGOs and/or affected communities. The same applies to ministerial regulations and high court rulings. The roots of poor legal implementation are deep and diverse. They include forces that may bias the decisions of judges and other officials, the related problems of power imbalances that weigh against women and other disadvantaged groups, courts that function poorly or lack independence, and the paucity of legal aid.

NGOs can, and frequently do, play an important role in helping to assure legal implementation. Their functions vary, sometimes challenging and at other times cooperating closely with government. In some societies, legal services NGOs even assume such traditional governmental functions as training judges or conducting specialized seminars. Quite often, NGOs bring to law-related work considerable familiarity with community problems. Indeed, NGO leaders who cut their teeth on community-based advocacy sometimes go on to join or advise government in positions that can help implement or influence policy.

Ford/Grantee Partnerships

Various insights emerge in this volume regarding the Foundation's partnerships with grantees. One of the most important has to do with the value of creativity and adaptability of NGOs and their funders. To make the law work for disadvantaged people, activists must be ready to respond with the most appropriate strategies, devise new ones, or shift them as challenges and opportunities emerge. In South Africa, for example, law-oriented organizations that were built around the goal of challenging apartheid have been able to adjust their operations to tackle other issues after apartheid's demise.

Moreover, many of the most successful law-related operations employ a mix of strategies to achieve their goals. In societies as diverse as India, Argentina, and the United States, grantees have integrated legal approaches with community organizing, civic education, and media campaigns, operating at both grassroots and national levels. In the process, they have developed sometimes unlikely allies to serve as critical partners in achieving their goals.

The chapters in this volume also suggest that the effectiveness of donors may be further enhanced by a willingness to provide support that is flexible, sustained, and guided by the judgments of grantees themselves. More specifically, under the right circumstances offering institutional support (covering such essentials as salary, office rent, and travel, etc.), and not only project support, can be a useful device. Grantees maintain that this flexible support has practical benefits. More narrow, donor-generated projects, although often a mechanism both grantees and donors use well, can sometimes impose upon grantees a time-consuming and counterproductive array of directions.

Much significant social change happens slowly, challenging grantees as well as funders to sustain their efforts over long periods of time without balking at occasional setbacks. The Foundation has funded some grantees for several years before their efforts were able to bear fruit. To the extent possible, Foundation personnel have sought to distinguish between those funding recipients who encounter problems because of insurmountable, internally generated obstacles, and the many others who exhibit considerable potential and just need more time to build their capacities, adjust their operations, or achieve results.

Foundation law-related programming attempts to be guided by the judgment of those on the ground, those closest to the problem. Grantees and the people they serve are typically in better positions than the Foundation to assess the opportunities and obstacles coming their way. At the same time, however, the Foundation has often been proactive in its grantmaking in such areas as facilitating peer networking, urging strategic planning, encouraging staff and board diversity, and building bridges between groups across organizational and geographical boundaries.

Chapter Previews: Part I, Case Studies

I. Battling Apartheid, Building a New South Africa

The partnership between the Ford Foundation and law-related groups in South Africa has been the most sustained—and, at its height, the largest—undertaking of Foundation law programming outside the United States. During the apartheid era, South African grantees mounted successful court challenges that persuaded judges to overturn key provisions of apartheid on the grounds of regulatory improprieties. University-based institutes aided the antiapartheid struggle through a variety of activities that included undertaking legal research, working with the labor movement, and organizing seminars that familiarized judges with human rights perspectives. Scholars based at these institutes played key roles in helping to develop the country's interim and permanent constitutions as apartheid was ending. With the transition to democracy, many new and continuing grantees have focused on social and economic rights, including land issues and the status of women. The Foundation has further sought to help increase access to the legal system by supporting university legal aid clinics—improving student skills and client services, and ultimately, it is hoped, diversifying the legal profession.

2. From Dictatorship to Democracy: Law and Social Change in the Andean Region and the Southern Cone of South America

The Foundation has supported law-related activities in Argentina, Chile, Colombia, and Peru through thirty years of dramatic political upheavals. After an early, largely unsuccessful attempt to transform legal education using U.S. methodologies during the 1960s, the Foundation in the 1970s began to focus its resources on local partners' initiatives. In the wake of military coups and political violence, Foundation support first helped endangered activists to find safe haven and intellectual independence at institutions overseas. Later, human rights grantees mounted court challenges and documented abuses of these repressive regimes, increasing international pressure on governments and providing a historical record of violations. With the return of democracy to Chile and Argentina and with new programming opportunities arising in Colombia and Peru, Ford in the 1990s supported efforts to use law to address a broader variety of issues—including government accountability, social justice, and environmental degradation. Grantees in the region have also developed innovative litigation strategies, including the use of new and previously ignored legal devices, suits to expand the law's boundaries, actions before regional tribunals like the Inter-American Commission on Human Rights, and effective media outreach to spread knowledge of significant cases in judicial circles and among the wider public.

3. Rights into Action: Public Interest Litigation in the United States

Ford Foundation support for law work started in the United States in the late 1950s, with funding for legal education, indigent defense, and legal services for the poor; it later focused on civil rights litigation on behalf of minorities, women, and immigrants. While grantees have employed a full range of strategies in their law-related work, this case study limits its focus to litigation efforts of Ford grantees during the last two decades. Despite its drawbacks, litigation has proven to be a powerful agent for change in the United States. It has addressed racial discrimination, reproductive health rights, inequities in educational opportunities and school financing, voting rights, immigration policy, Native American treaty obligations, and many other issues. With changes in the U.S. political climate, grantees developed legal strategies to oppose attempts to dismantle civil rights protections. They also supplemented litigation with public education and community mobilization efforts, and began to forge alliances with new partners, such as business, academic, and community groups whose activities complement courtroom efforts.

4. From the Village to the University: Legal Activism in Bangladesh

High rates of poverty and illiteracy in Bangladesh made the work of law-related grantees especially challenging and their efforts and accomplishments that much more noteworthy. In the early 1990s, the Foundation launched a public interest law initiative to expand NGO legal services, engage the bar in such work, and establish clinical legal education programs at the country's three leading law schools. The long-term aim was to help build a constituency for human rights and law reform. A key grantee strategy, adopted by a growing number of other NGOs, has been to use grassroots mediation outside the formal legal system, both to address economic and physical abuse of women and to help the poor resolve disputes. This approach employs community legal education and other devices to reform traditional Bangladeshi problem-solving forums, even as it utilizes them. On a national scale, grantees have won a string of high court victories regarding such issues as the environment, consumer rights, and police abuse.

5. Contributing to Legal Reform in China

When Ford launched its law grantmaking program in China in 1979, the country was just starting to emerge from an extended period of political upheaval that had effectively disabled the legal system for most of the 1960s and 1970s. In this environment, the Foundation helped to build a community of legal educators and scholars that could train future generations of lawyers and enable them to acquire new ideas and perspectives for their own thinking on institutional and legal change. It sponsored bilateral academic exchanges and supported over two hundred Chinese scholars from major law faculties to study or conduct research abroad. As Chinese legal reform has continued, that community of scholars has made important contributions. Subsequent Foundation-supported research has addressed concepts of human rights and specific reforms in criminal justice and administrative law that have been significant for Chinese citizens. In addition, grantees have contributed to judicial reforms and to the training of judges, which emphasizes judicial skills and values and the appropriate functions of the courts. Carefully targeted Foundation funding has also supported some of the earliest efforts to develop legal services, pursue test case litigation, monitor and improve the implementation of laws, and launch university legal aid organizations and practical legal education efforts.

6. Participatory Justice in the Philippines

After the 1986 fall of dictator Ferdinand Marcos, Philippine NGOs increasingly focused on social, economic, and environmental issues. Legal services grantees known as alternative law groups (ALGs) have played key roles in this trend. Typically working in partnership with other NGOs and with community associations, they have effected scores of legal reforms in such areas as urban housing, land reform, gender violence, and indigenous people's rights, and have helped get those reforms implemented on the ground. These grantees focus on grassroots efforts more than traditional courtroom strategies, employing paralegal development and other community-oriented approaches that strengthen local associations' capacities to participate actively in legal processes and to deal with legal issues on their own. They have also helped prepare training curricula for judges and prosecutors regarding violence against women, and trained both government personnel and citizens concerning issues surrounding decentralization. The Foundation today funds ALGs under its local governance program, reflecting the nexus of accountability, citizen participation, and human rights.

7. Eastern Europe: Funding Strategies for Public Interest Law in Transitional Societies

In building a public interest law movement in Eastern Europe after the democratic changes of the late 1980s, Ford grantees are working to overcome a great degree of what could be called legal nihilism. Under communism, domestic law was the tool of repressive states to varying degrees, and human rights activists rarely viewed the courts and legal system as a road to justice. The Foundation has worked with grantees to nurture public interest law groups that use new practices to expand public access to justice. Several approaches were undertaken to develop this new focus and introduce activists in the region to additional resources during its transition. As awareness of the law as a tool for social change has grown significantly in Eastern Europe, Ford grantees are now engaged in legal services, test case litigation, public legal education, and advocacy around such issues as ethnic discrimination, environmental protection, police brutality, domestic violence, and the rights of refugees, prisoners, and patients. University-based legal aid clinics that work with students are also in place. This case study examines the funding approaches used by the Foundation in collaboration with its grantee partners in four Eastern European countries: the Czech Republic, Hungary, Poland, and Slovakia.

Chapter Previews:
Part 2, Thematic Perspectives

8. University Legal Aid Clinics: A Growing International Presence with Manifold Benefits

Law school legal aid clinics serve many purposes: they offer free legal assistance for impoverished citizens, provide students with public service opportunities and practical legal skills, and build the profession of public interest law by encouraging students to pursue such work after graduation. Clinics have become a fundamental part of the legal infrastructure in South Africa, and are expanding in India and South America's Andean Region and Southern Cone. In Eastern Europe, new clinics are helping to build a generation of public interest law professionals. They have begun to emerge in places such as China and Russia, as well. While individual legal aid remains a central task for clinics—in many areas, they offer the poor the only free legal assistance available—a growing number undertake more ambitious work. These clinical programs litigate high-impact or test cases, and work with community groups to strengthen their legal knowledge, skills, and advocacy efforts.

9. Public Interest Litigation: An International Perspective

From Chile to Nigeria, Ford grantees outside the United States have worked to expand access to the courts and achieve court victories for social justice causes. They have used litigation to document injustice and to expose the inequities of repressive regimes. They have repeatedly gone to court to help implement constitutional principles and laws, and they have struggled to integrate international human rights norms into domestic law. In the course of that, they have fostered the development of new jurisprudence. Grantees often blend litigation with complementary political and organizing strategies to maximize impact. This chapter illustrates the use of litigation as a social change strategy in Nigeria, India, and parts of Latin America, the Middle East, and Eastern Europe.

10. Nonlawyers as Legal Resources for Their Communities

One of the most promising innovations in law-related work around the world is the increasingly widespread development of nonlawyers as vital participants in efforts to ensure government accountability, effective implementation of laws, and equitable and sustainable development. They often are paralegals—persons with specialized training and knowledge who provide important legal services to disadvantaged groups and frequently are members of those groups. Or they may simply be community residents who use the law collectively or individually to help themselves. Grantees train laypersons about the law for several reasons, the most basic of which is to build increased legal knowledge and skills within disadvantaged communities. Especially when coupled with community organizing, and/or with mainstream development efforts regarding health, livelihood, or other issues, improvements in knowledge and skills can effect attitudinal change and galvanize action on the part of the individuals and communities with which grantees work.

11. Laying the Groundwork: Uses of Law-Related Research

Research can be a powerful tool for the pursuit of social change. Foundation-funded research efforts around the world have, for instance, helped substantiate the factual bases for high-impact legal cases, demonstrated the need for law reform, contributed to policy development, laid the groundwork for new constitutions, and helped grantees galvanize public support for policy reform. University-based institutes have proven to be important forces for such research and resulting change. In Latin America and then South Africa, they provided institutional shelters that made it more difficult for repressive governments to quash opposition. Research does not constitute a stand-alone strategy, but in tandem with advocacy, litigation, and other tools, it can pave the way for social change and the advancement of human rights.

12. Weathering the Storm: NGOs Adapting to Major Political Transitions

Because of the sensitivity of legal work in changing political contexts, law-related nongovernmental organizations inevitably undergo significant strain at some points in their histories. Whether NGOs survive times of upheaval depends in part on their own adaptability and their donors' patience and flexibility. Foundation grantees have persevered through dramatic changes of government (from military dictatorships to democracy, for example) as well as more orderly shifts in political climate. Along the way, they have reevaluated their goals and retooled their strategies to take advantage of new opportunities, face new challenges, and address the changing needs of their constituents. This chapter describes some of the ways grantees have adapted to political transitions or climate changes in Russia, Eastern Europe, Peru, Argentina, South Africa, the Philippines, and the United States.

· · ·

An undeniable lesson emerging from GLPLI is that one size does not fit all, whether for grantee efforts or for the donors that support them. Different organizations working under different circumstances proceed along different paths toward such common goals as promoting human rights and development. Strategies can and should vary, depending on time, place, and organization.

Public interest law work will always be more a craft than a science. The Global Law Programs Learning Initiative and this book are attempts to catch just some of the successes, challenges, and innovations in action. This informal investigation points to the need for greater examination of the processes and results of diverse law-related efforts. Such study could only improve that work, expand its impact, and strengthen those who suffer under the burdens of poverty, prejudice, exclusion, and injustice.

PART I

Case Studies

I

Battling Apartheid, Building a New South Africa

STEPHEN GOLUB

Ford Foundation grantees in South Africa have contributed to a series of momentous undertakings. They challenged apartheid's legal apparatus in the 1980s. During the democratic transition and postapartheid era, they played vital roles in building a new South Africa by helping to craft interim and permanent constitutions and to construct an equitable legal system amid the rubble of past repression.

As a foreign organization, Ford has properly played only a supporting role in the legal battles against apartheid and for reform—battles which themselves form just a part of the broad sweep of South Africa's continuing national transformation. Nevertheless, financial support provided by the Foundation helped launch and strengthen lawyers' groups, university-based bodies, and other NGOs[1] that challenged apartheid's laws and continue to be crucial in consolidating a vibrant democracy.

Certain consistent goals and values run through Ford's law-related grantmaking in South Africa. This effort made its first significant mark in 1973. By 1993, it had an in-country presence with the opening of the Foundation's South Africa office. As former Foundation President Franklin Thomas recalls, "We were helping to reinforce black South Africans' notion that they had rights, that they could go to court, and that they could get a favorable court ruling enforced. That's no small thing in a country that tells you you're a non-person."

This grantmaking has been part of an ongoing stream of "promoting human rights, a human rights culture, and the rule of law," notes South Africa Program Officer Alice Brown. The program has flowed within that stream, she explains, even as it has evolved from helping to "fight apartheid in the 1980s to . . . working in a more targeted way today on diversity, gender, land issues, and social and economic rights."

This chapter by no means encompasses all of Ford's varied funding in South Africa. Law-related grantmaking has in fact been a pillar of Foundation work there, but other programs have supported higher education, community development, land reform, microenterprise development, natural resources management, and governance, sometimes in ways that have fruitfully interfaced with law grants. Nor does this chapter review the entire law-related grantmaking program. It focuses on three key areas of support. They are public interest litigation, clinical legal education, and a range of policy research, advocacy, and other activities primarily carried out by university-based institutes. Aside from a few more relevant exceptions, this chapter does not detail grantees' work in other important legal arenas, such as labor and land issues, individualized legal aid, mediation, grassroots legal education, diversifying the legal profession, and exporting models of law-oriented work beyond South Africa.

The chapter unfolds in two stages. The main body presents the context and evolution of the Foundation's law program in South Africa, emphasizing the three foci and identifying possible lessons springing from Ford's and grantees' work. The concluding section sums up relevant changes in South Africa, the contributions of Ford and its grantees to those changes, and some of the potentially useful insights that have emerged from that experience.

Building a Public Interest Law Movement

The racial classifications and related repressive mechanisms collectively known as apartheid imposed harsh realities on most South Africans. Apartheid denied the black[2] majority of the population the right to vote for the national Parliament, and to own or occupy most land. Devices such as the notorious "pass laws" (named for identification documents, or "passes") severely restricted their freedom of movement and residence rights. The government further enforced racial separation by such nominally legal measures as displacing entire communities, demolishing unauthorized dwellings without notice or court order, and creating artificial "homelands" for indigenous Africans (people of original African ancestry). Segregation and racially biased spending condemned nonwhites to vastly inferior public amenities, services, and education, where these were accessible at all.

Security laws and actions were equally egregious. Under the cloak of its own distorted notion of legality, the government regularly detained individuals indefinitely without trial. It regularly banned publications, organizations, and meetings, and conducted warrantless searches. The courts had no power of judicial review regarding acts of Parliament. In any event, they tended to view repressive legislation sympathetically. Finally, widespread official brutality was accorded impunity, and worked hand-in-glove with these ostensibly "legal" vehicles.

In two key respects, however, it would be misleading to paint apartheid and its oppression literally in terms of black and white. Apartheid classified the population in terms of four racial groups: White, Colored (mixed race), Indian, and African. The system further divided the African population into ten actual or potential "nations" along ethno-linguistic lines. Such classifications allowed the regime to maintain that the "white nation" was larger than most black ones.

Furthermore, apartheid enforced economic as well as racial inequities. The regime preached and practiced a policy of "separate development," to the detriment of all blacks. It further aimed to relegate indigenous Africans to homelands, in terms of residence or at least (for the many who worked for white businesses elsewhere in the country) citizenship. These homelands generally lacked natural resources, sophisticated commercial activity, and job opportunities.

Even under such circumstances, the ruling National Party (NP) government and the courts ironically boasted of upholding the rule of law. NP members of Parliament claimed in the 1980s that "the South African administration of justice and the judicature stand out as a symbol of hope and confidence" and that "every citizen of this country is assured that, whatever offence he commits against the laws of this country, he will have a fair trial."[3] The irony proved to be twofold as this distorted notion of the rule of law provided limited openings that Ford grantees and their allies eagerly exploited.

Though South African public interest law achieved a kind of critical mass in the 1980s, its roots reach back at least to the 1950s. Before Ford became involved other organizations were actively using the law to oppose apartheid. The Treason Trial Defense Fund enabled attorneys to successfully defend 156 anti-apartheid activists, arrested in 1956 for alleged high treason, in a trial that dragged on until 1961. Established in 1960, the South African Defense and Aid Fund (SADAF) initially focused on explicitly political cases, but later supported other civil and criminal litigation pertaining to apartheid. After the government banned SADAF in 1966, the London-based International Defense and Aid Fund quietly channeled external assistance to South African lawyers fighting apartheid.

Such efforts were not confined to trial work. Long before becoming a Ford grantee in the 1980s, the NGO Black Sash Trust provided legal advice to the population and protested unjust racial legislation. It was among several organizations that addressed apartheid-specific problems, access to government services, and other civil and criminal matters. Where necessary, such groups tried to connect indigent clients with volunteer lawyers or to the government's underfunded legal aid program.

These endeavors were more than Band-Aids, but far less than a cure for South Africa's grave legal ills. Limited pools of funds, organizations, and sympathetic lawyers made for a shredded patchwork of access to justice efforts. Black Sash Trust Chairperson Sheena Duncan recalls that "while we could get political offenders represented," the organization was unable to get pass laws, forced removal, and similar cases taken to court. No lawyers' group addressed apartheid's legal pathology in a comprehensive manner.

Although the Foundation previously had engaged with progressive South Africans, a Ford-funded 1973 conference on "Legal Aid in South Africa" became what many considered a watershed event. The conference at the law school of the University of Natal-Durban (hereafter University of Natal) included experts on legal services and clinical legal education in the United States, as well as South Africans like Duncan who were or would become leading human rights activists. Conference co-organizer David McQuoid-Mason reports that the event "definitely contributed to the growth of law clinics and new ways of doing legal aid here." Two other participants, John Dugard and Felicia Kentridge, went on to help found two organizations that would figure in the fight for justice. Dugard helped launch the Centre for Applied Legal Studies (CALS) and Kentridge the Legal Resources Centre (LRC). Dugard views the meeting as "the start of the idea of public interest law" in his country.

One participant's closing comments, unanimously adopted as a conference policy statement, proved particularly prescient. Sidney Kentridge, a leading commercial and progressive lawyer, noted that "we do have principles of common law which we can invoke" to prompt landmark judicial decisions, despite parliamentary legislation being beyond judicial review.[4] And he proposed the formation of a South African version of the U.S.-based Lawyers' Committee for Civil Rights Under Law—whose executive director had addressed the meeting—to carry out reform-oriented research. Eventually, CALS, LRC, and other grantees would adopt the approach identified by Sidney Kentridge. The conference organizers and Ford did not foresee this. What they did see and seize was the chance to bring together many of the country's best progressive legal minds, and to add some foreign intellectual seeds to those already germinating domestically.

The seeds planted at the 1973 conference sprouted slowly over the next several years. Their growth was spurred by the government's violent response to uprisings in Soweto and other black townships in 1976, and by the gathering storm of the anti-apartheid liberation struggle. They were partly fertilized by the Foundation's decision to support South African reform more actively in the late 1970s, by similar initiatives by the Carnegie Corporation and other donors, and by various visits that exposed South Africans to U.S. public interest law. "People were very excited by what was going on the United States," recalls LRC cofounder Geoff Budlender.

The Carnegie Corporation helped Dugard and others start CALS at the University of the Witwatersrand in 1978. Ford and the Rockefeller Brothers Fund also provided early and ongoing support to this legal research and advocacy institute. The following year Felicia Kentridge and Ford mobilized individuals and donors to help launch LRC, the country's first public interest law firm, under the leadership of National Director Arthur Chaskalson, already a preeminent commercial and human rights lawyer. Chaskalson proved vital in recruiting other legal luminaries to LRC's board of directors. This ensured a degree of tolerance by a conservative legal establishment and insulated the group against government intervention. Both within and outside South Africa, where government or bar opposition looms, the involvement of prestigious legal talent sometimes protects politically controversial groups.[5]

Flexible core support from Ford and other sources helped LRC and CALS adapt to evolving circumstances. Budlender praises the approach: "Once funders pick an area in which they'd like to be active, [they should] bank on ideas and people [who know the country best, and] choose key individuals and institutions and support them in what *they* want to do. Most funders come to you with a plan and you have to shift and move to accommodate them."

While South Africans deserve the credit for launching these two groups, a related evolution in Foundation thinking does merit mention. Former Ford Vice President William Carmichael notes that the Foundation's Latin America program had long before abandoned any assumption that "our natural client is the host government." The Foundation's other overseas programs were coming to this point of view by the late 1970s. In South Africa, certainly, reform-minded elements would be found almost exclusively in civil society.

Taking On Apartheid

The birth of CALS in 1978 and LRC the following year coincided with the start of the period historian Leonard Thompson dubbed "apartheid in crisis." A plethora of problems plagued apartheid. These included faltering economic growth; expensive maintenance of the system's multiple racial administrative structures; backlash from the brutal repression of the 1976 uprisings; and growing concern among whites (some altruistic, some self-interested) about apartheid's viability. Factors also included pressure from the ANC, the Pan African Congress, and other opposition groups; intensifying international isolation; a failed homelands policy; and an ever increasing racial imbalance due to white emigration and rising black birth rates.

Against the dismal backdrop of the late 1970s Ford aimed, in Carmichael's words, "to help black South Africans use the peculiar space allowed by the country's constitution to empower themselves." Grants were made for projects where law could be a vehicle for justice rather than just repression, helping to pave the way for a more democratic South Africa.

Foundation grantees contributed to the mounting reformist pressure by utilizing apartheid's legal system to address and illuminate its inequities. LRC, CALS, and their allies seized on the fact that though acts of Parliament were beyond judicial review, government ministries' implementation processes and regulations were not. As described below, they attacked apartheid by exploiting the system's internal contradictions.

Litigation at the Appellate Level

The pass laws were initial LRC targets. These embraced both acts of Parliament, which were beyond judicial review, and ministerial and local implementing regulations, which could be judicially challenged. Their many restrictions included barring blacks from residing in white towns and cities unless employed there, and prohibiting family members from living with such employees. LRC successfully tackled the second provision in the 1980 *Komani* case. It represented a black woman whom local authorities prohibited from joining her husband in Cape Town, where he legally worked and resided. The case did not challenge the underlying Black (Urban Areas) Act restricting black residence in white zones, because it was an act of Parliament. Rather, LRC convinced the Supreme Court that the act granted the authorities no power to issue regulations barring a wife from living with her husband under these circumstances.

LRC built on its *Komani* victory through an appeals case on behalf of a black person claiming permanent residence rights in Johannesburg. The basis was a legislative provision that granted such status to anyone who worked for one employer continuously for ten years. To frustrate realization of this right, the government had adopted a regulation limiting job contracts under these circumstances to one year. It therefore argued that ten years of steady employment were not, under the law, continuous. In the 1983 *Rikhoto* case, however, LRC persuaded the Supreme Court that a regulation could not negate a right granted by an act of Parliament, and that the substance (of ten years' employment) was more important than the form (of a series of contracts).

What was the upshot of the two cases? As Richard Abel writes in *Politics by Other Means*, his landmark study of anti-apartheid legal activism, "Although *Komani* and *Rikhoto* certainly were not the only causes, they did contribute to the gradual dismantling of the explicitly racist laws regulating movement."[6] In 1986, for example, the government repealed the pass laws and numerous related acts.

Despite its origins as an institution devoted to legal research, policy advocacy, and capacity building, CALS also played trailblazing roles regarding public interest litigation. In the 1985 *Orr* case, its attorneys represented a government doctor in asking the courts to bar police abuse of prisoners in the Eastern Cape province. Buttressed by medical records the doctor had collected there, which documented rampant torture of detained anti-apartheid activists and others, CALS won a Supreme Court order prohibiting the practices. The fact and allegations of abuse were nothing new in South Africa. What was new was the documentation by a white doctor employed by the government, and the lawsuit that helped focus national and international attention on the issue. It resulted in a front-page article in the *New York Times* and ongoing coverage by South African newspapers.

Orr certainly did not end torture by South African security forces. But it did demonstrate how skillful use of media could further litigation and, for that matter, many other public interest law efforts. Abel concludes that the case created a situation in which "judiciary and media reinforced each other: litigation created an uncensored space within which the press could criticize security forces; newspapers returned the favor by extolling the courts as the last bastion against tyranny." Although the police did not have to fear punishment, he writes, "mere publication of the torture significantly curtailed their power." It undermined their ability to operate in the shadows, and bolstered detainees' will to resist abuse. In Abel's words, "Sunlight was the real deterrent."

One issue in which both CALS and LRC became embroiled was that of the incorporation of indigenous Africans into so-called ethnic homelands. The brutal logic of the policy was to demarcate artificial entities in poor pockets of the countryside; eventually grant them nominal independence; revoke South African citizenship for persons living in or otherwise associated with them; and create a white majority South Africa that monopolized minerals and related wealth. Aided by CALS, the residents of the community of Moutse successfully challenged incorporation into what was to be the fifth independent homeland, KwaNdebele. In the 1988 *Moutse* case, CALS ironically appealed to one of the basic tenets of apartheid: ethnic exclusion. It won before the Supreme Court by arguing that Moutse's residents were ethnically and linguistically distinct from the rest of the homeland's population. The *Moutse* case, coupled with a subsequent LRC Supreme Court victory, helped turn the tide against the creation of new homelands.

The appellate victories of LRC, CALS, and their allies rested on a common strategy. They did not press judges to cut down apartheid as such. This would have failed. Rather, they exploited the courts' partial independence and rule of law rhetoric by focusing on narrower issues: that the South African and KwaNdebele governments had exceeded their authority to interpret and implement acts of Parliament, for instance. In Dugard's words, "The judiciary *had* a level of independence, but hadn't used it due to self-imposed subordination." CALS and LRC probed the interstices of apartheid's legalistic self-delusion to undermine that self-imposed subordination. They took what victories they could, holding their tongues in court on the system's grand injustice and instead illuminating its regulatory improprieties.

Why didn't Parliament overturn these judicial victories? The answer is circumstance as much as strategy, but even this may hold a lesson. When court decisions illuminated incontestable moral issues, such as torture or family unification, they increased the mounting domestic and international pressure for the government to abide by its own rule of law rhetoric and to explore alternatives to apartheid.

Litigation on the Ground

These landmark appellate victories by LRC and CALS were laudable, even historic. But they are best understood as part of a larger effort involving community activists, paralegals, and anti-apartheid NGOs. Community-based organizations (CBOs)[7] were at the heart of *Moutse* and many other cases. Black Sash referred both the *Komani* and *Rikhoto* plaintiffs to LRC. The two cases represented thousands of similar pass law problems, as well as many thousands of other apartheid-generated legal difficulties, that Black Sash and the broader paralegal movement helped South Africans address.

LRC's Budlender emphasizes that "Black Sash was our eyes and ears regarding pass laws and forced removals." It and other organizations identified trends in legal problems and needs, and turned up clients best suited for impact litigation. Yet Budlender would be the first to admit that Black Sash's functions did and still do extend far beyond finding litigants. Along with other NGOs, some Foundation funded, it trains and advises paralegals from CBOs across the country. Such paralegals, and the staffs of Black Sash and other groups, annually handle many thousands of legal problems that need not go to court—grievances subject to administrative redress, for example. Where paralegal work reveals systemic shortcomings, these organizations often convert what they learn into policy reform proposals.

Chaskalson, former LRC national director and now president of the new democracy's Constitutional Court, offers an additional insight regarding legal advocacy: "Legal implementation is crucial. We had hundreds of follow-up cases to *Rikhoto*, due to resistance by boards and bureaucrats who would not enforce the decision [which, under the old Constitution, lacked precedential value] because of minute differences between cases." Black Sash and other groups pursued many more on their own, through administrative avenues. Even in the face of such follow-up, government compliance with this and other Supreme Court decisions was far from complete. But had these organizations not doggedly sought compliance, and had the Foundation and other donors confined support to high-profile cases, they would have won the appellate battle and lost the pass law war.

Budlender stresses the value of selective "impact" litigation on an appellate level and follow-up compliance cases that push the government to implement high court decisions. But he also appreciates high-volume "service" litigation that more broadly seeks implementation of favorable laws, even if it does not hinge on appellate rulings. "Service work is important because you learn *and* you implement. And it keeps a lawyer from becoming too 'smart' or remote. The focus must be on changing social and material conditions on the ground."

One of Budlender's few regrets regarding LRC is that it failed to build a network of private practitioners that would have expanded the pool of legal talent available for such "on the ground" advocacy. That network could have, among other activities, litigated against enforcement of unjust laws. In an instance where CALS mobilized private lawyers to contest trials of blacks arrested under the Group Areas Act for living illegally in "whites only" zones, the resulting prosecutorial workload helped force the government to abandon enforcement.

Viewed most broadly, litigation was part of a political struggle waged on several levels. To various degrees in *Moutse* and related litigation, the Transvaal Rural Action Committee, the National Committee Against Removals, and Black Sash helped mobilize the local population, and conducted national advocacy and publicity drives. Chris Landsberg of the Centre for Policy Studies considers LRC's antiapartheid service work "crucial" not just in terms of defending detainees, but because it served as a liaison when the authorities denied families news about or access to imprisoned activist relatives. What's more, as former Ford Program Officer Aubrey McCutcheon points out, the lawyers' litigation and policy work would not "have had success if it had not been for the fact that they chose issues and aspects of the 'struggle' that already had great momentum within the mass liberation movement." An essential lesson of the pass law cases, says Richard Abel, was that "judicial victories are embedded in political struggles; they are neither self-realizing nor self-effectuating; appellate decisions are the beginning of the fight, not the end."[8]

As these dramatic disputes unfolded, Ford's South Africa staff was of necessity based at its New York City headquarters through the 1980s,[9] but remained heavily engaged with the law program and other activities in South Africa. They would visit frequently, for twenty or more person-weeks per year, often for about three weeks at a time. Though the Foundation generally prefers its overseas programming to be field based, its South Africa staff found that regular and lengthy visits enabled them to make funding decisions with confidence in their judgment and their grantees.[10] They would discuss progress and problems with grantees, explore potential programming opportunities, generally assess the evolving lay of the land, and encourage grantees as they labored under trying circumstances.

Such encouragement was appreciated by LRC, for example, because the group encountered both government opposition— reliable reports indicated that some officials considered LRC a communist front and contemplated banning it—and because its strategic litigation was the subject of some initial progressive scorn. There were those involved in the antiapartheid struggle who felt that such work legitimized the courts' institutionalized racism, and opposed LRC's and CALS's efforts in this regard. For example, the then-exiled opposition lawyer (and current Constitutional Court Justice) Albie Sachs initially questioned LRC's reformist orientation, "because I feared that people would see it as an alternative to the political struggle." He and many other skeptics later came to support this work.

It would be an overstatement to place NGO lawyers at the heart of the struggle that brought down apartheid. Larger forces were at play. And other individuals and organizations took greater risks. Still, time revealed the value of recognizing the authority of the courts in order to help undermine the foundations of apartheid.

University-Based Reform Centers

CALS was by no means involved only in litigation. Like other university-based institutes supported by Ford during apartheid, it also was heavily engaged in legal research, other applied research, policy formulation, and building partner organizations' capacities. As with litigation, these grantees rarely operated in isolation. They often were part of informal or formal coalitions organized around important issues. Former Program Officer McCutcheon coined a term that best summarizes their roles: "reform centers."

These centers proved to be significant sources of documentation for foreign law professors, policy analysts, and broader international audiences engaged in antiapartheid activism. Their contributions in these regards ranged from CALS's analyses of apartheid's legal structure to a University of Cape Town (UCT) Institute of Criminology study that documented torture of detainees, coincidentally lending weight to LRC's allegations in the *Orr* case. These roles were noteworthy, especially given that for much of the 1980s the United States, Britain, and other influential nations backed the South African regime's self-reforming self-portrait.

CALS's "justice and society" conferences approached human rights protection from another angle. The idea first came to Dugard in 1982 when he attended one of a series of Aspen Institute seminars that brought South African jurists to the United States. Partly with Foundation support, he launched an annual series of similar conferences in South Africa the following year. Forty to fifty judges and progressive lawyers each year discussed, among other topics, how judges could interpret law in favor of human rights. The conferences brought together an array of perspectives. "No point in getting people to preach to the converted," Dugard noted. The conferences also probably represented the first time that some judges had met black lawyers and other reformist attorneys outside of court. While the impact of the meetings is difficult to ascertain, Dugard feels that they contributed to progressive decisions by a number of judges who participated. Regardless, they hold instructive value as a model of how an NGO can possibly influence courts without taking a case to trial.

University-based institutes played particularly wide-ranging roles in assisting black South Africans' most organized and important domestic political force: the labor movement. Seeking to control and regulate illegal and increasingly disruptive black trade unions, Parliament passed the 1979 Labor Relations Act. This allowed unions to organize, register, strike, and take disputes to industrial courts. Though the government did not see them as such, unions were potentially powerful agents of democratic change. As part of a broad effort to strengthen them, the Foundation provided funds in 1980 for CALS to establish a Labor Law Project. CALS in turn helped launch two other Ford-funded, labor-oriented bodies in the mid-1980s: the Centre for Socio-Legal Studies at the University of Natal and the Labor Law Unit at UCT.[11]

Ford support for the labor movement might have seemed counterintuitive in certain respects, since union members were better organized and better paid than most South Africans. But working conditions in mines and other locations were abysmal, and pay was pitifully low in an absolute sense. Of even greater importance, the unions represented a crucial opportunity to introduce blacks to democracy and the rule of law in a society that practiced neither, while strengthening organized opposition to apartheid. As City University of New York (CUNY) law professor Penelope Andrews says in her evaluation of the three reform centers, "No democratic channels for voicing dissent existed anywhere, except in the trade union structures, and to a lesser extent, the church."[12]

Andrews concludes that the three centers' most significant contribution to labor "was the crucial negotiation skills that were imparted to trade unionists." By helping to build the unionists' skills and legal knowledge through training and advice, the centers enabled them to make use of the law. On the policy level, unions banded together to persuade the government to repeal the controversial 1988 Labor Relations Act. And through a kind of paralegal training, shop stewards learned how to handle day-to-day disputes such as unfair dismissals.

The centers also won notable court victories for both unions and individual members, and made labor an important arena for legal practice and instruction. Numerous conferences and scores of publications contributed to labor relations, law, and scholarship. Policy research and formulation were key parts of the mix. CALS studied other countries' laws regarding unfair labor practices, industrial health and safety, and other issues, and worked with the International Labour Organization to help integrate international standards into South African law. This blend of activities eventually contributed to a labor-management culture that included some consensus about the values of collective bargaining, political stability, and economic growth. South Africa's labor scene might have been much more chaotic and counterproductive in the 1990s if union leaders had not worked with reform centers in the 1980s. And the centers' assistance helped unions cut larger slices out of apartheid's inequitable economic and political pies.

The array of activities CALS undertook, notes Andrews, proved to be mutually reinforcing. Innovative litigation supported by solid research, publications on labor law, and the education and training of law students, lawyers, and trade unionists all helped labor leaders set their priorities, which in turn shaped CALS's further work.

Building a New South Africa

A turning point in South African history came early in 1990, when the government revoked its ban on the African National Congress (ANC) and other liberation groups. It removed restrictions on numerous other organizations and freed a host of political prisoners, most notably ANC leader and future South African President Nelson Mandela. Operating in this more hospitable climate, the Foundation expanded its assistance to institutions that have contributed both dramatically and subtly to the new South Africa.[13]

Creating a New Constitutional Structure

Ford support for relevant research and conferences helped important ANC figures and other South Africans contribute to shaping the country's new interim and permanent constitutions, which were respectively adopted in 1994 and 1997. Through a

modest 1989 grant to London's Institute for Commonwealth
Studies, for example, exiled ANC Legal and Constitutional
Affairs Committee (LCAC) member Albie Sachs was able to
research constitutionalism in South Africa. He returned home and
continued his work. Along with other individuals and organizations, Sachs advocated a Bill of Rights that was substantially
incorporated into the two constitutions.

The 1990–1994 transition to democracy enabled the
Foundation to provide broader, in-country support for constitutional studies, some carried out by returning exiles. Ford accordingly funded the University of the Western Cape (UWC) to host
several other members of the LCAC. While affiliated with UWC
for research purposes, in their private capacities they served as
senior members of ANC teams negotiating constitutional and
legal aspects of the transition with the government and other bodies. At UWC's Community Law Centre (CLC) and other units,
they were afforded "time and resources to think through policies
in connection with negotiations on the constitutions," says CLC
Director Nico Steytler. The UWC base also facilitated their meeting with international jurists, through the Southern Africa Project
of the U.S.-based Lawyers' Committee for Civil Rights Under
Law, and with community groups who helped ground their
research in grassroots realities. The community contact served the
additional purpose of putting formerly exiled leaders in touch
with the South Africa they had been forced to leave.

CLC undertook research, publications, and conferences
focusing on issues including the planned Bill of Rights. It looked
at local, regional, and national governance, judicial authority,
women's and children's rights, and ways of reintegrating the
bogus homelands into South Africa. CALS similarly played
important policy-oriented and political roles during the transition.
It assisted ANC discussions and negotiations regarding the Bill of
Rights, the new constitutions more generally, and the implementing regulations required by the interim constitution.

Foundation-supported international conferences also facilitated consideration of imminent constitutional change. Meetings in
the United Kingdom and the United States in the early 1990s
brought together prominent South Africans and other participants
from across the political spectrum to discuss the rule of law and

constitutionalism in a postapartheid South Africa. Many of these persons had never met before, or had done so under highly adversarial circumstances.

Expanding Focus: Social and Economic Rights

In addition to laying a constitutional foundation, building a new South Africa has involved grappling with apartheid's harmful legacies and seizing new opportunities presented by a relatively responsive government. What directions would public interest law take in a postapartheid state? As McCutcheon puts it, "The new constitution would come into place. Would law be used as a tool for advancing social and economic ends, or would it just be politics?" An early exploration of this question took place at a Center for Constitutional Rights symposium in New York, where South Africans and public interest law groups came together in 1992 to assess the next steps for their work.

With the rise of democracy and demise of apartheid in the 1990s, South African organizations and funding sources (including Ford) have focused work on the formulation and implementation of progressive laws, rather than challenging an unjust system. Though significant civil and political rights violations remain today, Foundation grantees and other groups continue to battle problems such as widespread police brutality, for instance—they are no longer condoned by the government. The broader threats to people's well-being and democracy's health are in the social and economic spheres.

In keeping with these realities, the LRC now focuses more on land, gender, and social service issues. In 1998, for example, it negotiated a landmark settlement for twenty-five hundred families seeking return to, or restitution for, land from which they were evicted under apartheid. One LRC field office successfully challenged a municipal pension scheme that was biased against women; drew on client and NGO contacts to identify and take on a debt collection agency that operated illegally; and helped to get the practice of debtor imprisonment declared unconstitutional. Over a recent eighteen-month period, typically without going to trial, another office helped gain redress for two thousand recipients of disability, pension, and child assistance grants whose payments had been reduced or delayed for months or years by a corrupt, complex bureaucracy. It still handles or monitors particularly significant police brutality cases, but also recognizes that official investigations and private lawyers (bringing damage suits) can help address this problem.

The Foundation's law-related grantmaking adjusted to new realities in South Africa with targeted support for specific social and economic initiatives, according to Program Officer Alice Brown. In the area of women's rights the Foundation has worked with an array of established and new grantees, including CALS's Gender Research Project (GRP), also supported by the Carnegie Corporation. As one of the only National Women's Coalition members with legal expertise, GRP contributed to the successful struggle to prevent customary law, which in some respects accords women lower legal status, from being exempted from equal treatment provisions of the final constitution. As a member of the Reproductive Rights Alliance, it has worked successfully on constitutional and legislative levels and pursued test case litigation to promote women's freedom of choice. Activities of a more recent grantee, the National Institute for Public Interest Law and Research (NIPILAR), have included serving as the legal arm for NGO coalition efforts that helped ensure the government's 1995 ratifications of the Convention on the Rights of the Child and the Convention on the Elimination of All Forms of Discrimination Against Women.

The Foundation was instrumental in the creation of the first national NGO to focus exclusively on law reform, advocacy, public education, and training related to gender violence. Ford identified and funded two South African activists, Joanne Fedler and Mmatshilo Motsei, to conduct field research in South Africa, other African countries, the United States, and Canada. Their study led to the 1997 launching of the Tshwaranang Legal Advocacy Centre to End Violence Against Women. Foundation personnel also facilitated networking and capacity building for the new group. According to Fedler, "There was lots of encouragement, providing contacts and attending to details, helping us to find people involved with similar work both within and outside of South Africa, and then assisting Tshwaranang to find additional sources of funding."

In contrast to their valuable exposure to other African nations, Fedler notes that their western visits led the two to conclude that "solutions that exist in First World countries are totally inappropriate for our situation here," citing detailed written information and telephone hot lines. (Many members of this NGO's target audience are illiterate and without telephones.) Motsei adds that it would have been better for the study's fieldwork to have concentrated exclusively "on Africa, with e-mails and Internet searches for the United States and Canada." In a related vein, Budlender and others feel that greater contact with non-Western NGOs would be valuable for South Africans.

Because land tenure and natural resources management are two of the other main socioeconomic concerns with which Ford's South Africa office is increasingly grappling, there is growing collaboration between Brown and Ford Program Officer James Murombedzi, whose portfolio covers these two fields. He is supporting LRC's Housing Unit, for example, and the two are co-funding land-oriented work by CALS and the Centre for Rural Legal Studies at Stellenbosch University. This builds on several years of cross-program collaboration. Such cooperation maximizes efficient use of resources. It also helps program officers with different kinds of expertise share insights and experiences regarding both specific grantees and the fields within which Ford personnel work. Thus the Foundation can more easily respond to South Africans in handling challenges that cut across its program categories.

With such interdisciplinary work in mind, an additional step might be to identify fortuitous grantee overlaps and facilitate informal grantee contact across the Foundation's grantmaking categories. (Considerable intraprogram facilitation, both formal and informal, already takes place.) University of Natal Legal Aid Clinic Director Asha Ramgobin notes that she learned only by chance of a Ford-funded microenterprise policy project elsewhere on campus. The irony is that microenterprise development is a focus of her clinic's work. Such overlaps among grantee efforts are common to many donor programs. While it might be counterproductive to set up burdensome systems for tracking such overlaps, greater informal attention to them could benefit donor and grantee efforts alike.

Building a New Legal Profession: Clinical Legal Education

Another important prong of Foundation activity has pertained to clinical legal education programs. Based at law schools, these blend practical classroom instruction with "law clinics" through which supervised law students provide legal advice to individuals. (In South Africa, students are not permitted to represent clients in court.) Ford began supporting South African law clinics in the late 1980s. It expanded its engagement in the 1990s to a total of eight out of the twenty-one law clinics in the country. Six of these, due to their racial compositions, received disproportionately little government funding under apartheid. The Foundation has ended this broad assistance after a decade of support, providing a large grant that enables the Association of University Legal Aid Institutions (AULAI) to selectively fund clinics' individual and collective proposals. But Ford has remained open to assisting the predominantly black law schools, which generally remain short of resources.

The legal aid clinics serve four primary goals. These are to supplement and complement other indigent legal services; to improve legal education by providing practical skills and experience; to encourage students to pursue public interest law careers, thereby enlarging and strengthening the public interest bar; and to increase the number and skills of black legal professionals. The clinics take varying approaches. Most build on practice-oriented classroom instruction to develop students' legal skills while serving low-income or indigent individuals from surrounding communities. Some have periodic outreach sessions in those communities. More typically, though, they offer "walk-in" clinics on campus, where individuals seek help regarding a wide range of legal issues such as government benefits, contracts, and family, labor, criminal, and customary law. A crucial element in successful operations is careful supervision of students. To be most useful and effective, students want and need opportunities to immediately seek advice from supervisors, even in the middle of meetings with clients.

A significant exception to the rule of individually oriented and broad spectrum client work is found at the University of Natal clinic. Like the others, it trains students regarding general legal skills. But based on consultations with CBOs, Ramgobin has set up three units for the bulk of the clinic's work. These are administrative and juvenile justice (police brutality, juvenile detentions); gender and children's rights (domestic violence, customary law issues, maintenance); and what she calls "development law" (access to land and housing, legal issues confronting small and microenterprises).

The Natal clinic also builds CBOs' legal capacities whenever possible. The clinic has represented groups of small businesses in negotiating rent and upkeep with the quasi-governmental corporations that are their landlords, while familiarizing these groups with laws and processes they can utilize on their own in the future. The University of Natal approach also differs from other clinics in the impact it seeks to have on students. Ramgobin characterizes this as "trying to get students to redefine what thinking like a lawyer is. . . . So, for example, with land claims, we have to get historians and town planners and lawyers working together."

The clinic is taking this approach in helping those who stand to benefit from the Restitution of Land Rights Act, which entitles those dispossessed under apartheid to reoccupy their land, or to receive alternative parcels or other compensation. In one small business dispute, it successfully used the implicit threat of negative publicity as an alternative to litigation and as a way to generate pressure on its clients' corporate landlord. Ramgobin views this as teaching "law students to think in a developmental way, instead of as a straitjacketed lawyer. This case, to a regular lawyer, is an eviction case. But it really is a case of economic power and the responsibility of an administrative agency."

Some other clinics' personnel do not embrace this approach. They feel they have their hands full with a broad array of individual clients whom they cannot turn away. One director argues that handling individuals' diverse problems is what best trains students for the general practice that many will undertake after graduation.

The University of Natal approach nevertheless appears promising precisely because it widens notions of what constitutes a legal career. Its community outreach can put students much more in touch with broader social realities than does traditional legal aid. It exposes them to the world of NGOs, CBOs, and development work. And it opens up an array of strategies for those inclined to practice public interest law. Finally, in South Africa it can offer opportunities to access government funds to carry out necessary services. The Natal clinic has done exactly that in winning contracts relating to land restitution and to policy development. This helps address the question of sustainability that law clinics, like most NGOs, must face.

In addition to building the skills of law students, the clinics have had a significant impact on the representation and advice available to South Africans. In some parts of the country, clinics are the only or main sources of assistance, particularly in the civil sphere. In the opinion of Tshwaranang's Lebo Malepe, "It would be disastrous if they were cut back."

Foundation support for clinical legal education included research geared toward improving clinic operations. In 1993, the late Shanara Gilbert, a CUNY law professor, studied various clinics' work to provide them and the Foundation with advice. In another research project, eight South Africans, mostly from historically disadvantaged law schools, conducted three-week missions to study clinical programs at CUNY and the University of Maryland. They later shared what they learned with other South African clinical personnel at an AULAI meeting.

Opinions from those involved in the United States visits ranged from ambivalent on the part of those who went there to negative by those who did not. UWC Director Beverley Franks found it useful to observe U.S. clinics in action and attend a University of Maryland seminar on supervision techniques. Before the Gilbert visit and U.S. exposure, Franks explains, "My background was in private practice and I had no idea what goes on in a clinic." On the other hand, she adds, "More clinicians would have been assisted in their growth by having someone visit here in an intensive way." Some who did not participate in the U.S. visit also feel that they could benefit best from an experienced foreign clinician's continued in-country advice and demonstration of techniques.

Clinical legal education has encountered other difficulties in South Africa. Certain of the historically black universities' programs have had trouble retaining leadership and getting their programs off the ground. Given their historical neglect by the apartheid regime and the current lure of big city legal practice—many of these schools are rather rural and isolated—the problems are understandable. Future clinical legal education assistance might usefully invest in developing a second tier of professionals who could easily take over in the event of directors' departures.

A third difficulty was the extensive delay in AULAI's acceptance of its large Ford grant that enables it to make subgrants to meet programs' individual and joint needs. Quicker action on this assistance, which puts important funding decisions in the hands of South Africans, might have occurred had a professional staff person been recruited to take on the organizational duties at AULAI.

A final and very positive facet of the Foundation's clinical legal education support is its overlap with efforts to diversify the legal profession in general and the public interest bar in particular. Ford has cemented the links between the two streams of funding by supporting black "candidate attorneys" at the clinics, the Constitutional Court, and elsewhere. This helps relieve a bottleneck in black admission to the bar, particularly among those who might move on to subsequent legal services work. Opportunities have historically been very limited for black graduates to pass through the "candidate" stage required before they may independently practice law. The Foundation also has supported important efforts by the Black Lawyers Association Legal Education Centre and other groups to expand black lawyers' options and training. Finally, both through its grantmaking and through grantee diversity reporting (which Ford grantees worldwide are asked to provide), the South Africa office has strongly encouraged NGOs to integrate their staffs and boards in terms of race and gender.

Conclusion

How have the Foundation and its grantees contributed to South Africa's progress? What are some of the insights and promising ideas that have emerged over the years? What challenges do they face today? This section offers brief answers to those questions.

Changes and Contributions

Of the many nations in which the Foundation operates, South Africa has undergone one of the most radical and beneficial transformations. Much of the world knows the story of its transition. Perhaps LRC National Director Bongani Majola best summarizes its meaning to black South Africans: "In the minds of many people, they can now go to sleep and wake up in the morning. For a long time, they would wake up in the middle of the night," fearing that police would barge through their doors.

Ford grantees have contributed to that transformation. LRC, CALS, Black Sash, and others exploited apartheid's legal loopholes, thus aiding the broader liberation struggle. They won significant high court decisions and aided grassroots efforts regarding pass laws, homelands policy, police brutality, labor organizing, and a host of other issues. Many persons affiliated with grantees have gone on to important government positions: president and several justices of the Constitutional Court; former ministers of justice and public service; numerous members of Parliament; and other senior executive posts in national and provincial governments. Now that they are in power, they are helping to institutionalize the respect for human rights and the rule of law.

Having contributed to constitutional deliberations, grantees today are helping to formulate and implement new policies, particularly in the social and economic spheres. For example, Ford-supported efforts to improve the status of women are proceeding on multiple fronts. These include the work of NIPILAR regarding international treaties, GRP concerning reproductive rights, and Tshwaranang as the first national NGO to focus on law reform, advocacy, public education, and training exclusively related to gender violence. Despite some problems, support for clinical legal education has upgraded the quality of education that many students receive, the quantity of legal help available to indigent South Africans (particularly given that few other outlets offer free legal assistance in some parts of the country), and the opportunities for black graduates to enter the bar in general and public interest work in particular.

Lessons and Insights

Perhaps the most universal lesson stemming from South African grantees' experience is a cautionary one: every nation in every era is faced with a unique set of challenges that require varying resources and responses. As University of Natal law professor Karthy Govender and others emphasize, an unusual array of circumstances came together in apartheid South Africa. "Students, unions, an international economic boycott, LRC, and many other forces applied smothering pressure on the government from every quarter," Govender says. Within the legal sphere, that government found itself fighting a multifront war. It faced mobilized communities backed by superb and well-positioned legal talent, under the glare of domestic and international publicity. Despite its heavy-handed and even brutal tactics, the government was constrained by a legal system to which it did, in fact, pay more than lip service, and was confronted by organized resistance throughout the country. One or more of those elements is lacking in many other unjust societies around the globe. And a different array of factors distinguishes today's democratic South Africa from many other countries striving to strengthen social justice. Nevertheless, with these caveats in mind, here are some of the lessons and insights that have emerged in South Africa:

Public Interest Litigation

1. Public interest litigation by LRC, CALS, and other organizations often proved successful when it sought relatively modest gains—exploiting the system's rhetorical adherence to the rule of law, rather than confronting apartheid directly. Despite some progressives' understandable initial doubts about working within the system, in South Africa those concerns proved unfounded. The litigation lent strength to antiapartheid activism, rather than draining energy from it.
2. The involvement of preeminent lawyers helped strengthen such litigation efforts. These figures provided political insulation against governmental and legal profession opposition.

3. A multifaceted legal services strategy, through which lawyers' groups have worked with other NGOs, CBOs, mass movements, unions, media, and other civil society forces, has proven successful in South Africa on a number of levels. These included building nonlawyers' legal knowledge and skills; basic service delivery by lawyers and paralegals; identification of widespread problems that can be addressed through test case litigation or other strategies; and, in turn, service delivery geared toward implementation of favorable legislation and appellate victories.

4. Mobilization of private practitioners to file large numbers of individual cases was effective in bringing pressure to bear on prosecutors seeking enforcement of unjust laws. This strategy was employed all too rarely. But where CALS utilized it against the Group Areas Act, it increased prosecutors' workloads to the point that the government abandoned enforcement.

5. Seminars for judges, such as those run by CALS, may exemplify an avenue for NGOs to expand judicial understanding regarding human rights and other priorities in ways that government-organized training often cannot.

University-Based Reform Centers

1. University-based institutes can be crucial havens for reformist forces. In South Africa, they provided institutional shelters that made it more difficult for the government to quash opposition. They later contributed to framing South Africa's interim and final constitutions, as well as legislation and other national policies.

2. These institutes also can partner with important organizations or sectors to engage more directly with reform-oriented activism in a multifaceted way. For example, at least three South African centers have worked with the labor movement to enhance negotiating skills, pursue litigation, contribute to law reform, and train union personnel regarding work-related legal issues.

3. Reform centers also contributed to the legal struggle against apartheid through research that developed data and strategies for challenging the apartheid regime in its own

courts and in the court of international opinion. Both during and after apartheid, they provided important conduits for integrating international legal experience into the South African context.

Building Law Clinics

1. Staff development and support can be crucial. Encouraging the growth of a second tier of leadership at a law clinic (or an NGO) could insulate it from the potential disruption of its director's departure.

2. A developmental approach to clinical legal education, as practiced at the University of Natal, might serve both South African students and client groups at least as well as traditional, individualized legal aid. It can broaden students' perspectives on legal practice and make communities more legally self-sufficient.

3. In view of the constant challenge of NGO and law clinic sustainability, the University of Natal clinic's success in securing government contracts merits mention. One such contract funds it to help process land restitution claims. This serves the community, provides students with valuable practical experience, and substantially supplements the clinic's resources. Though not detailed in this report, CALS's preliminary plans to sell services (such as environmental law training) to the private sector also have significant potential. Assuming it does not distort the organization's priorities, such activity could provide a useful service, augment the group's revenues, and enable it to pay enough to retain quality personnel.

Donor Programming Approaches

1. Institutional support to grantees such as CALS and LRC proved extremely helpful in giving them the flexibility to adjust to unanticipated obstacles and opportunities.

2. Strategic grants, even if small, can yield impact far beyond their budgets. Limited support to an exiled ANC official produced research that contributed to early deliberations on a new constitution. A modest grant enabled two activists to undertake relevant research and then to plan and launch

the country's first NGO focusing on the legal dimensions of battling gender violence. Small grants also helped historically black law schools initiate clinical legal education programs.

3. The experience of various grantees suggests that while U.S. exposure can be valuable, it often should not be the first option for expanding grantees' capacities and horizons. Generally, it is preferable to draw on in-country or non-Western expertise and models. And where hands-on instruction is helpful and local expertise is limited or stretched thin, as with clinical legal education, South Africans suggest that a long-term consultant working in-country may prove more useful than sending several South Africans abroad. The general rule should be to base international exposure on whether a given country offers a comparative advantage regarding applicable expertise, similar constraints, and adaptable solutions.

Looking Ahead

The demise of apartheid and the evolution of South Africa's democratic transition leaves the country and its NGO community facing a new series of challenges. None are quite as dramatic as those South Africans faced in the past. But they are far from mundane.

One challenge is the drain of NGO talent into the government. Some of South Africa's best minds have been drawn into the judiciary, various ministries, and elected positions. This has left parts of the NGO community in a difficult spot.

Funding is another challenge for NGOs: many donors have shifted their resources to the government. One way NGOs might deal with this is to access government funds, as the University of Natal clinic has done. For effective organizations with extensive track records, another possible approach is for donors to fund endowments. Ford provided such a grant to LRC as it closed out its nearly two decades of ongoing institutional support for the group. (It still makes project grants to LRC, however.) On the other hand, though an endowment can be a basis for a degree of long-term sustainability, interest on an endowment rarely fills the large hole left by the termination of annual institutional support.

Moreover, it is not a feasible option for the many organizations that have not evinced long-term stability and impact. A third approach adopted by LRC and other NGOs is to seek project-specific support. A trade-off here is that sometimes donors' project support can be very restrictive, denying NGOs the flexibility to set their own priorities and maximize effectiveness.

What does this indicate about many NGOs' financial prospects? Though they may have to become more entrepreneurial in seeking local resources, many will continue to need foreign funding. Even in the far more affluent United States and Western Europe, few NGOs are truly self-supporting.

South African NGOs merit continued support, partly because they continue to play important roles with respect to government. Law-oriented NGOs are an important part of this mix. A vibrant NGO community can work fruitfully with the state, but also help ensure that the government fully respects democracy's constraints. NGOs, including those with legal expertise, can crucially contribute to policy implementation. As LRC's Majola points out, "You can't rely on the state too much, because its capacity to implement programs and laws is limited." Another NGO activist takes a tougher line on the need to help or prod government officials to do their jobs: "I used to think that problems with clients obtaining pensions and disability grants were due to apartheid. But now I see the institutional culture [as an obstacle]."

Even where many NGOs do not directly address important problems, such as the widespread crime plaguing the country, the social and economic progress to which NGOs contribute may ameliorate these difficulties in the long run. It is not surprising that South Africa faces many such problems after decades of repression. Yet they do not diminish the great strides the country has made in the 1990s. For the nation to keep taking such steps, the civil society forces that have contributed so much to date will need to remain a central part of the democratic future.

Notes

1. To avoid splitting possible definitional hairs, for the purposes of this study NGOs include university-based entities.
2. The term "black" has been employed in various ways in recent

South African history, some more inclusive than others. As used here, it is employed interchangeably with "non white" and refers to all South Africans of African, mixed race, and Asian descent.

3. As quoted by Richard L. Abel, *Politics by Other Means: Law in the Struggle Against Apartheid, 1980–1994* (London: Routledge, 1995), p. 13.

4. *Legal Aid in South Africa: Proceedings of a Conference Held in the Faculty of Law, University of Natal, Durban, from 2nd–6th July, 1973* (Durban, South Africa: University of Natal Faculty of Law, June 1974), p. 265.

5. David McQuoid-Mason pursued a similar strategy with his controversial (and eventually Foundation-funded) Street Law program. He obtained political protection for this effort, which teaches young people about legal issues most pertinent to their daily lives, by securing backing from the legal establishment and participation by a prominent jurist.

6. Abel, p. 60.

7. As the terms are employed here, CBOs are locally run and operated organizations, with personnel typically drawn from their communities. They sometimes are characterized by the voluntary natures of their staffs and by community-based memberships. In contrast, NGOs tend to be more professional outfits with paid staffs. Some NGOs train, service, or otherwise assist CBOs. These are only rough delineations, however. The two concepts clearly can overlap.

8. Abel, pp. 64–65.

9. The Foundation did not open a South Africa office until 1993 for at least two reasons. It in no way wished to be beholden to or constrained by the apartheid regime, which would have decided on whether and under what conditions Ford could retain a presence there. And, on the advice of South African colleagues, it held off early in the transition to democratic rule. This was to avoid prematurely contributing to an impression that the tenuous democratic transition was proceeding in an irrevocable manner, and that the international community could lighten its pressure on the government.

10. Nevertheless, being based outside South Africa was difficult. During the mid to late 1980s, Foundation staff often encountered problems and lengthy delays in obtaining visas. On at least one occasion, a visa request was denied.

11. While its orientation and operations were different and will not be detailed here, another key Ford-supported player in the labor field was the Independent Mediation Service of South Africa.

12. Penelope Andrews, "Grant Evaluation Reports Prepared for the Ford Foundation," 1994, p. 4.

13. In some key respects, this assistance predated the events of 1990. Though not law oriented, the work of the Institute for a Democratic Alternative in South Africa merits mention. This Foundation grantee brought together prominent Afrikaner and ANC leaders for meetings outside the country in the mid and late 1980s.

Appendix: People Interviewed for This Study

Catherine Albertyn
Head, Gender Research Project, Centre for Applied Legal Studies, Johannesburg

Paulin Breed
Dean, Faculty of Law, University of the North, Pietersburg

Alice Brown
Program Officer, The Ford Foundation, Johannesburg

Geoff Budlender
Director-General, Department of Land Affairs, Pretoria and Former National Director, Legal Resources Centre, Johannesburg

William Carmichael
Former Vice President, The Ford Foundation, New York

Arthur Chaskalson
President, Constitutional Court, Johannesburg, and former National Director, Legal Resources Centre, Johannesburg

Mahendra R. Chetty
Attorney, Legal Resources Centre, Durban

Thisbe Clegg
Financial Director, Black Sash Trust, Cape Town

Dennis Davis
Former Director, Centre for Applied Legal Studies, Johannesburg

John Dugard
Former Director, Centre for Applied Legal Studies, Johannesburg

Sheena Duncan
Chairperson, Black Sash Trust, Johannesburg

Joanne Fedler
Former Executive Director, Tshwaranang Legal Advocacy Centre
to End Violence Against Women, Johannesburg

Beverly-Ann Franks
Director, Legal Aid Clinic, University of the Western Cape, Cape
Town

Karthi Govender
Deputy Director, African Centre for the Constructive Resolution
of Disputes, Durban

Karthy Govender
Associate Professor, Faculty of Law, University of Natal-Durban

Bheki Gumede
Street Law Coordinator, Centre for Socio-Legal Studies,
University of Natal-Durban

Gary Howard
Candidate Attorney, Campus Law Clinic, University of Natal-
Durban

Val Kathuravaloo
Attorney, Law Clinic, University of Durban-Westville

William Kerfoot
Attorney, Legal Resources Centre, Cape Town

Bongani Khumalo
Director, Community Law and Rural Development Centre,
Durban

Boogie Khutsoane
Head, Gender Rights Department, National Institute for Public
Interest Law and Research, Pretoria

Philippa Kruger
Director, Campus Law Clinic, University of the Witwatersrand,
Johannesburg

Chris Landsberg
Deputy Director, Centre for Policy Studies, Johannesburg

Pius Langa
Justice, Constitutional Court, Johannesburg, and former
President, National Association of Democratic Lawyers,
Johannesburg

Harold Letsela
Paralegal, Law Clinic, University of Durban-Westville

Peggy Maisel
Visiting Professor, Faculty of Law, University of Natal-
Durban

Bongani Majola
National Director, Legal Resources Centre, Johannesburg

Lebogang Malape
Director, Legal Research and Policy, Tshwaranang Legal
Advocacy Centre to End Violence Against Women, Johannesburg

Erin Martin
Country Program Director, National Democratic Institute for
International Affairs, Cape Town

Aubrey McCutcheon
Former Program Officer, The Ford Foundation, Johannesburg

David J. McQuoid-Mason
Professor, Faculty of Law, University of Natal-Durban

Asha Moodley
Office Administrator, Legal Resources Centre, Durban

Richard Thabo Moloko
Executive Director, National Institute for Public Interest Law and Research, Pretoria

Mawethu Mosery
Director, Centre for Socio-Legal Studies, University of Natal-Durban

Mmatshilo Motsei
Executive Director, Agisanang Domestic Abuse Prevention and Training, Johannesburg

James Murombedzi
Program Officer, The Ford Foundation, Johannesburg

Munira Osman
Supervisor, Administrative and Juvenile Justice Unit, Campus Law Clinic, University of Natal-Durban

Asha Ramgobin
Director, Campus Law Clinic, University of Natal-Durban

Albie Sachs
Justice, Constitutional Court, Johannesburg, and former member, Legal and Constitutional Affairs Committee, African National Congress

Vincent C. Saldanha
Attorney, Legal Resources Centre, Cape Town

Michael Savage
Executive Director, Open Society Foundation for South Africa, Cape Town

Chuck Scott
Media and Training Officer, Centre for Socio-Legal Studies, University of Natal-Durban

Siphiwe Sikhakhane
Director, Legal Aid Clinic, University of the North, Pietersburg

Nico Steytler
Director, Community Law Centre, University of the Western Cape, Cape Town

Franklin A. Thomas
Former President, The Ford Foundation, New York

Alison Tilley
Legislation Monitor, Black Sash Trust, Cape Town

David Unterhalter
Director, Centre for Applied Legal Studies, University of Witwatersrand, Johannesburg

Yousuf Vawda
Director, Law Clinic, University of Durban-Westville

Naomi Webster
Director, Marketing and Programs, Tshwaranang Legal Advocacy Centre to End Violence Against Women, Johannesburg

Marc Wegerif
Director, Nkuzi Development Association, Pietersburg

Theresa Yates
Associate, Nkuzi Development Association, Pietersburg

Group Interviews/Activities

Observation of University of Natal-Durban and University of Witswatersrand law clinic activities

Selected faculty members, Faculty of Law, University of the North

2

From Dictatorship to Democracy: Law and Social Change in the Andean Region and the Southern Cone of South America

HUGO FRÜHLING

Since the 1970s, the Ford Foundation has supported organizations that use the law to promote democracy, defend human rights, and pursue socioeconomic change in the Andean Region and the Southern Cone of South America. With this support, along with that of other donors, the many individuals from the region, through their courage and leadership, have expanded human rights practice and public interest law, despite often difficult and sometimes dangerous circumstances.

Through its Santiago-based office, Ford provides support to groups in Chile, Argentina, Peru, and Colombia. Activities of Ford grantees include clinical legal education; monitoring of human rights violations; and litigation combined with advocacy, research, and media outreach to ensure greater accountability of governmental and societal institutions and to promote social justice.

This chapter traces the origins and evolution of the Foundation's law-related efforts in the region through three stages of development: the 1960s law and development movement; human rights program work, which began in the 1970s; and the public interest law grantmaking program initiated in the 1990s. The paper discusses the linkages between these efforts and describes the historical circumstances that shaped them. A concluding section offers insights and lessons gained from the strategies implemented by grantees and by the Foundation as a donor.

The Law and Development Movement

During the 1960s, the Ford Foundation first became involved in legal activities in the developing world by supporting what was known as the "law and development movement." Numerous U.S.-based institutions participated in this effort, including law schools, foundations, and government agencies concerned with international development. In 1966, the Ford Foundation provided $3 million to establish the International Legal Center (ILC) in New York City as a vehicle for mobilizing legal assistance to developing countries.

These early activities were mostly framed as a complement to foreign development assistance. U.S. law and development scholars perceived the need for developing countries to modernize their courts and legal systems to respond to the growing pressures of poverty and underdevelopment. These legal experts believed that the U.S. model of the lawyer as problem solver would be particularly useful for developing countries. As a consequence, much of the Foundation's involvement with this program focused on the reform of legal education, which some of the Foundation's advisors saw as the key to long-term change within the entire legal system.[1]

Legal experts encouraged the use of the case method, a U.S. model for legal instruction that exposes students to actual cases from which they identify legal rules. The Foundation's support created fellowship opportunities that allowed law professors and students from the region to study at American law schools or to attend summer law and development programs. Programs supporting research and the training of law professors were also launched with Ford funding in Chile, Colombia, and Peru.

For the most part, the strategy was not successful. In 1971, a Foundation review of its law and development activities returned an appraisal critical of its impact. Moreover, several American law professors, as well as former administrators of the program, criticized the law and development movement for its reliance on a liberal American model alien to the local legal culture.

Although the movement for law school reform stalled in Chile and Colombia, similar reforms produced more enduring impact at the Catholic University Law School of Peru. Rocio

Villanueva, a former Catholic University student who now heads the Women's Rights Program at the Ombudsman's office in Lima, recalls that her law professors who studied as visiting fellows at the University of Wisconsin Law School returned home to have a positive impact on their students. "The so-called 'Wisconsin Boys' proved to be an excellent investment for Peru," she says. "They created new teaching materials and taught us to question authority." Similarly, Marcial Rubio, a vice rector at Catholic University, observes, "Look at the few, modern and functioning legal institutions in Peru. They are staffed by lawyers from the Catholic University."

The reform movement's failure in Chilean law schools was partly due to the fact that the universities suffered from military intervention. In 1974, backed by the new military junta, the most conservative law professors took over the law schools. Both in Chile and Colombia, reform efforts were largely resisted by the bar and the most established academics of the law schools. In contrast, in Peru, law school reform was encouraged by the political climate created by the social changes that were implemented by the military government then in power, and due to the academic freedom that existed in the universities.

Moreover, the U.S.-sponsored reform efforts had very limited success in advancing the rule of law and legal change beyond law schools in Chile, Peru, and Colombia, because they were hampered by misguided conceptions about the relationship between legal training and Latin American legal systems. American professors tend to describe Latin American legal culture as traditional and formalistic, that is, composed of lawyers who are trained to mechanically apply the law. The truth was that, in the case of judges, they sometimes justified their ideological biases by saying that they did not have the authority to change the law. In other cases, their formalism in applying the law was a reflection of the diminished position of the judiciary within the political system. The problem, then, was one of practical politics perhaps more than the legal teaching methods.

Despite its shortcomings, the law and development movement produced the first studies on the functioning of the legal system in Latin America. Beyond that, some lawyers in the United States and Latin America who participated in the movement continued collaborating, establishing law clinics and legal services for the poor. One such example is the Inter-American Legal Services Association (now the Latin American Institute of Alternative Legal Services), founded in Washington, D.C., in 1978. In the 1980s, it moved its headquarters to Bogotá, Colombia, and from there provided networking services to legal services organizations in Latin America.

What are the lessons from the law and development experience? Perhaps the first is that successful law-related programs should rely on local academic and legal institutions whose capacities could be enhanced by adapting foreign institutions' experience. Much of the law and development movement, in unfortunate contrast, was built around the ideas and abilities of American law professors, who received most of the funding. This certainly weakened internal support for legal education reform in Chile and Colombia. The legal programs that the Foundation funded subsequently relied much more heavily on the knowledge and participation of in-country professionals, with the aim of correcting these perceived weaknesses of law and development programs.

Another lesson from the law and development experience is that programs aiming for substantial transformations require institutional openness and long-term support of people who share common beliefs. The institutional hospitality, as well as the reform-minded professors, at the Catholic University Law School in Peru are excellent examples. In Chile, however, the more traditional professors held considerable power, and those taking part in the reform process were sharply divided by their country's political problems, a conflict that seriously hampered their ability to defend law school reform.

Protecting Human Rights

Context and Origins

Although Argentina, Chile, Colombia, and Peru generally share a common historical and legal heritage, their levels of socioeconomic development differ greatly. Argentina is the most prosperous, followed by Chile and Colombia. Peru is the poorest of these countries. Political violence has significantly affected all of these societies in recent decades, but their historical and political evolutions have differed during these times. During the 1970s, democratically elected governments in Argentina and Chile were overthrown by highly repressive military regimes that suppressed political pluralism and basic rights. One of the bitter legacies of this period is the "disappeared"—people who were assassinated by the regimes in power but whose remains were never found. The official accounts place the number of disappeared in Chile at 1046, while their number in Argentina might be ten times higher. Argentina moved away from authoritarianism in 1983, while Chile moved toward democratization in 1990. By then, a vigorous nongovernmental sector, which had challenged many authoritarian policies, was in place in both countries.

Peru had been ruled by a reform-minded and much less repressive military regime from 1968 to 1979, when a transition to democracy began. Soon after, in 1980, the Shining Path (a Maoist organization) initiated a terrorist campaign in the Ayacucho region, assassinating local officials and community leaders. In response, the state unleashed violent repression against what it labeled as "subversives"—individuals believed to be members of Shining Path or its sympathizers. The country was immersed in a wave of unprecedented violence until Shining Path leader Abimail Guzman was captured by police in 1992. By 1993, political violence diminished, but hundreds of people who had been unfairly tried for their alleged participation in terrorist activities remained in jail.

Whereas Peru's insurgencies were largely suppressed, Colombia's decades of war have continued. Besides the violence provoked by long-active guerrilla groups that control half of the country's territory, Colombia also suffers human rights violations committed by military and paramilitary forces fighting the guerrilla groups and attacking other social and political organizations. These problems are worsened by the corrupting influence of a large criminal drug economy. Despite its political and institutional crises, however, Colombia has been ruled by constitutional civilian governments for the last four decades.[2]

Clearly, the violent histories of these four countries have raised serious obstacles to democratic development. State-sponsored and societal violence posed serious challenges to dedicated lawyers and other activists, who have faced threats of arrest, assault, or even death while seeking to promote human rights and social change.

The Foundation's human rights grantmaking in the region can be traced back to the 1973 overthrow of democratically elected President Salvador Allende in Chile, and the 1976 military coup in Argentina. Until then, Chile had been one of the region's most stable constitutional democracies, and during the twentieth century it had experienced only one brief period of dictatorship, from 1927 to 1931.

The Foundation's immediate response to the Chilean coup was an emergency effort to protect threatened intellectuals. Ford increased its budget for fellowships, enabling more individuals to undertake graduate study abroad. In subsequent years, the Foundation focused its efforts on helping to create and preserve local research groups that were critical of governmental social and economic policies, and which became the only independent centers of thought and research.

By the mid-1970s, the Ford Foundation had established an international human rights program in its New York headquarters. That program was considerably expanded after Franklin Thomas became the Foundation's president in 1979, undertaking a reorganization that identified human rights as one of six priority issues of the Foundation.

By 1983, the Foundation had defined two major human rights programmatic areas in the Andean Region and the Southern Cone: civil and political liberties, and access to social justice and legal services. The main objectives of this work were to strengthen the ability of local, nonpartisan human rights organizations to investigate, document, and publicize human rights abuses and to promote rights awareness among disenfranchised groups. This section of the case study describes only the civil and political liberties area, which dealt with the defense and promotion of the basic rights to life and freedom.

In the 1980s, most Ford funding for civil and political liberties in these countries went to human rights NGOs to improve their abilities to monitor and document human rights violations, and to disseminate this information both domestically and to the outside world. Because strong, credible human rights organizations were already functioning in Argentina and Chile, most early Foundation grants were concentrated in these countries. In Chile, the Foundation supported the legal work of the Vicariate of Solidarity, the documentation efforts of the Chilean Commission of Human Rights, and the research efforts of the Academy of Christian Humanism, among others. In Argentina, Ford gave support to the legal program of the Center for Legal and Social Studies (CELS), and to Grandmothers of the Plaza de Mayo. The Grandmothers were searching for their grandchildren, born in prison to their "disappeared" children, and given up for adoption without the families' consent.

One of the first grants outside the Southern Cone was made to the International Commission of Jurists. This Geneva-based NGO, which undertakes human rights research, training, and advocacy, organized a commission of prominent jurists from the Andean region to establish linkages among local human rights groups. From its headquarters in Lima, Peru, the newly established Andean Commission of Jurists rapidly developed research programs and training courses in international human rights law for judges and prosecutors from the region.

In 1985, the first grant to a local Peruvian group was made to the Legal Defense Institute (IDL), a group of young lawyers who provided legal assistance to prisoners of conscience and developed human rights education in rural areas. This group later joined with others to create the Human Rights National Coordinator of Peru, a network of forty-nine NGOs that publicly rejected both governmental repression and the violent tactics of the Shining Path.

Until 1988, no human rights grant had been made in Colombia, despite the widespread and widening abuses there, because Foundation staff could not identify an independent organization that documented human rights abuses. The Foundation took a proactive approach, helping to establish the Colombian branch of the Andean Commission of Jurists, which sought to present cases of human rights violations before international human rights bodies such as the Inter-American Commission of Human Rights. A few months after the commission started, Chilean human rights expert and former Amnesty International

Deputy Secretary General José Zalaquett spent two weeks in Bogotá as a Foundation consultant. He provided advice based on his previous experience as head of the legal department at the Committee of Cooperation for Peace in Santiago.

Building Capacities, Credibility, and
Legal Strategies of Human Rights Groups

Ford characteristically sought nonpartisan grantee partners, believing that attribute was critical for credibility and effectiveness. To increase their credibility, human rights groups emphasized the quality of the information they released to the media and to other groups. This information was widely disseminated by international human rights organizations and by the press, which helped raise international pressure on the Argentine and Chilean military regimes to modify their repressive policies. Reports on Chile by the Inter-American Commission of Human Rights cited information produced by the Vicariate of Solidarity. Resolutions of the United Nations Commission on Human Rights stating concern for the human rights situation in the country expressly considered reports provided by Chilean NGOs. International human rights groups such as Americas Watch (now Human Rights Watch/Americas) made consistent and effective use of information provided by the Chilean Commission of Human Rights, the Vicariate of Solidarity, and CELS.

The development of these and other local human rights groups was made possible by the efforts of activists, relatives of the victims of repression, and, especially in Chile, leaders in the Roman Catholic Church. In the days following the September 1973 coup in Chile, clandestine opposition to government repression developed, as exemplified by the individual actions of Catholic priests who sheltered persecuted individuals and sought asylum for them in foreign embassies. Three weeks after the coup, with the support of other religious denominations, the Catholic Church initiated a group to defend Chilean citizens, the Committee of Cooperation for Peace (COPACHI).

One of COPACHI's first steps was to organize a legal aid department to defend political dissidents being tried before the military courts. With support from the World Council of Churches and other donors, the committee's activities grew rapidly. Tension between the government and COPACHI came to a head in late 1975, when government pressure forced the committee to dissolve. The Church responded by quickly creating the Vicariate of Solidarity as an integral part of the Catholic Church. The Church's status as a national institution in the predominantly Roman Catholic country helped shield the Vicariate from military repression. The Vicariate vigorously investigated and documented human rights violations and brought numerous legal actions. It first received Ford funding in 1978.

In Argentina, where the Church hierarchy did not protect or promote human rights programs, organized human rights efforts emerged more slowly. The late Emilio Mignone became involved in the human rights movement in July 1976 when his daughter was detained and disappeared. Soon after, he was invited to participate in the Permanent Assembly for Human Rights, an Argentine NGO that was gathering information on disappearances and other abuses. "At that time," he recalled, "we met at churches and in other places that were loaned to us." In 1979, together with three other friends whose sons or daughters had also disappeared, Mignone proposed that the assembly assume the legal representation of victims of repression. More cautious members rejected the idea, and in March 1980, Mignone and the others formed CELS. From its inception, CELS sought to defend victims of human rights abuses, and it established strong international relations with organizations such as the International Commission of Jurists. CELS became a Ford grantee in 1981.

International human rights organizations and local groups developed a mutually beneficial relationship. Efforts to build connections between various grantees also increased the impact of human rights work in the region. The Foundation supported transnational linkages by funding regional conferences, training courses, and workshops. Lawyers from Argentina and Chile visited Peru to provide local organizations with information about reporting methodologies. Conferences organized by the Academy of Christian Humanism in 1985 and 1987 brought together human rights activists from Argentina, Chile, Peru, Brazil, Colombia, and the United States to discuss their work.

Ronald Gamarra, head of the IDL legal department in Peru,

explains, "When the Institute was founded, there already existed the precedents of Chile and Argentina. We frequently went to the Vicariate. Our first evaluator was Roberto Garreton [head of the judicial department at the Vicariate]." A lawyer at the Colombian Commission of Jurists also mentioned their long-standing and enriching relationship with Garreton.

Most grantees interviewed for this study described contacts with Ford program officers as regular and open. None seemed to consider this as intrusion in their work, nor were there manifestations of ideological mistrust of the Foundation or its goals.

As repression grew in the countries covered by this report, a variety of organizations filed legal actions on behalf of the victims of human rights violations. These legal actions have included legal assistance at military court proceedings in Chile and Peru; petitions of habeas corpus for people detained under states of siege in Argentina, Chile, and Peru; defense of people accused of terrorist actions and state security violations before military and civil courts in Chile and Peru; and presentation of cases from all four countries before the Inter-American Commission of Human Rights, as well as UN bodies.

While a detailed examination of the impact of these actions is beyond the scope of this study, several examples illustrate a lesson from this experience: one of the most effective strategies in the defense of human rights under these authoritarian and repressive regimes was the legal representation of victims of repression.

Immediately after the coup in Chile, defense lawyers supported by the churches began providing legal defense to people tried before martial law tribunals for alleged crimes such as treason and sedition. At first, these lawyers' arguments had very little effect. Some lawyers interviewed agreed that in a few cases they might have influenced the military judges to impose more lenient sentences. Others believed that at times their most important contribution was giving defendants some contact with the outside world.

However, arguments presented by the defense gradually achieved greater impact. In August 1974, the Chilean army's legal advisor instructed all division commanders to review sentences imposed by the military courts and to correct legal mistakes or omissions. These reviews usually resulted in much lighter sentences.

In a very different context, in 1992 IDL began to defend people accused of membership in terrorist organizations before Peruvian military courts. Gamarra describes the situation: "Our work in the military courts was very complicated. We had to argue before three different courts: the military judge, the Council of War, and the Supreme Military Council. The lawyer had no contact with the defendant, but nevertheless we were successful in 10 percent of the cases." In defending people before civil courts, IDL claimed a success rate of 90 percent.

Most people affected by repression were arrested without charges under state-of-siege regulations. Human rights groups were not nearly as successful in any of these countries with the presentation of habeas corpus petitions on their behalf, which required authorities to release or produce in court a person who had been detained or arrested. Between 1973 and 1983, Chile's Supreme Court rejected all but ten of fifty-four hundred habeas corpus petitions filed by COPACHI and by its successor, the Vicariate. Results in Argentina were similar. This is not surprising, given the batteries of legal instruments with which the military regimes armed themselves to detain people without expressing a reason. However, in 1979, relatives of 1,542 persons who had disappeared in Argentina presented a collective habeas corpus petition before the Supreme Court, explaining that previous presentations had been rejected despite the fact that it was clear these people had been detained under state authority. In Mignone's words, "The court declared that deprivation of justice existed in Argentina and that the judges could not apply the law due to lack of collaboration from the executive. They sent the decision to Argentina's [then-President] Videla who replied with a shameful note saying he agreed but that no collaboration would be forthcoming. Human rights activists felt the courts became more open to human rights arguments after the incident.

In Chile, habeas corpus petitions were also useful for gathering and disseminating information about human rights abuses. Victims of repression or their families made sworn statements about governmental actions that were presented to the courts. The complaints gave an empirical measure of the detentions and torture. If the Vicariate simply reported the number of judicial complaints filed, which was a recognized part of the legal process, it could not convincingly be accused of involvement in an "international smear campaign" against the military regime. Information coming from these sworn testimonies was included in monthly and annual reports that the Vicariate prepared and distributed worldwide. These reports catalogued human rights violations, changes in the forms of repression, and legal actions the Vicariate had filed in response. This information was widely used by international human rights organizations to increase pressure on the Chilean government. On the basis of Vicariate documentation and other sources, the UN General Assembly annually condemned human rights conditions in Chile from 1974 until 1988.

In the late 1980s, several human rights groups began presenting individual cases before the Inter-American Commission on Human Rights, which could find states responsible for rights violations. The Colombian Commission of Jurists was one of these groups, specializing in representing victims. Its deputy director, Carlos Rodriguez, says, "When we began, the Inter-American Commission had only handed down one decision concerning Colombia. Today, and after ten years of work, there are seventeen decisions." Bringing cases to the Inter-American Commission has had an important impact in publicizing human rights violations and in informing domestic judiciaries of human rights standards that should be applied in national courts.

Adapting to Political Changes

In 1983, dictatorship had given way to democracy in Argentina. The transitional leadership adopted measures to prosecute members of the military juntas who were involved in past human rights violations. A few years later, in 1987, the civilian government enacted a law that suspended those prosecutions. Chile remained under the control of a military dictatorship, but repression eased as the country prepared for a 1988 plebiscite, which voted to end the military regime. The human rights situation in Colombia and Peru was much more complex after 1985, as civilian governments seemed unable to curtail abuses by their own security forces and by guerrilla groups.

The return of elected governments in some countries of the region opened the door to new advocacy strategies. A 1985 Foundation-supported study concluded that human rights activists could best respond to new developments by learning from recent transitions from dictatorship to democracy; identifying strategies for confronting past human rights violations; understanding how human rights groups could relate to governments in a more collaborative way; and stimulating greater interest in human rights beyond the human rights community.

Former Ford Program Officer Michael Shifter recalls that at the core of the Foundation's new strategy was "to make human rights much more central to the societies." This was done partly by supporting programs that helped human rights groups reach out to professional associations, the media, and intellectuals. Another route was to help organizations as they devised new strategies toward violations that were not politically motivated and that were committed by government officials or other societal actors in the transitional democracies.

The Foundation in partnership with its grantees made several efforts in this direction beginning in the late 1980s. In each country, one or two leading organizations that had built institutional capacity were awarded larger, longer-term grants to ensure their viability. These institutions produced reliable data on human rights violations and opposed violence by all parties to various conflicts. The so-called flagship institutions were CELS in Argentina, the Vicariate of Solidarity and the Chilean Commission of Human Rights in Chile, the Colombian Commission of Jurists in Colombia, and the Andean Commission of Jurists and IDL in Peru.

At the same time, support for human rights research programs was expanded in two aspects. First, grants were awarded to research centers, universities, and bar associations not previously involved with these issues. Second, the research was now broadened to include studies on violence, administration of justice, and policies addressing past human rights violations. For instance, the Diego Portales Law School in Chile received support in 1991 to undertake studies on judicial reform processes in Latin America as well as on Chilean criminal justice procedure. As Jorge Correa, former dean of the school, explains, "The work we did with Ford Foundation project support helped highlight the shortcomings of the Chilean legal system as we were trying to influence its reform." Members of the research team later drafted the new Criminal Procedure Code and assisted the Justice Ministry in preparing, among other legislative measures, a law that would create a Public Prosecution Office. In Colombia, several political science professors from the National University who participated in Foundation-supported human rights research projects in the late 1980s played a significant role in the debates leading to a new constitution in that country in 1991.

Groups that advocated on the types of human rights violations of the 1980s and early 1990s are still a small part of these societies, but human rights discussions now involve a much wider variety of people and institutions, including the universities, Congress, and even the judiciary. A considerable number of judges have attended national and international human rights courses organized by grantees. In recent years the Andean Commission of Jurists has received nine hundred applications from judges, prosecutors, and academics from the region to attend its annual course on International Protection of Human Rights.

Ford Foundation staff also supported older human rights groups as they shifted their strategies from opposition to military dictatorships to monitoring and promoting rights under the new democracies. This meant sustaining them through the sometimes slow process of adapting to the new context, using law and courts to address a new range of nonpolitically motivated rights violations. The case of CELS is illustrative. CELS president Mignone, as well as Foundation staff, agreed on the need to develop new programs even as the group remained deeply engaged in human rights issues lingering from the military dictatorship, including the debate over the pardoning of military officers who had committed human rights violations. However, the Foundation recognized that CELS remained one of Argentina's most important civil society organizations and that it deserved continuing support. In 1996, CELS began a new international human rights program to bring international standards to bear on issues such as police violence, access to public information, violations of due process, and gender discrimination. Under new leadership since 1996, the group has continued to evolve and adapt its strategies to post dictatorship realities.

Political changes in the region have created conditions for a human rights practice that goes beyond denunciation of violations and confrontations with the government. Legal activists interviewed for this study stressed the need to maintain open channels of communication with all sectors of society. They hope to have an impact beyond the usual circles of supporters for human rights.

Examples of this new strategy can be found in both Colombia and Peru, where human rights organizations have engaged with governmental authorities in discussions on human rights. Peru's IDL is an example. Despite its criticism of the government's antiterrorist legislation, IDL has worked closely with a special government commission reviewing cases of people sentenced for terrorism. By mid-1998, 438 such individuals had been pardoned by President Alberto Fujimori.

Public Interest Law Grantmaking

Origins of a Program

The rationale for increasing support for the use of legal actions to pursue human rights and social justice goals in the region was explained in a 1997 Ford document: "To enhance probity, impartiality, and transparency in public functions, judicial institutions are being looked upon to assume new prominence in regulating the state and in mediating the whole relationship between government and civil society."[3]

NGOs and activists in the region, like Foundation staff, viewed law as an increasingly important instrument for rendering public institutions accountable. In recent years, a number of legal reforms passed in the four countries have recognized new constitutional rights, allowed third parties to initiate legal actions, and created ombudsman offices. In 1991, Colombia approved a new constitution which recognized the concept of "popular actions," discussed later in this chapter. The constitution also established the possibility of class actions. The 1993 Peruvian constitution reaffirmed traditional constitutional rights and added the right to request information from governmental entities, the right to a healthy environment, and the right of any person to his or her ethnic or cultural identity. The new constitution also introduced other institutional reforms, such as referenda, popular legislative initiatives, and ombudsman offices. A year later, the new Argentine constitution recognized the constitutional right to a healthy environment, the rights of consumers, and the right of protection against discrimination. It also recognized the writ of *amparo*, which gives any person the right to file a legal action before a judge requesting an end to any infringement of his or her constitutional rights. Such actions can now also be presented by the ombudsman or NGOs.

While these constitutional amendments create new opportunities for legal and social change, certain institutional and legal factors have undermined these reforms. The most significant problem is the judiciary's lack of legitimacy. Martin Abregu of CELS states, "The impact of a leading case in Argentina is not the same as in the United States. Here, the judiciary can reach the most unthinkable result because of ignorance or corruption." In Peru, environmental lawyer Manuel Pulgar agrees: "Judicial corruption and the fact the government has interfered with judicial independence complicate [matters] greatly. However, we do not rely on litigation alone. We use the press, present petitions to the administration, and lobby the boards of corporations investing here."

Most people involved in public interest law efforts in the region believe that two basic activities are required to overcome the obstacles a conservative judiciary presents: education of judges on public interest law concepts, as well as on specific issues being brought to court; and greater public advocacy, including media outreach and community mobilization, which can help define and promote public accountability and the public interest.

The Ford Foundation's efforts to promote these objectives—and the rule of law and democratic society they would support—are manifested in grantmaking that began in 1995 and is overseen from the Foundation's Santiago office under a democratic governance rubric. That program supports community organizing, advocacy, research, training, and litigation efforts that seek to ensure accountability of both public and private institutions, and to defend and promote collective rights. For example, Ford grantees are today promoting the rights of women and other vulnerable groups, as well as the right to a clean environment. Often they collaborate to create a new dynamic for change. For instance, the Diego Portales University is coordinating a consortium of public interest law clinics at universities in Argentina, Chile, and Peru.

Those familiar with Ford's public interest law grantmaking say it evolved from the human rights struggle of past years. "The human rights movement showed that legal and social change were possible in these countries," says Ford's former representative in Santiago, Alex Wilde. Argentine political scientist Catalina Smulovitz agrees: "The trials against the military junta showed people that results could be achieved through the judiciary." The human rights efforts of the 1970s and 1980s and the more recent public interest law developments intersect in another way: law professors from the Diego Portales Law School in Santiago, who are very active in the human rights movement, are using law to promote rights on an increasingly broader set of issues. NGOs, such as CELS, have filed test cases in areas such as discrimination against vulnerable groups and access to public information.

Ford's public interest law grantmaking is also connected to the work addressing alternative models of legal services that has sought to strengthen civil society by promoting greater access to justice. These groups engaged in efforts to organize excluded groups, teach them about their rights, and help them to obtain entitlements collectively. During the 1980s several such legal services organizations received support from the Foundation. One was the Colombian Communities Foundation, which worked with indigenous communities to defend a range of their interests, including respect for indigenous culture and title to traditional lands.

By the mid-1980s scholars and organizations outside of the human rights movement began working in other areas not covered by the then existing legal services groups. In 1986, a group of young Peruvian lawyers joined together to create the Peruvian Society for Environmental Law (SPDA), now a Foundation grantee. SPDA was dedicated to using the law in the service of environmental protection, by conducting public interest litigation, training, and public awareness campaigns. A number of legal scholars and lawyers in Argentina, Chile, and Colombia had also been exploring use of the law in the defense of the public interest.

The public interest law movement in the region developed around a strong conceptual base, demonstrating how research can lead to practical effects in seeking social justice and improving people's lives. In 1988, German Sarmiento, a well-respected Colombian lawyer, published a book arguing that the country's nineteenth-century civil code recognized the existence of "popular actions." Any citizen could file such an action if "national goods of public use" (for example, roads, public areas, and the ocean) were affected by governmental or private actions. Sarmiento's thesis inspired a group of Colombian lawyers to create an NGO, Foundation for the Defense of the Public Interest (FUNDEPUBLICO), later a Ford grantee, which gained public attention by filing popular actions in environmental cases. Attorney Ernesto Michelsen, FUNDEPUBLICO's director, explains: "In 1989, a very important law on urban reform that recognized the concept of popular actions was passed by Congress. In 1991, a new constitution expanded the concept of popular actions to include not only the protection of public spaces, but also public health, public safety, administrative probity, and the environment."

Another influential thinker in the area of public interest law was Carlos Santiago Nino, an Argentine constitutional law professor and philosopher who taught in Argentina and the United States, and whose writings introduced students and lawyers to the possibilities of using the law for social justice purposes. In 1995, a group of young Argentine lawyers who had studied or taught at universities in the United States decided to establish the Association for Civil Rights, modeled after the American Civil Liberties Union. One hundred lawyers from Buenos Aires gathered at the inaugural meeting of the association and more than one-third became permanent members. They have since brought test cases to court in collaboration with other NGOs.

Thus, by the early 1990s, some experience in the use of public interest litigation mechanisms already existed in the region. Strong expressions of interest were coming from other organizations—some of them already grantees, like the Diego Portales

Law School—that wanted to utilize litigation in the promotion of collective rights. Ford Program Officer (and now Representative) Augusto Varas opened a dialogue involving local grantees, lawyers, and other experts in the field. With Foundation support, academics, NGOs, and other institutions are now working closely to produce legal research, file test cases before the courts, and communicate the results of those cases through the mass media. And, as described below, they are training concerned groups in the use of new legal mechanisms that have recently emerged in these countries.

Public Interest Strategies

This section describes four main strategies under Ford's program framework and used by grantees of its public interest law grantmaking: impact litigation; fostering a public interest legal community; cultivating law students; and improving communications and advocacy skills. All of these strategies are anchored by Ford's ongoing efforts to strengthen civil society organizations that work on behalf of the public interest. The existence of a vigorous civil society aware of its rights and of the legal instruments that can be used to ensure public accountability is seen as a prerequisite to any public interest law project's success. Most of the organizations funded have stressed the need for some form of community participation, integral to the four strategies.

For example, Citizen Power, an Argentine organization that holds public officials accountable to citizens through monitoring and advocacy, has used community involvement to help identify cases that could have public impact. NGO representatives were part of an advisory board that met regularly during the implementation of a project testing the usefulness of existing legal mechanisms through court challenges. As Roberto Saba, then director of Citizen Power, explains, "At first, they did not come with cases, but they gave us a picture of discrimination affecting every sector of society. Now they are providing us with a lot of cases." In the first such case, Citizen Power and the Association for Civil Rights filed a writ of *amparo* in 1996, demanding the enforcement of the Law to Protect the Disabled. The case was won, and in Buenos Aires, courts were made accessible to disabled people.

Citizen Power also worked with NGOs to launch workshops

and training activities in the use of legal and procedural instruments that could promote the public interest. It collaborated with an environmental organization and a women's rights group to prepare two manuals on collective actions to defend rights in those areas. Afterwards, training in the use of these instruments was provided to law students as well as activists.

Public interest litigation can create conditions for public mobilization. SPDA and other organizations have provided legal support and contacts with international organizations to stop a Chilean firm from building a large pasta factory on the edge of the wetland known as Pantanos de Villa, Lima's only protected natural area and a haven for migratory wildfowl. In this example, SPDA's involvement complemented the political protests of residents.

For Corporation for Legal Training for Citizenship and Democracy (FORJA), litigation is just one component of a multi-faceted community effort. First, local associations of FORJA-trained and organized paralegals undertake an opinion poll among the community organizations to discover priority problems. In one locality, for instance, the target was the poor quality of local medical clinics. Next, actions are planned by neighborhood committees and sometimes the problem is brought to the attention of the local press. In this example, local residents formed a Local Health Council, which is monitoring the measures taken by the authorities to improve the management of the clinics. The matter would be taken to court only if necessary.

The community organizing aspect of these projects has faced problems. For instance, FORJA has encountered unwillingness by some municipal mayors to cooperate with their evaluations, as well as passivity on the part of some local groups. Naturally, the level of community interest depends on the issue at stake.

Strategies used by groups have become more developed over time. The four described below have been adapted to local contexts, and continue to expand and evolve.

Litigation

Varas points out that most grantees select cases that involve a public interest issue (usually not a conflict between two private parties); have potential for serving as a model for the future; primarily deal with the interpretation of constitutional rights; will draw public and media attention; and utilize, where possible, interpretation of international human rights agreements.

Early cases targeted relatively noncontroversial issues to generate broad public support and to avoid negative reactions that might even result in legislation that could create additional obstacles to filing of this type of legal action. The several discrimination cases involving disability filed by Citizen Power and the Association for Civil Rights received wide support from the public and press because the plaintiffs inspired public sympathy.

Other litigation efforts have targeted the very centers of power. In Colombia, FUNDEPUBLICO has expanded its class action portfolio to include cases of official corruption. These suits were based on a Constitutional Court decision permitting such actions in the event of collective injury, such as government corruption. FUNDEPUBLICO's victories in this area have included a notable case involving the irregular privatization of state mining interests.

All lawyers interviewed recognize that they face several obstacles in their work, such as court delays, occasional judicial ignorance, and even corruption. Moreover, lawyers involved in public interest law issues are still a minority within the legal profession. Their assessment, as well as that of independent observers, is that by selecting viable test cases they are making inroads, gaining press attention, and providing vulnerable groups with a measure of access to justice. Rodrigo Uprimy, an auxiliary judge of Colombia's Constitutional Court, states, "These types of class actions are significantly different from the highly partisan rhetoric used to defend human rights in Colombia. They are more accessible to the common citizen."

Despite the ongoing challenges, grantees have won significant courtroom rulings. For example, Argentina's CELS asked the administrative court, a branch of the judiciary that deals principally with reviewing the legality of governmental actions, to order the Minister of the Interior to release information on the number of people detained by the Federal Police in Buenos Aires. The petition was granted, and the police gave all the information requested. In another pertinent case, CELS lawyers sought to force the national government to fulfill its duties to make available a vaccine for an illness that could affect three million people. The lower court dismissed the case after the Ministry of Health announced that it would eventually produce the vaccine. CELS appealed, and the court of appeals ordered the public agencies involved to keep the court informed of progress on the vaccine's production.

Public interest lawyers hope that another benefit of their work will be a better educated judiciary. For litigation to be successful, there is a need to familiarize judges with the concept of public interest law, as well as with judicial decisions in other countries regarding new collective rights such as the right to a clean environment, consumer protections, and socioeconomic rights. This can be partially achieved through the legal arguments presented to the judges. As Michelsen explains, "We are performing an educational role, directed towards the judges and other public authorities. The enactment of a new constitution in 1991 and the legal rules that regulate this constitution are relatively new and complex. Sometimes even the authorities find it difficult to interpret these rules in the right way." Judge Uprimy maintains that actions that force the judges to apply constitutional norms, which may have various interpretations, also encourage implementation of a new methodology of interpretation that has significantly changed judges' perspectives on human rights.

Building a Legal Community

Another important Ford effort has been to create and expand a community of lawyers interested in public interest litigation. From the inception the grantmaking program on public interest law stressed the need to develop a multinational network of academics, institutions, and legal practitioners that shared information regarding their practice with counterparts in the region. The work of this network seems to have profited because of the fact that it was established just as some members were first beginning to engage in public interest litigation. According to Martin Bohmer from Argentina's Palermo University Law School clinic, which is part of the network, this helps ensure the affinity and shared interest of all participants, as well as their commitment to common goals in countries with different political contexts.

The network effort coordinated by the Diego Portales Law School started with a pilot in late 1995. During its first stage, four local workshops were held in Bogotá, Buenos Aires, Lima, and Santiago, while an international and comparative law seminar also took place in Santiago. This stage was instrumental in identifying further steps to involve law schools more permanently around public interest law initiatives. As a result, in December 1996, a second phase was initiated in Argentina, Chile, and Peru. The program established a network of university clinics on public interest law, involving litigation, clinical exchange, and research. Professors and students work within each country and also interact in regional meetings with their counterparts in other countries. Professors heading these clinics are encouraged to spend three to four weeks at a U.S. law school clinic with extensive public interest law experience.

Abregu of CELS says that the international exchange has been very productive in terms of encouraging participants to reflect on what they were doing or had accomplished. Exchanges between clinics have led to uniform criteria for selecting test cases and have drawn attention to the use of the international law covenants applicable to the issues. Bohmer believes that these international linkages among law schools create a common language among activists, lawyers, and academics. However, one law professor interviewed considered the national meetings of clinics to be more useful, given the different stage of development of public interest litigation in each country.

At the same time, both NGOs and law schools involved in the program are expanding their contacts with government officials, as well as with lawyers in private practice. For example, the Office for the Defense of the Rights of Women (DEMUS), a Peruvian grantee, has developed a fruitful relationship with the Ministry of the Interior and has implemented training courses for the police in Lima. DEMUS also collaborates closely with the ombudsman's office in a Ford-funded research project on gender discrimination in the law. In Chile, the law clinic from the Catholic University of Temuco signed agreements with governmental organizations such as the National Women's Service, the National Consumers' Service, and the National Corporation for the Development of Indigenous People in order to investigate

cases involving gender discrimination, consumer rights violations, and racial discrimination.

Grantees have also involved private lawyers in their efforts.
In August 1997, the Catholic University of Lima law clinic established cooperative agreements with the Peruvian Society of
Environmental Law (another Ford grantee), and a private law firm
well known for pro bono litigation. In July 1997, Chile's Diego
Portales law clinic organized a meeting with several lawyers in
private practice to inform them about their work. The lawyers
offered advice on the process of selecting cases, discussed possible courtroom collaborations, and suggested that the law school
offer a course on public interest law for judges. In another promising collaboration, an agreement was developed between
FORJA, the Chilean bar, and the National Foundation to
Overcome Poverty to engage private lawyers in providing legal
representation in public interest law cases. Those involved have
suggested these collaborative experiences are advances in the
movement to promote the rule of law in Latin America.

Training Law Students

Grantees also help fill the need for public interest lawyers by
investing in the education of new lawyers who are better trained
and more socially aware. In contrast with the law and development experience, the aim is not to transform law school teaching
methods, but to encourage the formation of public interest law
clinics that attract a small number of interested students to work
with NGOs in the preparation of test cases that could have social
impact. Through their participation in the clinics and contact with
NGOs, it is hoped that these students will remain engaged in public interest law, or at least become legal practitioners who are
aware of the problems of poor and disadvantaged communities.

As of this writing, a network of eight Foundation-supported
public interest legal clinics exist in Argentina, Chile, and Peru.
Although the number of students in each clinic is quite limited,
professors in charge of the clinical work hope that the number
will increase as the arena of public interest law becomes better
known.

The launching of law clinics benefited from international

experiences. The Palermo University law clinic was created by Martin Bohmer, a former graduate student at Yale University Law School, who gained familiarity at Yale with the role and functioning of law clinics. Yale law students visiting Buenos Aires helped Bohmer plan the clinic's launch.

Many of those in the consortium of law clinics believe that participants have gained useful comparative insights from the several decades of U.S. clinical experience to which they have been exposed. The U.S. participants in consortium seminars have shared with the network members aspects of clinical organization and student involvement in litigation, as well as their own clinical teaching methodologies.

These clinics are important for several reasons, observers say. They improve access to justice by providing legal representation on important policy issues that may not receive attention from any other public or private agency. Second, they improve the legal training process, since the students involved must carry out complex legal and even interdisciplinary research in order to bring a test case to court. The teacher's involvement in the process can also have a positive impact on his or her teaching abilities. These clinics also provide the students with exposure to NGOs, since all the universities have established agreements to cooperate with NGOs to bring cases with public impact.

Yet the reality is that current conditions force most new lawyers into private practice with little chance of practicing what they learned in the field of public interest law. Few NGOs or public interest law firms today offer new lawyers positions after graduation. Still, the graduates' clinical experience might at least lead them to offer their own services on a pro bono basis in public interest cases.

Influencing Public Opinion

Lawyers involved in public interest law work are aware that the communication component of each project is essential. In the Continental European legal systems prevalent in the region, one court's decision does not necessarily carry weight in other courts, so the possibility of influencing future judicial decisions comes at least partly from public pressure.

A working relationship between the mass media and such NGOs is crucial, and many discussed here have media units, which have been successful in publicizing their work. The drawback of press coverage is that it usually focuses on only the most dramatic aspects of a case and educational opportunities to showcase effective legal remedies are sometimes lost. Members of Citizen Power have discussed two strategies to help ameliorate the problem. One is promoting their own philosophy through opinion pieces published in various media. Another is holding seminars for journalists about public interest law generally and the litigation in question, stressing the potential contribution to a democracy of citizens who can act directly to defend and promote their rights.

Conclusion

Changes and Contributions

The vision and courage of Ford grantees described above have led to significant successes in their efforts to further human rights and social justice. By the late 1990s, a cohesive and growing community of organizations and lawyers was involved in advocacy, education, community organizing, litigation, and policy work in the public interest. Discussions about human rights issues in these countries have become more informed and more open than in the past. Academics, law faculties, NGOs, and professional organizations have joined this dialogue. More important, these programs have produced concrete improvements in the lives of affected populations.

These achievements must be balanced by considering some obstacles still faced by the grantees. The human rights and public interest law communities are still small, and their influence on policy limited. While Ford support has contributed to a better and more frequent use of legal and social actions that demand accountability from the government and large enterprises, many lawyers still report that citizens remain distrustful of judiciaries, and are reluctant to use all the legal instruments available.

Following are some of the insights and lessons that have emerged from this study.

Lessons and Insights

Legal Strategies

1. Even under repressive regimes, law-related NGOs can have substantial impact in promoting democracy and human rights. Legal representation of victims of repression was one of the most important strategies under authoritarian regimes in the region. Lawyers provided support to the victims and their relatives, gathered and disseminated factual information on the patterns of repression, and prepared cases to be presented before international human rights bodies. Their work generated significant international pressure that helped lead to diminished state repression.

2. Law-related NGOs pursuing human rights concerns can go beyond denunciation and confrontation with the government and foster communication with all sectors of society. NGOs can be effective beyond their usual circles of interaction.

3. Research on controversial issues can serve several important functions. It can affect policy and stimulate debate on institutional reform when more direct reform strategies are untenable, as in Chile during the early 1990s. Support for research also broadens the community of people actively engaged in human rights issues.

4. In the countries covered by this chapter, efforts to enhance public accountability have effectively combined the use of various strategies. Litigation, in particular, is best accompanied by other activities, due to the extensive time required and the possibility of losing the case. Moreover, even if the case is won, there is no guarantee that similar cases will be decided the same way in nonprecedent-based legal systems.

5. Most of the organizations funded have stressed the need for some form of community participation. Community-based groups can help legal activists and scholars identify

cases and facilitate training activities to popularize the use of public interest law. Litigation can also aid public mobilization by providing legal advice and support to community groups that are challenging strong commercial and political interests.

6. Initially, lawyers bringing public interest litigation in this region have focused on popular causes to enhance the potential for positive press coverage and to encourage broad public support.

7. Despite the institutional obstacles that public interest litigation faces in the region, the possibilities for cases to be won on their own merits are increasing. Many cases filed by grantees discussed here have resulted in favorable rulings or created pressure to implement reforms.

8. Public interest litigation can be one means to educate the judiciary. Moreover, training seminars can help raise judges' awareness of public interest law concepts and acquaint them with court rulings in other countries regarding new legal developments.

9. University law clinics have exposed future lawyers to public interest law, provided support to groups that lack resources to hire lawyers, and raised issues often neglected by the broader legal community, such as environmental problems and gender discrimination. Clinics have also improved the training of law students by requiring them to conduct research in support of test cases.

Donor Programming Approaches and Roles

1. Donors can best support law-related efforts by choosing grantee partners who remain nonpartisan while consistently demonstrating commitment to causes for which they advocate. Those NGOs that rejected violence and produced impartial reports on human rights conditions have earned credibility for their work both domestically and internationally.

2. Donor efforts to facilitate contact among grantees at the regional level have proved useful in increasing both the local and regional impact of their work. The network of regional law clinics cited in the case study particularly

benefited from participation of all members at the inception of the network.

3. Donors providing long-term and continued support can help grantee organizations through important transitions as evidenced in this region by the successful transformations of CELS and others.

The strategies pursued by Ford grantees discussed here have promoted the rule of law and helped build a civil society more aware of its rights and the legal instruments available to defend them. This work is vital if countries in the region are to continue on the path toward democracy.

Notes

1. James A. Gardner, *Legal Imperialism: American Lawyers and Foreign Aid in Latin America* (Madison, Wisconsin: University of Wisconsin Press, 1980), p. 66.
2. Michael Shifter, "Colombia at War," *Current History,* March 1999, p. 116.
3. *Public Interest Actions in the Andean and Southern Cone Region: An Overview of the Emerging Field of Public Interest Law in Latin America* (Santiago, Chile: The Ford Foundation, 1997), p. 3.

Appendix: People Interviewed for the Case Study

Martin Abregu
Director, Center for Legal and Social Studies, Buenos Aires

Eduardo Aldana
Professor, Los Andes University, Bogotá

Carlos Basombrío
Former Director, Legal Defense Institute, Lima

Enrique Bernales, Sara Sotelo, and Denisse Ledgard
Lawyers, Andean Commission of Jurists, Lima

Martin Bohmer
Professor, Palermo University Law School, Buenos Aires

Diego Carrazco, Juan Pablo Olmedo, Pedro Vera, and Sebastian Cox
Staff, Corporation for Legal Training for Citizenship and Democracy (FORJA), Santiago

Alejandro Carrio
President, the Argentine Association of Civil Rights, Buenos Aires

Camilo Castellanos
Director, Latin American Legal Services Association, Bogotá

Gaston Chillier and Marcela Rodriguez
Staff, Center for Legal and Social Studies, Buenos Aires

Marcel Claude
Director, Terram Foundation, Santiago

Gino Costa
Deputy Ombudsman for Human Rights, Ombudsman's Office, Lima

Lorena Fries and Veronica Matus
Staff, Women's Development Corporation (La Morada), Santiago

Ronald Gamarra
Lawyer, Legal Defense Institute, Lima

Felipe Gonzalez, Felipe Viveros, and Jorge Correa
Law Professors, Diego Portales Law School, Santiago

Gorki González
Professor in charge of the Public Interest Law Clinic, Catholic University Law School, Lima

Miguel Huertas
Adjunct to the Executive Secretariat of the National Coordinator of Human Rights, Lima

Ernesto de la Jara
Director, Legal Defense Institute, Lima

Beatriz Kohen and Roberto Saba
Professionals in charge of the Public Interest Law Program,
Citizen Power, Buenos Aires

Francisco Leal
Vice Rector, University of Los Andes, Bogotá

Desiderio Lopez and Daniel Medina
Advisors, Defensor del Pueblo (Ombudsman), Bogotá

Ernesto Michelsen
Director, Foundation for the Defense of the Public Interest
(FUNDEPUBLICO), Bogotá

Emilio Mignone
Former President, Center for Legal and Social Studies, Buenos
Aires

Hector Moncayo
Former President, Latin American Institute of Alternative Legal
Services Association, Bogotá

Luis Moreno Ocampo
President, Citizen Power, Buenos Aires

Alicia Oliveira
Lawyer, Center for Legal and Social Studies, Buenos Aires, now
Ombudsman of the City of Buenos Aires

Juan Pablo Olmedo and Clovis Montero
Staff, Terram Foundation

Carlos Rodriguez
Deputy Director, Colombian Commission of Jurists, Bogotá

Rosa Rosenblitt and other staff
Grandmothers of Plaza de Mayo, Buenos Aires

Marcial Rubio
Vice Rector, Catholic University, Lima

Judge Alicia Ruiz
and other lawyers who participated in a research project on women's rights directed by Haydee Birgin at the Local Development Studies Center, Buenos Aires

Michael Shifter
Former Program Officer, Andean Region and the Southern Cone, The Ford Foundation

Catalina Smulovitz
Professor of Political Science, Torcuato Di Tella University, Buenos Aires

Adolfo Triana
Director, Colombian Communities Foundation, Bogotá

Rodrigo Uprimy
Auxiliary Judge, Constitutional Court, Bogotá

Augusto Varas
Representative, The Ford Foundation, Santiago

Roxana Vasquez
Director, Office for the Defense of the Rights of Women (DEMUS), Lima

Manuel Pulgar Vidal
Director, Peruvian Society of Environmental Law, Lima

Gustavo Villalobos
Former Chief of the Legal Department, Vicariate of Solidarity, Santiago

Rocio Villanueva
Specialized Defender of the Rights of Women, Ombudsman's Office, Lima

Alex Wilde
Former Representative, Andean Region and the Southern Cone, The Ford Foundation, Santiago; now, Vice President, Communications, The Ford Foundation, New York

José Zalaquett
Professor of Law, University of Chile, Santiago

3

Rights into Action: Public Interest Litigation in the United States

HELEN HERSHKOFF & DAVID HOLLANDER

This chapter examines the Ford Foundation's support of groups that use litigation to promote equality and justice for racial minorities, women, and immigrants in the United States. Since becoming a national foundation in the 1950s, Ford has played an important role in supporting the efforts of inspired civil rights lawyers to develop a network of organizations dedicated to using law to improve conditions and to promote equality for historically marginalized groups. Through seed funding, core financial support, and capacity-building grants, the Foundation has helped to sustain these organizations during the changing political climate of the late twentieth century. Although the Foundation supports a broad set of strategies in its U.S. law programming—including public education, community organizing, and coalition building—this case study focuses on Ford's support of litigation to effect social reform. Moreover, although Ford's promotion of law-based work spans the nearly half century of the Foundation's history, this case study focuses on the 1980s and 1990s, and is current as of mid-1999.

Ford's support of groups undertaking public interest litigation in the United States draws on a moral commitment shared by the Foundation and its grantees to social justice and to rule of law values. It also rests on the pragmatic view that judicially precipitated reform can help to remove discriminatory barriers, to expand opportunities, and to improve conditions for historically underrepresented groups. The Foundation recognizes, however, that the concept of social change is ambiguous; the literature on public interest litigation offers no single definition of "success." Some commentators criticize public interest litigation as a failed strategy that short-circuits the political process and produces few, if any, long-lasting successes. Reading the same evidence, other commentators declare victory for civil rights litigation, but urge a refocusing of effort on public education, legislative reform, and political mobilization. Still others point to litigation's unintended adverse consequences—including bitter political opposition—and emphasize the need for consensual solutions to divisive social problems. Finally, some observers recognize the limits of court-initiated reform, but recommend its continued support as part of a multipronged strategy to expand social justice and to preserve victories against erosion and assault.

This case study addresses many of these concerns. Looking at the work of some of the Foundation's grantees over the last two decades, the study illustrates the process of public interest litigation in the United States and identifies some of the factors framing its strategic use. The study does not claim to be scientific or comprehensive; it does not discuss, for example, Ford's significant support of legal services for the poor during this period. Nor does the case study provide an audit of grantee work. Rather, through a sampling of the Foundation's law grantees—in women's rights, minority rights, and immigrant and refugee rights—the authors glean lessons from the use of litigation to change public policy; to enforce, implement, and monitor change; and to mobilize and empower members of historically disadvantaged groups. The authors conclude that public interest litigation has been and remains integral to a holistic social change strategy that may also include community mobilization, leadership and economic development, media outreach, policy analysis, and empirical research.

The chapter first provides a brief institutional history of Ford's support of civil rights litigation in the United States and then describes the adjudicative campaigns of particular grantees in such diverse fields as school finance reform, reproductive choice, and land-use planning. Within specific U.S. contexts, the study then discusses the strengths and weaknesses of litigation as a social change strategy and explores how grantees have used media and other public education activities to mitigate some of the potential risks and disadvantages of court-based activities. Finally, the study draws some general lessons that may be of use to advocates, donors, and policy analysts in considering when, whether, and how to use public interest litigation as a way to support social change. The chapter concludes with a brief look at future challenges, emphasizing the need for continued and sustained philanthropic support of public interest litigation as part of a social change strategy for historically marginalized groups.

Brief History of Ford's
U.S. Law-Related Grantmaking Program

Ford's support for law-based programs in the United States began in earnest in the early 1960s, with a primary focus on legal services for the poor. During that time, the Foundation launched its comprehensive "Gray Areas" program to combat urban poverty at the grassroots level by providing a wide array of legal, educational, medical, and other social services. The Gray Areas initiatives became the model for many of the Great Society programs, including the Legal Services Corporation. In 1965, Ford helped to establish the Center on Social Welfare Policy and Law, with the goal of using test case litigation to precipitate systemic change in the welfare system. Under the leadership of Edward Sparer, later a professor of law at the University of Pennsylvania, the center had a hand in many of the landmark poor people's due process cases of the late 1960s, and also provided backup services to frontline neighborhood legal services offices around the country.

McGeorge Bundy, who became the Foundation's president in 1966, spearheaded a substantial increase in the Foundation's grantmaking to minority rights groups in the United States, from only 2.5 percent of its annual giving in 1960, to 36.5 percent in 1968. A significant portion of this increase during the eight-year period went to litigation designed to ensure equal access to voting, education, employment, housing, and the administration of justice. The increasing emphasis on civil rights litigation reflected Bundy's view that the law "must be an active, not a passive force" for social change. Substantial grants went to the National Association for the Advancement of Colored People Legal Defense and Educational Fund, Inc. (LDF), and to the Mississippi office of the Lawyers' Committee for Civil Rights Under Law. Litigation comprised a key part of these groups' multipronged strategy, which also included support for improving minority leadership; promoting policy-oriented research on race and poverty; and expanding the availability of legal resources to disadvantaged communities.[1]

Recognizing the distinct needs of other ethnic groups and interests, Ford provided grantees start-up funds during the years 1968–1972 to establish seven new civil rights groups: the Mexican American Legal Defense and Educational Fund; the Southwest Council of La Raza; the Native American Rights Fund; the Puerto Rican Legal Defense and Educational Fund; the Women's Law Fund; the National Committee Against Discrimination in Housing; and the Legal Action Center. The Foundation also provided a seed grant to the Center for National Policy Review, which monitored federal agency action under civil rights and equal opportunity legislation. In providing funds to help create this broad civil rights network, the Foundation's aim was to support organizations, rather than particular cases, leaving decisions about actual lawsuits and specific strategies to the grantees themselves, a policy that continues to the present.

In 1979, Franklin Thomas became president of the Foundation. His tenure coincided with internal budget reductions, caused by the recession of the 1970s, and began just one year before the election of Ronald Reagan as U.S. president. Observing that the Foundation's law initiatives addressed some of society's most "sensitive and unyielding problems," Thomas emphasized that the quest for equality and justice remained "incomplete." He reaffirmed Ford's support for civil rights groups that use law for social reform, focusing the Foundation's domestic law programs on three goals: to advance the substantive legal agenda of the civil rights community; to enhance legal services for the poor; and to build the capacity of minorities, women, refugees and immigrants, and the poor to advocate on their own behalf.

During Thomas's tenure, "support for public interest law became a means to impact the lives of vulnerable groups in which the Foundation had a growing interest, rather than an end in and of itself," explains Lynn Walker Huntley, former director of the Foundation's Rights and Social Justice Program. In continuing to support the national civil rights groups that it had helped provide funding to establish, the Foundation underscored the importance of their organic links to community, as well as their established track records of success. At the same time, Ford encouraged these grantees to develop new strategies, especially in the areas of education, employment, and housing, and to take greater account of the overlapping significance of race, class, and cultural characteristics.

Theodore M. Shaw, associate director–counsel of LDF, observes that 1980 marked "the end of a period in which civil rights litigation was viewed expansively and offensively, and [the beginning of] another in which by necessity it was viewed less expansively and defensively." The nation's political retrenchment from certain social programs presented the civil rights community with challenges on several fronts. The government had earlier been an ally of civil rights advance in court, through research, and by enforcing and monitoring antidiscrimination laws. After 1980, the Justice Department frequently opposed civil rights groups in court. As the President made appointments to the federal bench, the judiciary increasingly reflected the nation's ambivalence toward civil rights. New and well-funded opposition groups filed their own lawsuits seeking to reverse earlier gains. At the same time, financial cuts in programs for the poor and in legal services highlighted the importance of including issues of poverty, as well as race, in the broader civil rights agenda.

Political opposition and legal challenges—in such key areas as employment opportunity, reproductive choice, and fair treatment of immigrants—badly strained the financial capacity of Ford's grantees. By providing core and occasional project-based support, the Foundation afforded grantees maximum flexibility in designing and administering law programs as the social and political contexts of their work changed. Although grantees report that a triage mentality dominated their efforts throughout the 1980s, many groups—seemingly against all odds—scored important court victories on antidiscrimination issues and also secured the extension of civil rights law.

To address this evolving situation, many groups also began to explore new issues and to complement litigation with public education and community mobilization activities. The American Civil Liberties Union (ACLU) and others expanded voter registration efforts, and also focused attention on the discriminatory barriers raised by the use of standardized tests in jobs and schools. In addition, during this period, the Foundation helped expand and sustain the civil rights infrastructure of nongovernmental organizations. In the early 1980s, Ford funding enabled the National Women's Law Center to become a freestanding organization, and helped establish groups with litigation capacity to represent refugees and immigrants. The Foundation provided support to encourage churches (or faith communities) to respond to the needs of the black community, and gave funds to enable groups to conduct research about Latinos and to build public support for and leadership skills within that community.

The election of Bill Clinton as president in 1992 did not stem challenges to civil rights. A conservative federal judiciary was now in place. Federal legislators—especially after the 1994 election—passed a series of laws that sharply diminished the federal "safety net" for poor people, imposed tough restrictions on immigrants, cut funding for legal services, and blocked access to judicial review even for certain constitutional claims. Ford increased its financial commitment to preserve and promote the interests of the disadvantaged, maintaining high levels of core support for some groups, and moving to project-based support for others.

Recognizing Asian Pacific Americans as the nation's fastest growing minority group, Ford helped to establish the National Asian Pacific American Legal Consortium in 1993. At the same time, Ford placed increased emphasis on intergroup relations among minorities, identifying important issues for additional support and fostering coalitional efforts on matters of broad concern. For example, in anticipation of the myriad legal issues that would be presented by the 1990 census, and out of concern that minorities would be adversely affected when voting districts were redrawn, the Foundation initiated a $2 million campaign for grantees to support education, monitoring, advocacy, technical assistance, and litigation in the area of voting rights.

Throughout these years, other national and local foundations also gave support to public interest litigation and related strategies. Some foundations provided grants for targeted projects. At the national level, a few key donors provided sustained support; they included the Rockefeller Foundation and the Carnegie Corporation.

In 1996, Susan Berresford became president of the Ford Foundation. As executive vice president of the Foundation for many years, she was well placed to provide strong support for civil rights and to lead Ford into the next century. In the final years of the 1990s, the Foundation encouraged grantees to rethink their basic missions, urging even greater attention to the relationships among race, gender, and class that could especially impact historically marginalized groups. As federal powers began devolving to the states, Ford also helped grantees explore ways to work in state government policy contexts that potentially afforded new opportunities for community involvement. Finally, Ford encouraged grantees to forge linkages with the academic community, business, and community groups to develop new partnerships for social reform.

"It is essential that the Foundation take a long-term approach to funding public interest litigation in the United States, while at the same time encouraging grantees to pursue new directions and strategies," says Anthony Romero, the Foundation's director of Human Rights and International Cooperation. "That's why the work we're doing now is as pressing as when we first started in the 1960s."

A Sampling of Grantee Activities:
Three Dimensions of Court-Based Strategies

More than 150 years ago, Alexis de Tocqueville observed, "There is hardly a political question in the United States which does not sooner or later turn into a judicial one." One of the great advances in American society in the last half century has been the creation of a network of civil rights organizations that enables historically marginalized groups to participate in this national judicial process. Legal advocacy can encourage democratic possibilities that are often blocked by discrimination and disadvantage. Civil rights groups thus use litigation strategically to create leverage for their constituents, promoting political and social goals that afford disadvantaged minorities a stronger place in society.

By the start of the 1980s, civil rights groups had largely secured a set of rights aimed at ensuring the formal perquisites of social and political equality. But poverty and inequality persisted, and Congress and the courts resisted efforts to remedy entrenched private practices that blocked movement toward further economic and social equality. After years of trying to use court decrees to reform public institutions—whether by desegregating public schools or improving health and safety conditions at mental hospitals—advocates accepted that litigation is a blunt tool requiring years of tedious enforcement proceedings. Indeed, because legal categories do not always correspond to social needs, litigation sometimes seemed to impede or distort policy goals. Moreover, the public's tendency to view litigation as a "winner takes all" game contributed to a sense that civil rights efforts fueled unnecessary divisiveness, which contributed to backlash. Finally, whether because of "docket fatigue" or other reasons, the federal courts no longer appeared receptive to egalitarian arguments, increasingly raising procedural barriers to relief that impeded further progress. The changed political climate of the 1980s required grantees to reconsider not only many of their substantive goals, but their strategies as well.

Yet, even as grantees devoted more resources to public education, community organizing, and administrative advocacy, they did not abandon litigation as a tool to advance civil rights. As Marcia Greenberger, copresident of the National Women's Law Center (NWLC), explains, "A concrete case could provide a way of highlighting the importance of a legal principle in the context of a real set of facts and actual people affected by the outcome. A case could serve to rally press and public attention to the legal principle at stake." In some instances, civil rights groups resorted to litigation to block the government's enforcement of unfavorable laws, such as efforts to challenge the 1986 immigration restrictions and Proposition 187 (a California referendum that attempted to bar undocumented immigrants from basic health and educational services). In other areas, grantees turned to state courts and to state constitutions for new sources of civil rights protection. In many instances, traditional civil rights groups could no longer control when and where they would raise particular issues in court; opposition groups frequently filed their own lawsuits, and grantees had to intervene in such actions to preserve past victories. As civil rights groups matured, they struggled with mixed success to mitigate the risks of litigation, and their litigation goals evolved over time to accommodate new realities of public opinion and judicial philosophy.

Public Interest Litigation and Public Policy Reform

Ever since the National Association for the Advancement of Colored People (NAACP) first mounted its litigation campaign against segregation, the public has associated the courts with the power to change social life. Civil rights groups use different techniques to trigger the process of judicially precipitated reform. Test cases can establish precedents that will apply to many individuals. Class actions with many, often thousands, of plaintiffs allow the interests of a broad group of people to be addressed in one proceeding. Individual lawsuits have the potential to declare new rights and to extend a legal principle into new areas. In addition, civil rights groups must sometimes litigate defensively to preserve reform or to block harmful policies. And in some cases, Ford grantees appear as amicus curiae—as "friends of the court"—to explain or emphasize important issues.

The court-based struggles of Ford grantees show that litigation is an imperfect strategy constrained by many factors. Yet, in certain situations, it remains unclear whether noncourt strategies can prove successful without support from—or the threat of—litigation. Even when a lawsuit fails in court, it can help publicize issues, mobilize constituents, garner resources, and legitimate an outsider's position, thereby endowing disadvantaged groups with forms of political capital.

This section looks at three adjudicative campaigns mounted by Ford grantees that, among other things, have helped reform public education, advance reproductive choice, and extend fair treatment to immigrants.

Using State Courts to Reform Public Schools. After the desegregation battles of the 1950s and 1960s, it became apparent that despite the end of formal segregation, schools in the poorest areas, many primarily composed of minorities, lacked resources to provide their students meaningful educational opportunity. American schools are largely financed by local property taxes, with the result that significant disparities exist between rich and poor school districts. Litigation efforts in the 1960s and early 1970s to reform school finance systems faltered when the U.S. Supreme Court refused to locate a right to education in the Constitution, and efforts to effect reform through state legislatures likewise achieved very limited success. In the 1990s, students in one poor Alabama school district still used decades-old textbooks predicting that one day man would walk on the moon.

Ford's long-standing commitment to education reform began with grants in the 1950s to study the effects of segregation, and continued with multimillion-dollar support for research, training, advocacy, and litigation in the 1970s. In the late 1980s, a Ford grant enabled the ACLU to work with school finance economists to develop an empirical base for a new litigation strategy aimed at enforcing a state constitutional right to an adequate education. Unlike the U.S. Constitution, every state constitution explicitly requires the establishment of free public schools. The ACLU's goal was to leverage these state constitutional clauses into an enforceable right to a quality education.

Since 1989, the ACLU has commenced state court challenges in Alabama, Connecticut, Louisiana, Maryland, and New York, and, as amicus curiae, in Massachusetts and California. While the outcomes vary from state to state, courts have typically upheld the principle of educational equity and adequacy. In Alabama, the court invalidated an earlier state constitutional amendment that eliminated any state right to free public education, on the ground that it was a blatant attempt to circumvent the historic 1954 U.S. Supreme Court desegregation ruling, *Brown v. Board of Education.* (*Brown* declared unconstitutional state laws that allow public school districts to separate students by race.) In a later ruling, the Alabama court defined the content of Alabama's state constitutional education right in terms of nine capacities that the state must develop in all children through appropriately funded programs of instruction. In Maryland, the lawsuit precipitated a historic negotiated agreement among the parties, requiring management reform and increased state funding for public schools. In Connecticut, the court's order triggered a statewide planning process on how best to improve school quality through regional integration.

The ultimate goal of assuring quality education for every child in America has remained the same all along. When legislatures failed to do what was necessary to make that goal a reality, public interest lawyers stepped in. Says ACLU Legal Director Steven R. Shapiro, "Education litigation has become increasingly sophisticated, moving from the desegregation cases, to fiscal equity, to educational adequacy. The problem has changed over time, but the ACLU has a real commitment not to abandon the field."

Litigating for Reproductive Choice. The U.S. Supreme Court's 1973 decision in *Roe v. Wade,* establishing a woman's right to make reproductive choices, marked only the beginning of a long political struggle in the United States. Given the profound moral issues that abortion presents, the Court's decision provoked bitter opposition from churches and in Congress. With the help of Ford and other donors, Janet Benshoof established the Center for Reproductive Law & Policy in 1992 to advance women's reproductive rights. Benshoof has been litigating for reproductive choice since her days as a staff attorney at the ACLU Women's Rights Project. "In 1977," she says, "I was given a grant by John D. Rockefeller III to ensure that *Roe v. Wade* was implemented in all fifty states—a task that he thought, and I naively agreed, could be finished in a year! It wasn't long before we realized that advancing women's reproductive freedom would involve a life-long commitment."

Commentators sometimes refer to abortion as the classic example of litigation moving ahead of community norms and causing a political backlash. Opposition to abortion is deeply felt and highly mobilized. Benshoof observes, "There is no other issue in which the other side has galvanized so much money." Nevertheless, the center stands firm in its belief that litigation is an essential component of that struggle in the United States.

Simon Heller, the center's director of litigation, says the center's main work involves Supreme Court advocacy to preserve

Roe and the structure of reproductive rights that it protects. In support of that goal, the center also undertakes varied strategies, including litigating "service" cases that secure pro-choice policies for individual women to make sure that policies are enforced "on the ground." Yet as Anika Rahman, its international program director, cautions, "Litigation is likely ultimately to fail if there isn't along with it a public education campaign effort. At the end of the day, the most important thing is to ensure that the general public supports your goals and objectives."

An important center priority has been to restore full reproductive rights to low-income women in the wake of the elimination of federal Medicaid funding for abortion. Within days of being contacted by a poor woman in Montana who had become pregnant after being raped, the center flew its lawyers to Montana and obtained a state court injunction, mandating that the state pay for the abortion she sought. Center staff used the case, based on the state constitution, to educate the public through the media about the extreme circumstances poor women can face. Eventually, complete restoration of Medicaid funding for reproductive choice in Montana was achieved. By 1996, 40 percent of women in the United States lived in states that provided public funding for abortion.

Defending the Rights of Immigrants. The civil rights revolution that began with *Brown* has never fully penetrated the realm of immigration law. Because noncitizens are a highly marginalized group, lacking even the right to vote, legislatures and courts often do not always respond to their needs. Beginning in 1982, Ford provided support to maintain and expand an infrastructure of national and regional legal organizations that help monitor and ensure the equitable enforcement of immigration laws. Among them is the ACLU Immigrants' Rights Project, a grantee since its founding in 1983. "There's enormous judicial deference in the area of immigration that doesn't exist in other civil rights areas," says Lucas Guttentag, its director, explaining that courts typically accept the policy judgments of the other branches of government in the immigration area. "But there have been significant advances. And I think the question is, where would we be without that litigation effort? And where we would be is absolutely nowhere."

With plaintiffs generally poor, legal fees limited by the federal attorney's fee statute, and the issues to be litigated unusually complicated, the vast majority of reform litigation in the area has been brought by immigration lawyers dependent on foundation support. By necessity, much of the work is defensive or reactive. Yet grantees have scored some dramatic victories. In the early 1980s, several class actions successfully challenged aspects of the asylum process. Under a landmark case initiated in the 1980s involving Haitian refugees, a court ordered the government to reprocess 5,000 asylum applications in a way that would comply with fundamental due process. The 1982 landmark case of *Plyler v. Doe* established the principle that it is unconstitutional to deny undocumented children a free public education. Later, in a case involving Salvadoran refugees, the United States Immigration and Naturalization Service was barred through a settlement in 1991 from manipulating refugees into abandoning their right to seek political asylum.

In 1996, a tidal wave of unfavorable federal legislation hit the immigrant community. Popularly backed federal legislation to control illegal immigration and to reduce welfare rolls also eviscerated the rights of legal immigrants. The combined effect of three extremely complex and overlapping new laws left the underfunded immigration law community reeling. Organizations such as the ACLU and the National Immigration Law Center, an organization providing expertise on the rights of immigrants to public entitlements, divided up areas of responsibility in responding to the laws. On the litigation front, the ACLU, with other groups, challenged some of the new statutes' provisions that block immigrant access to judicial relief. Other advocates persuaded Congress to restore some of the categories of public assistance that the 1996 act eliminated. Many states have since agreed to replace some of the eliminated federal funding with state funds.

Taryn Higashi, Ford Foundation Refugee and Migrant Rights program officer, explains: "Lawyers have been central to all these strategies because immigration laws are so complicated. . . . Even though many issues are driven and shaped by public opinion and politics, without a lawyer to parse the laws, you just can't move." Because of Ford and other donor support, stable immigrants' rights institutions, staffed by seasoned experts who knew and trusted one another, were in place when the crises hit, and they cooperated to meet the immigrants' legal needs.

Public Interest Litigation to
Implement, Enforce, and Monitor Change

Public policies and laws are not typically self-executing. Time and again, a law is passed, or a judicial decree is issued, and little or nothing changes. Part of the problem is that legal norms are often expressed in general or open-ended terms, leaving implementation of statutory requirements to the discretionary decisions of many individuals, officials, and bureaucrats. Moreover, on some issues, opposition organizes and actively hinders implementation.

"If there's anything we've learned it's that it's not enough to be instrumental in creating a principle or policy," says Nancy Davis, former executive director of Equal Rights Advocates (ERA), a Ford grantee that litigated with other organizations to gain women and minorities equal access to employment as San Francisco firefighters. "Being around to make sure that it's enforced and that it has some teeth is absolutely critical." And indeed ERA was forced to monitor the settlement in the firefighters' case for many years.

"You can't relax on the law front," warns Burt Neuborne, John Norton Pomeroy Professor at the New York University School of Law, "because the moment you relax on the law front, they'll push you back to the old system of law. . . . Within a lifetime—within one single lifetime—much of what we've gained from the fifties to now could be gone."

Implementation and monitoring can be expensive, tedious, and long-term activities. Yet litigation can also be a cost-effective strategy. Litigation groups have won much-needed injunctive relief, and reaped millions of dollars in back pay awards and damages for clients with no other recourse to claim their rights.

Some people express reservations over using litigation to make law, even when other strategies have failed. However, public interest litigation is very often used as a tool to enforce laws and to seek compliance with decrees already on the books. As the following three examples—involving desegregation, Native American treaty obligations, and women's rights—show, there is sometimes simply no alternative to litigation as a means of monitoring and obtaining compliance with legal requirements.

Maintaining Desegregated Public Schools. History recounts massive resistance by the Southern states to the landmark 1954 desegregation ruling of *Brown v. Board of Education,* and official indifference, and worse, in the North. LDF, a longtime Ford grantee, has returned to court hundreds of times to ensure that *Brown* is implemented. Janell Byrd, who joined the Washington office of LDF in 1984, explains that litigation to enforce *Brown* has tried to eliminate both "the legal structure of racial segregation" and "the racial caste system" that supports it. LDF's docket thus aims broadly at ending "the wide variety of practices that go 'hand-in-glove' with racial segregation (including inferior educational resources in terms of school facilities, books, technology, and teachers), as well as the exclusion of minorities from mainstream society and its opportunity structures."

Enforcing desegregation decrees thus forms part of a broader strategy: desegregation cases create opportunities for African Americans to participate in important community decisions. As Elaine Jones, LDF president and director-counsel, explains, "Desegregation is about funneling resources to your children. It is not just about white and black students sitting together in a classroom. It provides a lever for decision making by the black community."

In its litigation, LDF emphasizes that desegregation improves educational policy. "During the period of the most effective school desegregation, roughly 1970 to 1990, the academic achievement for African Americans, while not closing the gap with whites, showed dramatic improvements," LDF's Byrd points out. In Alabama, for example, LDF recently resisted efforts by Chambers County to amend its desegregation plan with a proposal that would have allowed a significantly white, newly established city in the rural part of the state to secede from the county school system, which is predominately black, and to take with it a disproportionate share of the county's educational resources. In the process of enforcing the existing desegregation order, LDF was able to bring about significant educational improvements involving course offerings, teacher resources, and school facilities.

As of 1997, more than two hundred school desegregation orders remained in effect throughout the nation. Despite the trend toward resegregation, LDF has successfully maintained integration and improved school quality in the seventeen southern states where it has brought hundreds of proceedings to enforce *Brown*.

Enforcing Native American Treaty Obligations. Native Americans have historically faced systematic mistreatment in the United States and a loss of ancestral lands. In one of its efforts to break up Indian tribes and tribal lands, Congress in 1887 provided for the allotment of a portion of tribal lands managed by the United States to individual members of the respective tribes. The federal government undertook to hold the proceeds from those lands— income from leases allowing grazing, farming, logging, or mining—in trust for the individual tribal members. By all accounts, the government utterly failed in its obligations.

Many of the account holders are among the poorest people in the nation. Two hundred fifty million dollars flow through the system every year. In all, billions of dollars, held in trust for as many as half a million individuals, are at issue. Much of the money is impossible to trace because of government negligence. The gross mismanagement of the trust funds, the *Wall Street Journal* reports, "is so complex and so potentially expensive to fix that it has been kicked from one administration to another since the 1920s." Although the problems had long been recognized, and the legal rights of the individuals were clear, the injustice continued and grew. As Elouise Cobell, a lifelong resident of the Blackfeet reservation in Montana, says: "They forced us to rely on a system that everybody knows didn't work. When we complained about it to the Bureau of Indian Affairs, to the Interior Department, to Congress, and to administration after administration, it fell on deaf ears."

In 1996, the Native American Rights Fund (NARF), a Ford grantee since its creation in 1972, filed a class action lawsuit, with Cobell as lead plaintiff, on behalf of the account holders. In February 1999, Federal District Judge Royce Lamberth held gov-

ernment officials in contempt of court for failing to produce
records pertaining to the trust funds. A few months later, the court
rejected the government's request to dismiss the lawsuit, finding
that government officials have a duty to the account holders to
"act as a proper trustee . . . as mandated by Congress." John
Echohawk, NARF's executive director, says of the decision, "This
is the first time a Federal court has ruled that the Federal trustee
in this context of trust funds will be held to the standards of a private fiduciary, just like any other American. Because of that, this
is watershed, landmark litigation." A trial on the merits began,
still later, in June 1999, with government lawyers admitting that
the U.S. was unable to account for what it owed the Indian benefi-
ciaries.

Advancing Educational Opportunity for Girls and Women. "With law
on your side, great things are possible," says NWLC's
Greenberger. NWLC has been using law to expand opportunities
for women since 1972, when it began as the Women's Rights
Project of the Center for Law and Social Policy. A freestanding
organization since 1981, NWLC's programs are grouped in four
broad areas: education, health and reproductive rights, employment, and family economic security.

NWLC has used an ambitious and complementary strategy of
litigation, administrative advocacy, and public education to
define, enforce, and expand federal protections, in particular
under Title IX of the Education Amendments of 1972, which
guarantees gender equity in educational programs funded by the
federal government. According to Greenberger, sticking with an
issue is key: the positive development of Title IX protection in the
area of school athletics programs is a case in point. NWLC has
been involved in virtually ever major Title IX athletics case, and
every U.S. court of appeals that has considered the issue has come
out in favor of broad protection against gender discrimination in
athletic programs. In 1997, on the twenty-fifth anniversary of
Title IX, NWLC highlighted the problem of continued athletic
scholarships discrimination by filing complaints against twenty-
five colleges and universities with the federal enforcement
agency.

Its work to expand notions of gender equality have also

included protection of female students against sexual harassment. In the first student-to-student sexual harassment case the U.S. Supreme Court has ever considered, *Davis v. Monroe County Board of Education*, the Justices ruled in 1999 that under federal law a public school system is responsible for protecting a student from repeated and vicious sexual harassment by a fellow student. The case was brought by the family of a fifth-grader, who, over the course of five months, was repeatedly threatened, grabbed in inappropriate places, and sexually harassed by a boy in her class. Despite repeated complaints and pleas for help to her teachers and principal, the school system failed to protect the ten-year-old girl, explains Verna Williams, the NWLC attorney who successfully argued the case before the Court.

"The Court's decision holds schools responsible for the safety of their students," says Greenberger. "This ruling extends to students basic protections against sexual harassment that prevents them from getting the education they deserve and have a right to expect."

These examples illustrate how grantees constantly have to return to court to turn "law on the books" into "law in action." "Public interest litigators know that securing the initial court order is only the first step of many to cement a victory, even with the best judge," says Mary McClymont, senior director of Ford's Peace and Social Justice Program. "Time and continued vigilance are essential to achieve the change sought, and that's why institutional support to litigating groups to enable them to keep going during the compliance stage is so critical."

Public Interest Litigation and Political Mobilization

In a fundamental sense, public interest litigation aims at empowering historically disadvantaged groups so that they can freely and equally participate in the political process and protect the rights they secure. A court-based strategy can encourage community mobilization by raising consciousness, providing resources, and creating allies. In addition, litigation adds legitimacy to community groups when they confront government action, and helps publicize their goals. Yet just as the threat of "see you in court" gives communities important leverage, so national litigation groups benefit from the experiential knowledge of grass-roots groups. The importance of community mobilization to long-term social change thus cannot be overstated. Helen Neuborne, deputy director of the Foundation's Human Development and Reproductive Health unit, says, for example, "Many people believe that the national women's groups did not do enough grass-roots organizing after their victory in *Roe v. Wade,* that they went too far, too fast and lost support from their constituents."

Law groups are not always equipped to do organizing and community mobilization activities. Part of the difficulty, as one activist lawyer acknowledges, is "the difference in class and race between lawyers and the people they serve." Cindy Morano, senior organizer of Wider Opportunities for Women, a community organizer who has worked with lawyers throughout her career, explains, "Because lawyers and community organizers have different skill sets," legal skill does not predict organizing ability.

As a national foundation, Ford does not make many small grants to local groups. Over the years, however, it has developed mechanisms to channel funds to groups with expertise in community-based activities and has encouraged innovative legal strategies that are more broadly linked to community mobilization goals. Such techniques enable grantees to acquire information from affected communities and to keep these communities informed and engaged.

Some grantees have complemented their litigation programs with proactive "transactional lawyering" activities that involve community groups in nonlitigation legal strategies. As Alan Jenkins, Ford's Racial Justice and Minority Rights program officer, explains, these alternative lawyering approaches are intended "to help craft solutions where an adversarial approach is unlikely to succeed." He underscores, however, that while these nonlitigation efforts are important in mobilizing and sustaining political support, they carry their own set of limitations.

Finally, a holistic approach to social change requires coordination among different and diverse organizations. LDF Staff Attorney George Kendall explains the problem well: "Some of the most important issues that we need to win cannot be won without encouraging and sustaining cooperative efforts between national organizations. They require multipronged campaigns—legal, public education, legislative—to succeed. Such efforts are beyond the means of any one organization; we will have success in the future on these must-win issues only if the donors recognize the necessity to provide funding on such collaborative efforts."

The remainder of this section examines three diverse community-based strategies that grantees used to complement or spearhead their litigation work.

Coordinating Litigation with Community Organizing. In 1994, Los Angeles County was a vast urban area of approximately four thousand square miles and more than nine million people. Most residents traveled long distances to work, for medical care, and for other routine activities. The many working poor who could not afford an automobile were completely dependent on public transportation provided by the county's Metropolitan Transportation Authority (MTA). Buses carried 94 percent of the MTA's passengers. Eighty percent of the bus riders were people of color; their average household income was less than $15,000. Despite the fact that its buses carried nearly all its riders, the MTA devoted more than 70 percent of its budget to rail programs, which primarily benefited affluent riders. Its fleet of buses was the most overcrowded, oldest, and least reliable in the nation. In the summer of 1994, the MTA announced plans to spend tens of millions of dollars in discretionary funds—which could have been spent on buses—on a light-rail line. At the same time, it announced plans to raise bus fares and discontinue inexpensive monthly passes, in order to make still more money available for rail facilities.

That fall, LDF sued the MTA on behalf of the Bus Riders Union (BRU) and a community organizing group that had helped create the BRU, citing Title VI (a federal antidiscrimination statute) and equal protection violations. LDF won a preliminary injunction against the fare increase and the elimination of passes. More than eighteen months of litigation followed, with four lawyers working nearly full time on behalf of the bus riders. A mountain of evidence was assembled, clearly showing the disparities in funding of bus and rail transportation. Public opinion began to crystallize in favor of increased bus service, and the *Los*

Angeles Times also became a forceful advocate for greater equity in public transport.

In 1996, the MTA agreed to a consent decree requiring it to implement several of the plaintiffs' main goals, including lower and controlled bus fares and reduced overcrowding. A joint working group of representatives of the MTA and the BRU was formed—giving bus riders an official, ongoing role in Los Angeles County public transportation policy. LDF closely monitored compliance with the consent decree, and went back to court several times. Finally, in October 1998, the MTA board voted to buy 2,095 new buses over the next six years, and days later the head of the MTA, in what the *Los Angeles Times* called "a sharp break with the [MTA's] long absorption in rail transit," called for the creation of a vast network of rapid bus lines.

More than four years after the litigation commenced, and over two years after the consent decree, Los Angeles bus riders were on the verge of seeing major change. "This work could not be done without the BRU," says Richard Larsen, an LDF attorney who has been on the case from the beginning. "They know the consent decree, they know the issues, they know the MTA. They articulate their causes well." BRU's community involvement was essential to mobilize interest in and support for this issue. But without the staying power of an established institution like LDF, the bus riders would never have had their day in court. The injustice done to the people who depend on buses for transportation became clear only through the focusing power of litigation—as discovery generated the mass of evidence that BRU relied on to change public opinion and public policy.

Forming New Groups for New Constituencies. In 1991, Ford and other foundations funded a collaboration of three regional Asian American legal groups under a single umbrella, the National Asian Pacific American Legal Consortium. Using a range of strategies including litigation, community education, and leadership training, the consortium, under Executive Director Karen Narasaki, has led its constituents from the margins to the center of civil rights advocacy.

The consortium has tried to learn from the experience of older public interest law groups, while remaining keenly sensitive to its particular constituency. Many Asian Americans are recent immigrants, Narasaki says, with "an understandable mentality of saying, 'Well, I left my country for a good reason. This country is better than what I had there. So who am I to complain?'" The consortium has focused heavily on community education and outreach, as well as developing leadership skills. "We don't do litigation just to do litigation," Narasaki explains. "It has to be capacity building somehow. Whether you're doing grassroots organizing around the case, or using the case to educate the media, there has to be something more than the actual litigation itself."

To help build a sense of community, the consortium has chosen hate crimes as a principal focus for its work. "One of the reasons is that it's been a defining issue for the community as a whole," Narasaki says. Asian American communities are extraordinarily diverse, with dozens of ethnicities and languages. To Narasaki, "the fact that these kinds of crimes exist is the clearest, most easily understandable reason why Asians have to come together in a coalition." The coalition has tried to listen to its constituents, and to bring its resources to bear on issues that are high on the list of their concerns. But Narasaki emphasizes the critical role that lawyers play in the community that her organization serves. Many grassroots leaders face English language barriers and are unfamiliar with the political system. Having a law degree confers legitimacy in the corridors of power. "I tell lawyers and law students that I really think that for the Asian American community, we're the bridge," Narasaki says.

Organizing a Community-Based Political Strategy. Luke Cole, of the California Rural Legal Assistance Foundation, a former Ford grantee, has organized in the Central Valley in California around issues of environmental justice, in opposition to polluting enterprises in neighborhoods populated by the poor and disenfranchised. Cole argues that "taking environmental problems out of the streets and into the courts plays to the grassroots movement's weakest suit" since "most poor people find the legal system foreign and intimidating." Cole calls instead for "a community-based political organizing strategy [that] can be broad and participatory."

Cole travels frequently from his office in San Francisco to help build networks of activists in the Central Valley. He says that mobilization "has to happen at an individual level in community after community after community." The strategy faces many obstacles. Philanthropic support, never adequate, has diminished. Political resistance has forced environmental justice clinics at law schools to close or has blocked law students from appearing in court. Concerted opposition from industry and other groups has evoked critical media coverage and legislative setbacks. In California, for example, a significant court victory requiring the provision of Spanish language materials in environmental hearings was nullified by the legislature. Lacking a legislative presence in the state capital, grassroots activists were not even aware of the adverse legislation until after it had become law.

"If we had the power in the legislature, we would be able to know about these bills that are going through and are undoing our gains and stop them," Cole says. "The fact that we had won this little local battle largely on legal grounds was unsustainable because we didn't have a statewide political presence. So what we need to do is build on those local struggles, and knit them together into some type of larger network that then demands accountability. That's a very labor-intensive process." The California Rural Legal Assistance Foundation has not abandoned litigation, but knows that it is a tool that must be supported by broad public education and mobilization to realize lasting social change.

Addressing the Limits of Litigation

The problems with litigation are many. As Antonia Hernandez, president and general counsel of the Mexican American Legal Defense and Educational Fund, says, "We see litigation as the tool of last resort. It is costly. It is long. And it is chancy. And particularly since 1980, the courts have not been our friends. But it's the realization that you have the ability to litigate that gives you the credibility to use the other strategies effectively. And so to us, it's a continuum—each tool, each strategy coming together for an end."

Perhaps the most telling criticism of litigation as a strategy is that court decrees do not automatically trigger a change in people's attitudes. "When courts declare something, some number of people tend to believe it is the right thing to do," says Jack Greenberg, former LDF director–counsel. "And the court's order gets incorporated into their conduct and their behavior changes over time." But, he emphasizes, court orders do not necessarily win over a majority. Sustained public education campaigns are thus essential to frame public debate and to prevent distortion of progressive values. Most public interest law groups, however, spend their limited resources on lawyers first, with communicators and educators a distant second. By contrast, newly established opposition groups, created in reaction to civil rights advances, have committed sizable resources to public communications.

Media work demands a complex balance of coordination, policy analysis, and focus. "A successful media strategy requires obtaining a baseline of public attitudes through polling and research, and putting forward a message consistent with those values that does not compromise the movement's values," says Kathy Bonk, executive director and cofounder of the Communications Consortium Media Center.

For some grantees, use of new information and communications technologies, acquired under targeted Ford grants, offers greater sophistication and effectiveness in reaching both the media and the public. ACLU senior counsel Christopher A. Hansen cites changes at the ACLU since 1994 as an example: "We have e-mail listservs where all our press releases go out, so we reach many more reporters on a much more regularized basis. All of the documents on our cases get posted on our website and are available to the general public."

Public education is also directly connected to legal implementation. The monitoring and enforcement of laws and judicial decrees depends on networks of private lawyers available to work cooperatively with public interest law groups. Public education materials, including legal education manuals, provide critical resources for this effort. Many groups, however, lack the time and budgets for this effort. Elizabeth M. Schneider, an expert on battered women's issues and a professor at Brooklyn Law School, says that public interest groups that work on this issue "have no way to put out ideas or distribute necessary materials to lawyers around the country." A public education strategy, she suggests, thus also requires linkages with the academic community, as well as with students—the next generation of social change activists—in order to develop and refine cutting-edge thinking and better frame public debate.

Over the last two decades, some grantees have had to create a communications infrastructure from the ground up, with high start-up costs for personnel and computer technology. Other organizations have focused on intergroup coordination as a way to leverage resources and visibility. Some groups have "reinvented" themselves to adapt to the changing political climate. Still other groups have recast their membership structure as a way to further public education. No single group has taken all of these steps, and no single approach is necessarily the most effective. This section looks at the innovative efforts of three grantees—LDF, Americans for a Fair Chance, and the Women's Legal Defense Fund—to overcome some of the limitations of litigation and to influence the broadest possible public.

Creating a Communications Infrastructure.   During the 1990s, LDF has focused on rebuilding its communications capacity to respond to the new political climate. Former LDF head Greenberg recalls the early days of the civil rights movement: "The NAACP had hundreds of thousands of members. It sent out the word through *Crisis* magazine, and bulletins, and newspapers. LDF lawyers met regularly with lawyers in every city imaginable. Especially in the black community, the lawyers were the leaders."

During these earlier years, training programs and fellowships helped LDF to "spread the word" by allowing it to cultivate new civil rights attorneys and to foster a network of community-based, cooperative lawyers. Institutional capacity dwindled, however, as resources shrank. By the 1980s, budget cuts forced LDF to close its Division of Legal Information and Community Services, which collected and analyzed data, produced studies and investigative reports, organized state coalitions, and collaborated with academics, policy analysts, activists, women's groups, union leaders, and Latino and Native American groups.

LDF lawyers now emphasize that they are public relations entrepreneurs, as well as litigators. "In the 1980s," recalls Theodore M. Shaw, a veteran LDF attorney, "we would say, 'We're lawyers, we litigate; we're not publicity hounds. Those who count recognize what we do.' We did not have any internal person who would work with the press on our issues."

Since 1992, LDF has used general operating funds to retain a Washington, D.C., public relations firm to help develop media support for its issues. LDF took a major step forward in 1997 when Ford provided a special two-year grant to start a communications department. LDF has expanded its communications capacity, but sees much work ahead. Elaine Jones, current president and director–counsel, explains: "We need to have in-house communications capacity. We need to develop literature. We need a day-to-day contact person with the press. We need to do media work across the country."

Collaborating to Mobilize Public Support.   Aside from abortion rights, affirmative action has perhaps elicited the most serious backlash against post–World War II social justice gains. Some observers believe that civil rights groups were put on the defensive by the intensity of the opposition. With legal and policy challenges to federal affirmative action programs, six civil rights groups, supported by the Ford, Rockefeller, Carnegie, C.S. Mott, and Cummings foundations, joined together in 1995 to establish a collaborative public education campaign to support affirmative action. After conducting research, including focus groups, the member groups decided to create a formal organization, Americans for a Fair Chance (AFC).

AFC's initial goal aimed at implementing a strategic communications plan in six states where affirmative action was under attack. The strategy involved identifying a wide range of potential allies, partners, and messengers—not just the traditional minority groups, but other constituencies with a stake in diversity such as veterans, students, and business—and providing them with sophisticated materials for disseminating a pro–affirmative action message. AFC has initiated public education efforts around particular legal challenges (it chose Michigan as a target state in part because of pending litigation there), but its primary focus is on general public education. AFC's message—"It's Fair. It Works. It's Necessary"—appears on widely distributed fact sheets. Its campaign has been acutely sensitive to ensuring opportunities for all ethnic groups, as well as for women, and to promoting cooperation within the civil rights community. In the future, AFC leaders would like to see their model replicated on the local level around the country, enabling grassroots membership organizations to put forward a unified message.

Refocusing Institutional Identity. In the mid-1990s, the Women's Legal Defense Fund undertook, with Ford support, an institutional review. Focus groups revealed that the Fund's constituents were unhappy with its very name. "They think we're too litigious as a society, just plain don't like litigation as a strategy," says its president, Judith Lichtman. "But if you described what we do as having a seat at the table, representing their interests, being in Washington for them on a set of issues they care desperately about—like the Patient's Bill of Rights—they loved it. Holding public officials accountable once they get elected or appointed, they loved it."

So, on February 24, 1998, the twenty-seven-year-old Women's Legal Defense Fund was reborn as the National Partnership for Women & Families. With the name change came a new focus. "We learned that if you try to be all things to all people, you end up fooling around the edges of a lot of people's agendas, and driving little of an agenda yourself," Lichtman says. "Imposing an internal discipline and programmatic focus was very hard, harder than the name change." The partnership now formally takes a backseat on issues where sister organizations have greater expertise, such as educational equity, a specialty of the NWLC, and has instead consolidated its work into two main program areas—Work and Family, and Women's Health—areas where it had earlier developed significant expertise and a long history of success.

Recently, the partnership was approached by the American

Medical Association (AMA), the American Trial Lawyers Association, and leading labor unions to chair a coalition to mobilize public support for a "patient's bill of rights." "That could not have happened with the old name," Lichtman says, "and I know that because the trial lawyers and the AMA told me. So a user-friendlier name opened up new advocacy opportunities for us." The partnership has not abandoned litigation, but believes it is now positioned to accomplish more through non-court activity.

Conclusion

The work of these public interest law organizations over the last twenty years suggests that the courts remain an important source of leverage for historically disadvantaged groups, lending them credibility, influence, and access to power. Public interest litigation sometimes produces dynamic policy impacts that extend far beyond the specific terms of a judicial decree, supporting social reform even if defendants refuse to comply with a court's order. Looking forward, civil rights law will continue to play an important role in the struggle for social justice, even if defensive strategies must be used. The holistic approach that characterizes the work of Ford grantees speaks to the cyclical nature of social progress, in which victories are almost always followed by backlash and retrenchment. Losses often create new opportunities, but resources must be available to mine them effectively. This section offers some lessons that might be learned from the experiences of the grantees whose work this case study has surveyed. The lessons presented offer ideas and guidance for those working in this field; they can be adapted to many situations, but are not intended necessarily to be replicable formulae.

Lessons and Insights

Litigation-Related Strategies
   1. Litigation remains the "big stick" that enables organizations dedicated to social change to be taken seriously. Although litigation may not produce transformative change

for all groups and on all issues, a steady development of legal principles can support incremental reform essential to social justice aims.

2. Litigation has a mixed, but important, impact. It can affect policy in different ways and to different degrees. As in the ACLU's school reform cases, a judicial decision can play an agenda-setting role by highlighting a legal issue and making it a priority for the other branches of government to resolve. In addition, a court can delineate rights and obligations—as in LDF's desegregation cases—providing bargaining leverage to otherwise politically excluded groups that enhances their ability to secure reform. A court can also give programmatic content to legal norms. Sometimes a judicial decree holds the line and preserves past victories. The success of a litigation strategy on one issue or in one area does not predict success for other groups or at other times. Some factors, however, appear to be crucial prerequisites to litigation success: appropriate and capable institutional mechanisms; adequate funding; dedicated leadership; and broad community support.

3. Monitoring and enforcement mechanisms can greatly enhance the impact of judicial decrees. Formal victory does not automatically translate into on-the-ground change. Without monitoring and enforcement, reform prospects are seriously diminished. Experience has shown that few judgments are self-executing, and that much work, sometimes including further litigation or the threat of it, is required to turn a court's rhetoric to reality. Moreover, monitoring brings to the surface experience and practice that can then be integrated into new forms of institutional design.

4. Litigation goes hand in hand with other strategies. Litigation can provide a pressure point for change, but systemic reform demands interactive and synergistic efforts to mobilize public sentiment. The need for such complementary work does not negate the role of lawyers.

5. An effective social change strategy requires a mix of organizations—some devoted to single-issue causes, others multi-focused—as well as mechanisms to link different

groups. On the one hand, an effective social change strategy requires the continued support of national civil rights groups. But an interlocking network of complementary institutions—state-based lawyers, grassroots community activity, and academic think tanks—is also vital. Finally, as conditions change, efforts must be made to include new groups and issues in the civil rights infrastructure.

Programming Approaches and Donor Roles

1. Encouraging groups to work together can be an effective donor role; forcing partnerships can be counterproductive. Coalition building takes time and resources; funds for this purpose allow groups to leverage capacity, but do not substitute for other forms of financial support. Collaborations are best developed in close consultation with participating groups. Unwanted partnerships can divert time and attention from important activities.

2. Law groups and the communities that they serve need long-term core support as well as capacity-building grants. Viable institutions, rooted in their communities, with strong ties to other organizations, must be in place before a crisis hits. Core support allows grantees to develop technical expertise, credibility, and a long-term perspective on problems to which they can commit serious attention over time. They can thus function as "repeat players," giving grantees an advantage when they litigate or seek allies on common issues. Withdrawal of support can impede a group's effectiveness and even end reform efforts altogether.

3. It is unreasonable to expect most public interest law groups to become self-supporting. Despite the availability of membership fees for some groups and attorney's fees in some cases, it is implausible to expect these groups to be weaned of donor support. Donors can, however, encourage grantees to broaden their bases of support and to explore innovative, entrepreneurial forms of financing linked to public education and mobilization goals. Project support that helps organizations identify alternative sources of support can further this effort; among them are endowment

campaigns that might offer long-term grantees substantial financial independence.

Looking Ahead

The next stage of social justice work requires a new articulation of goals, as public interest law groups work to forge "a more perfect Union" for all Americans. The changed political climate, together with increasingly narrow access to federal courts, highlights the need to continue integrating litigation into a broader social change strategy. National civil rights groups must develop new linkages with grassroots organizations, with the business community, and with government. And support must be available to nurture a new generation of intellectuals who can help to shape future civil rights discourse, to mobilize favorable public sentiment, and to encourage innovation.

Combined philanthropic efforts are needed to establish a space for social activists to meet, to confer, to consider past strategies, and to plan future endeavors with social scientists, affected communities, and others. To combat an apparent loss of faith in civil rights ideals, Ford and its partners could usefully sponsor empirical research to demonstrate the continuing importance of these ideals to a nation that strives to be fair, as well as efficient and productive. New forms of public advocacy and public education, from radio talk shows to popular movies to web-based materials, will need support to generate community sentiment in support of social justice goals. At the same time, support for litigation and legal advocacy will remain as necessary and important as at any point in the Foundation's history.

Notes

We thank students at the New York University School of Law—Steven Cottreau, Jeffrey Hauser, Sameena Majid, Karin McEwen, Christopher Pushaw, Jennifer Simon, Cassandra Stubbs, Elizabeth Stull, Megan Tipper, and especially Ben Wizner—for helpful and enthusiastic research assistance.

1. In 1970, the Foundation launched an ambitious "Public Interest Law" initiative designed to support improvements in areas such as consumer rights, health care, and pollution. The program began with a grant to the Center on Law and Social Policy; over the next decade nine other public interest firms received support as well. In 1980, the Foundation awarded "terminal grants" to these public interest recipients and withdrew from involvement in the program.

Appendix: People Interviewed for This Study

Lorna Babby
Staff Attorney, Native American Rights Fund, Washington, D.C.

Janet Benshoof
President, Center for Reproductive Law and Policy, New York

Louis Bograd
Staff Counsel, American Civil Liberties Union, Washington, D.C.

Kathy Bonk
Executive Director, Communications Consortium Media Center, Washington, D.C.

Janell Byrd
Staff Attorney, NAACP Legal Defense and Educational Fund, Inc., Washington, D.C.

Luke Cole
Director of the Center on Race, Poverty and the Environment, a project of the California Rural Legal Assistance Foundation, San Francisco, CA

Dayna Cunningham
Rights Officer, The Rockefeller Foundation, New York

Ron Daniels
Executive Director, Center for Constitutional Rights, New York

Nancy Davis
Former Director, Equal Rights Advocates, San Francisco, CA

Robert Dinerstein
Professor and Associate Dean for Academic Affairs, Washington College of Law, American University, Washington, D.C.

Alan Divack
Archivist, The Ford Foundation, New York

Susan Drake
Executive Director, National Immigrant Legal Support Center, Los Angeles, CA

John E. Echohawk
Executive Director, Native American Rights Fund, Boulder, CO

Theresa Fay-Bustillos
Vice President of Legal Programs, Mexican American Legal Defense and Educational Fund, Los Angeles, CA

Shepard Forman
Director, Center on International Cooperation, New York

Susan Goering
Executive Director, ACLU of Maryland, Baltimore, MD

William Goodman
Legal Director, Center for Constitutional Rights, New York

Patricia Grayson
Director of Development, NAACP Legal Defense and Educational Fund, Inc., New York

Jennifer M. Green
Staff member, Center for Constitutional Rights, New York

Jack Greenberg
Adjunct Professor, Columbia University School of Law, New York

Marcia Greenberger
Co-President, National Women's Law Center, Washington, D.C.

Diane L. Gross
Program Director, Americans for a Fair Chance, Washington, D.C.

Lucas Guttentag
Director, Immigrants' Rights Project, American Civil Liberties Union, San Francisco, CA

Christopher A. Hansen
Senior Staff Counsel, American Civil Liberties Union, New York

Keith M. Harper
Senior Staff Attorney, Native American Rights Fund, Washington, D.C.

Simon Heller
Director of Litigation, Center for Reproductive Law and Policy, New York

Antonia Hernandez
President and General Counsel, Mexican American Legal Defense and Education Fund, Los Angeles, CA

Irma Herrera
Executive Director, Equal Rights Advocates, San Francisco, CA

Taryn Higashi
Program Officer, Refugee and Migrant Rights, The Ford Foundation, New York

Jaribu Hill
Director, Center for Constitutional Rights-South, Greenville, MS

Lynn Walker Huntley
Director, Comparative Human Relations Initiative, Southern
Education Foundation, Atlanta, GA

Alan Jenkins
Program Officer, Racial Justice and Minority Rights, The Ford
Foundation, New York

Linton Joaquin
Litigation Director, National Immigrant Legal Support Center,
Los Angeles, CA

Elaine Jones
President and Director-Counsel, NAACP Legal Defense and
Educational Fund, Inc., New York

George H. Kendall
Staff Attorney, NAACP Legal Defense and Educational Fund,
Inc., New York

Lewis Kornhauser
Alfred and Gail Engelberg Professor of Law, New York
University School of Law, New York

Richard Larsen
Staff Attorney, NAACP Legal Defense and Educational Fund,
Inc., Western Regional Office, Los Angeles, CA

Judith Lichtman
President, National Partnership for Women & Families,
Washington, D.C.

Vivian Lindermayer
Development Director, Center for Constitutional Rights, New
York

Stephen Loffredo
Associate Professor, City University of New York Law School,
New York

Geraldine D. Mannion
Chair, Democracy Program and Special Projects, Carnegie
Corporation, New York

Mary McClymont
Senior Director, Peace and Social Justice Program, The Ford
Foundation, New York

Cindy Morano
Senior Organizer, Wider Opportunities for Women, Oakland, CA

Karen Narasaki
Executive Director, National Asian Pacific American Legal
Consortium, Washington, D.C.

Burt Neuborne
John Norton Pomeroy Professor of Law, New York University
School of Law, and Legal Director, Brennan Center for Justice at
New York University School of Law, New York

Helen Neuborne
Deputy Director, Human Development and Reproductive Health,
The Ford Foundation, New York

Barbara Olshansky
Assistant Legal Director, Center for Constitutional Rights, New
York

Robert Peregvy
Senior Staff Attorney, Native American Rights Fund, Washington,
D.C.

Anika Rahman
Director, International Program, Center for Reproductive Law
and Policy, New York

Rene A. Redwood
Executive Director, Americans for a Fair Chance, Washington,
D.C.

Anthony Romero
Director, Human Rights and International Cooperation, The Ford
Foundation, New York

Charles F. Sabel
Professor of Law and Social Science, Columbia University
School of Law, New York

Elizabeth M. Schneider
Professor of Law, Brooklyn Law School, Brooklyn, New York

Steven R. Shapiro
Legal Director, American Civil Liberties Union, New York

Theodore M. Shaw
Associate Director–Counsel, NAACP Legal Defense and
Educational Fund, Inc., New York

Linda Thurston
Staff, Center for Constitutional Rights, New York

Verna Williams
Vice President and Director of Educational Opportunities,
National Women's Law Center, Washington, D.C.

Stephen Yale-Loehr
Attorney, Ithaca, New York

4

From the Village to the University: Legal Activism in Bangladesh

STEPHEN GOLUB

Bangladesh has made significant strides in replacing dictatorship with democracy, reducing poverty, slowing population growth, and overcoming the traumatizing legacy of its bloody 1971 secession from Pakistan. Yet, significant problems remain. The World Bank calculates that 35 percent of the population is "very poor." The United Nations Development Programme index of human development indicators ranks it 150th out of 173 countries. Three-quarters of the country's women and half of its men are illiterate. There is little enforcement of laws promoting gender equality, constitutional assurances notwithstanding. Violence against women—including domestic abuse, rape, and vigilante attacks— is common, as are police beatings and other human rights violations. The barriers of illiteracy, poverty, violence, and social stigma keep many from seeking or obtaining legal redress for their problems.

In view of these conditions, how can dedicated lawyers, NGOs and law professors use the law to address problems plaguing their society? This chapter examines some of their strategies. It describes work funded and facilitated under the Ford Foundation's Public Interest Law Initiative (PILI) in Bangladesh in the 1990s. The full impact of that work will be known only over time. But some results and lessons already are emerging.

Launched in 1992, PILI constituted Ford's first and only law-related program in Bangladesh. It supported clinical legal education for law students and legal services for disadvantaged populations. It sought to broaden the community of activists providing such services by constructing a pipeline of programs that would channel motivated individuals into that community on a full-time, part-time, or pro bono basis. These legal activists would in turn form a constituency for long-term systemic reform geared toward increasing access to justice. Beyond the closing of Ford's Dhaka office in 1997, many of these activities continued to be supported through some extended funding by Ford and by other donors.

PILI wove together three strands of funding. One supported the operations of four preexisting legal services groups that, to varying degrees, conduct research, grassroots service delivery (featuring advice, nonformal education, mediation, and litigation), and policy advocacy. The Bangladesh National Women Lawyers Association (BNWLA), Ain O Salish Kendra (ASK), and the Madaripur Legal Aid Association (MLAA) focus mainly on women's rights; the Bangladesh Environmental Lawyers Association (BELA) works mainly on environmental justice. ASK and MLAA, respectively, also serve the urban and rural poor (not just the women in those sectors). This chapter pays particular attention to how MLAA and many other NGOs have adapted traditional Bangladeshi mediation techniques to advance women's rights and resolve disputes—an innovation growing in popularity across the nation.

Another strand of PILI funding created and financed a new organization, the Bangladesh Legal Aid and Services Trust (BLAST). Launched under the initiative of the leadership of the legal profession's apex body, the Bangladesh Bar Council, BLAST now has a nationwide network of offices. In addition to legal aid, the organization conducts mediation, policy advocacy, and public interest litigation.

The funding initiative's third component helped the country's three major law schools—at Chittagong, Dhaka, and Rajshahi universities—start clinical legal education programs. These law clinics initially focused on classroom-based training that was more skills oriented than theoretical. The programs later arranged for students to obtain practical experience regarding fieldwork and court procedure. This experiential learning has included internships with former Ford grantees and other NGOs.

To complement its funding for the law clinics and legal services work, Ford very selectively supported foreign consultants, international conferences, and grantee site visits abroad. Two successive Dhaka-based American attorneys taught classes, advised the clinics' professors, and prepared course materials. Foundation staff facilitated cooperation among grantees, helped formulate and launch BLAST and the law clinics, and coordinated work with other donors, particularly The Asia Foundation (TAF) and the Norwegian Agency for Development Cooperation (NORAD).

This case study presents the context, nature, and evolution of PILI and of the grantees' operations. In addition to discussing the three branches of the initiative, the chapter also illuminates innovative NGO adaptation of traditional Bangladeshi mediation processes. It then sums up changes to which grantees have contributed, lessons and insights springing from PILI, and thoughts on future challenges for this work in Bangladesh.

Context of PILI-Supported Work

The vision for PILI was described in a 1994 document prepared by Ford's Bangladesh office: "The long-term goal of the Dhaka office's ongoing public interest law initiative is to promote the establishment of a more equitable and effective legal system that will provide redress and relief to the great majority of Bangladeshis who now have little or no recourse to justice. As a first step, Dhaka staff have embarked on a strategy designed to encourage the practice of public interest law. If successful, this initiative [PILI] should forge an increasingly broad-based community of like-minded activists committed to changing the existing legal structures and conventions."

This section fleshes out the underlying assumptions and implications of that reasoning. It first provides some brief background on legal problems facing Bangladeshis. It particularly focuses on the status of women, since they constitute most grantees' main client group. The discussion then probes roads not taken by Ford, as a way of explaining early strategic choices.

The 1991 return of democracy to Bangladesh, after nearly nine years of military control, did not secure the rule of law. Women are most severely affected. As a report prepared for the

United Nations Children's Fund (UNICEF) points out, "Women often face difficulties in pursuing their rights within the legal system, due to the lack of implementation [of laws against murder, rape, assault, child marriage, and many other abuses]. Social norms tend to ostracize [female] victims rather than perpetrators of crimes."[1] Other reasons for the lack of implementation include the long delays and occasional political influence afflicting the courts; many traditional mediators' ignorance of the law, including relatively progressive provisions of religious law; the corruption and attitudinal obstacles affecting both courts and traditional mediation; weak police performance; and widespread poverty and legal ignorance among the population, both of which block effective access to a complex and prohibitively expensive (for most Bangladeshis) legal system.

Furthermore, not all of the country's laws embody equity. Although its constitution grants women equal treatment in public life, this protection does not extend to intrafamily matters such as marriage and inheritance, which are based on Islamic law. Thus, while the Muslim Family Law Ordinance of 1961 generally incorporates the most liberal provisions of the four Sunni schools of *sharia,* some of these provisions still relegate women to a lower legal status.

Gender violence is widespread. Surveys indicate that the greatest reported cause is husbands' frustration with wives for not serving dinner promptly. Another key reason is men's demands that their spouses' parents pay dowry. This fee, paid with money, livestock, or other resources, is determined at the time that a marriage is negotiated. (Most marriages in Bangladesh are arranged not by the bride and groom, but by their parents.) Though barred beyond a modest amount by the 1980 Dowry Prohibition Act, the practice remains common. Cash-strapped parents are willing to pay dowry because it frees them of the long-term financial burden of maintaining a daughter, and is often the only way they can secure a modicum of a decent life for her. The parents' initial dowry payment may be followed by a husband's repeated demands for additional sums. The threat or reality of domestic violence may accompany these demands.

Another common legal issue is underage marriages. Despite the Child Marriage Restraint Act of 1929 (which was strength-

ened in the 1980s), girls frequently are subject to arranged marriages long before reaching the legal age of 18, and sometimes
before reaching puberty. Parental endorsement of the practice
remains common. It stems in part from fears that their daughters
will engage in sexual activity, whether forcibly or not. Such activity would ruin a young woman's marriage prospects. Driven by
these economic and cultural forces, youths are sometimes wed
without even meeting until the marriage ceremony. Ironically but
not surprisingly, parents' efforts to arrange economic security for
their daughters through early marriage is often counterproductive.
According to Bangladesh scholar Eirik Jansen, "The older the
bride is at the time she enters into a marriage and the better education she has, the greater are the chances for a stable marriage."[2]

Desire for dowry is but one of many factors driving widespread disregard of the law. Though men may legally have more
than one wife at a time, this is subject to requirements of the
Muslim Family Law Ordinance. These requirements include permission by the current wife before a new marriage can take place,
and equal treatment for all spouses. The men involved rarely
honor such provisions. Husbands also deny their wives legally
mandated maintenance in the event of divorce. And they fail to
pay dower, the sum that the marriage contract stipulates that the
husband should give the wife over the course of the marriage. A
major problem is that many marriages are carried out without formal registration. This works to the husbands' advantage because
this initial lack of documentation makes it far easier for them to
avoid their legal responsibilities, such as child support and alimo-
ny, later.

Given the depth of women's legal problems in Bangladesh,
and the Foundation's concerns about them, why were they not the
sole focus of PILI from the start? In fact, women's rights were an
implicit priority of the initiative. (This was also true of most of
the Foundation's other work in Bangladesh, even where that work
was not explicitly law oriented.) But to build awareness of gender
issues among male students and attorneys, it was first useful to
engage them with human rights issues in general. Ford Program
Officer David Chiel and his Bangladeshi colleagues reasoned that
once students and attorneys were drawn into legal aid, they
inevitably would address domestic violence and other issues

affecting women. In fact, women turned out to be the large majority of their clients. The more general human rights focus also
would allow PILI to concentrate on other important legal needs
regarding peasants, the urban poor, and the environment.
Furthermore, this would help create new and different opportunities for women lawyers (as with BELA's environmental activists)
to begin playing leading roles in other fields, and not just
women's rights.

These were laudable objectives. But if the aim was to help
build a better legal system, why focus just on legal activists? Why
not build up the bench, bar, and other institutions that constitute
or control the system? In fact, when Chiel arrived in Dhaka in
1992 as the first Foundation program officer there with specific
law-oriented responsibilities, he expected to work with governmental bodies. He investigated collaborating with the judiciary,
the police, and other mainstream institutions, but a wide range of
Bangladeshis advised that a civil society focus would represent a
better route to meaningful reform.

At the same time, Foundation staff were exploring working
with NGOs that did not in fact become part of the initiative. One
such organization increasingly failed to evince any energetic dedication to reform. A promising alternative direction was assistance
for umbrella efforts to pull together a sector-specific community
of NGOs. But this foundered on personal and ideological rival-
ries. Though the Foundation invested considerable energy in heal-
ing these rifts, the effort ultimately failed. One possible lesson is
that however important an issue is in fact and a coordinating body
is in theory, grantees' effectiveness may hinge as much on the
personalities at play as on the issues they strive to address.
Another is that donors may sometimes be better advised simply to
facilitate informal grantee interaction, as opposed to formal structures and coordination.

Building a Community and Constituency for Reform

At the same time that the Foundation was investigating the
above approaches, it was pursuing an alternative, constituency-
creating route. It aimed to help bring together an increasingly

broad-based community of like-minded activists that would address specific legal issues over the medium term while eventually pushing for systemic, long-term reform.

The four preexisting legal services groups—ASK, BELA, BNWLA, and MLAA—constituted an excellent core for that community of activists and held the promise of greatly contributing to law reform. They already had demonstrated dedication and impact, with the potential to do much more both individually and jointly. The Foundation decided to increase funding in this regard.

A secondary reason for Ford's focus on legal services and law reform through NGOs in Bangladesh was its related work in other countries, which gave it international experience and contacts in this field. PILI supplemented its funding by drawing on these contacts. It supported occasional overseas training and exposure for grantee personnel through the London-based organization INTERIGHTS and three U.S.-based groups: the Advocacy Institute, the International Human Rights Internship Program, and the National Institute for Citizen Education in the Law. A BNWLA leader returning from training at the Advocacy Institute, for example, found that for the first time she saw the value "of finding friends within the bureaucracy, of having to analyze the budget and specific policies. So if we want a repatriation program [for women forced or lured into prostitution abroad], we have to look at the [national] budget and lobby for money for this." Acknowledging that the government was not necessarily immediately open to NGO budgetary input, this NGO leader saw potential in the relatively new notion that advocates and officials could work together in a constructive and focused manner.

If these legal services groups were to become the core of a "broad-based community," they needed to become more of a community themselves. As of the early 1990s, they were, in fact, relatively atomized. Ford grantmaking efforts concerning resource management and women's empowerment already supported a few of these groups. Other donors funded a handful of similar efforts. But their work and interaction were relatively limited. To address this problem, the Foundation devoted energy to facilitating grantee interaction. Before his untimely death in 1997, BELA's secretary general, Mohiuddin Farooque, described attending "a meeting organized by Ford and TAF at which some

legal services NGOs met for the first time." Ford also helped link
MLAA Executive Director Fazlul Huq to BLAST when the latter
needed a leader familiar with grassroots legal aid.

In some instances, building links meant breaking down walls
beyond the NGO community. Exposing law students and professors to legal services organizations through joint meetings helped
dispel what one professor called the stereotype of "well-paid
NGO types all driving Pajeros [expensive, four-wheel-drive vehi-
cles]." Conversely, the meetings helped overcome legal services
NGOs' fears that law student internships would drag their organizations into bitterly partisan politics associated with some student
groups.

The Foundation itself was part of another community that
also played an important role regarding legal services. This was
the community of donors. Ford's Chiel was aware of fruitful
Ford/TAF co-funding of Philippine legal services groups. He
found that Ford, TAF, and NORAD similarly shared program priorities in Bangladesh. This cooperation allowed the three donors
to exchange ideas and impressions, to the mutual benefit of their
programs. They each funded different aspects of the work of
MLAA and Banchte Shekha, a women's movement that integrates
innovative legal services into its broader health, education, community mobilization, and livelihood programs in the country's
Jessore District. Initial support from TAF enabled grantees to
grow to a point where they could absorb larger Ford grants usefully. And by co-funding BLAST, TAF shared Ford's risk in making its initial grant to the group when nationwide legal aid work
could have proven controversial.

What have these grantees accomplished, both collectively and
individually? A few examples will suffice here; subsequent parts
of this chapter offer others. ASK and MLAA organized a 1992
Ford-funded conference that highlighted progressive rulings by
India's Supreme Court. The force of that intellectual example may
have helped pave the way for the Bangladesh High Court to
award BELA a landmark 1996 decision on standing to bring suit.
In that case, the Court also ruled in favor of BELA's argument for
proper resettlement and compensation for people displaced by
government flood control measures.

BELA's success with this issue may also stem from its productive efforts to involve high-level justices in seminars it organized. It made the NGO less of an alien presence in court, so that its arguments were more likely to be heard on their merits and less likely to be viewed as emanating from the legal profession's periphery. Other legal services NGOs might similarly benefit by efforts to bridge the gap between them and potentially sympathetic jurists. Senior private litigators in many countries often have the advantage of personal or professional familiarity with appellate judges. BELA's approach represents a step toward leveling the judicial playing field in a legitimate way. It enables NGOs and jurists to better understand each other's perspectives, without crossing the line to undue influence.

Strategic selection of cases has been another hallmark of BELA's approach to litigation. It has, for instance, sought to open up judicial perspectives on the environment by employing environmental arguments in seeking to block political activists from putting up wall posters in certain areas. Some judges resented the posters, because they were sometimes plastered on the jurists' property. Though not all NGO lawyers have agreed with this "poster" tactic, the approach demonstrates the need to pick and choose cases based on the prospects for jurisprudential advances. This can help to establish precedents for addressing broader issues.

Both in connection with and independently of litigation, grantees and other Bangladeshi groups use the media to enhance public awareness of the issues that concern them. ASK, BNWLA, and others have used high-profile cases to try to educate the public regarding systemic problems, such as police brutalization of women, and to generate pressure for a government response to particularly egregious crimes, such as trafficking of females for prostitution. Over the long haul the combination of litigation, media work, and advocacy may also spur governmental action regarding the underlying conditions that spawn abuses.

Another constituency-building strategy involves cultivating diverse connections around the country. Toward this end, BELA established links with local lawyers, journalists, NGOs, and political leaders in several parts of Bangladesh. And, of course, a nationwide legal aid network is at the core of BLAST's operations.

Moreover, as BELA's Farooque advised, "Never take anyone as a permanent enemy or as a permanent friend." Government officials or private parties who oppose public interest groups on one issue may support them on another. This has been BELA's experience regarding environmental matters and MLAA's in trying to educate and modify the positions of local religious leaders. MLAA's Huq emphasizes that "you can't ignore these people. . . . They've listened when we've pointed out to them that parts of our country's family law [that protect women's rights] were drafted by Islamic scholars."

Grantee leaders assert that, particularly in Bangladesh's heavily politicized environment, they strive for nonpartisan identities in offering services, building constituencies, and assembling coalitions. MLAA has backed away from working with a national group embroiled in partisan politics. And where being nonpartisan is not possible, it falls back on a bipartisan approach. MLAA and BLAST have addressed the presence of politically active members on their boards of trustees by ensuring that the nation's two major political parties are represented.

Employing Mediation in Legal Services: The Nature and Importance of the Strategy

As the preceding discussion suggests, former grantees are pursuing a variety of legal advocacy strategies. This report cannot fairly weigh their relative contributions to social justice in Bangladesh. It can, however, illuminate a few potentially useful lessons by highlighting how the Madaripur Legal Aid Association has made innovative use of an especially important strategy.

Shalish, loosely translated to mean mediation, is an indigenous practice that uses outside parties to facilitate the resolution of disputes. But it also can include strong elements of arbitration, in which the outside parties go beyond facilitation to heavily influence the outcome. MLAA has adapted shalish to better address the needs of women and other disadvantaged groups. It is the main way in which MLAA directly serves the over one million citizens of the Madaripur District of Bangladesh and, to a lesser extent, an additional million-plus residents of neighboring areas. The evolution and nature of its systematic, methodical approach merits some attention, particularly because it has been a model for other NGOs.

Formally founded as a court-oriented legal aid group in 1978, MLAA began using mediation in 1983 partly out of frustration with the expense and delay of the judicial system. In addition, many clients wanted their problems addressed as simply as possible, and MLAA could serve more through alternative dispute resolution. Ford and other donor assistance, including the NORAD-supported construction of a residential training facility in the early 1990s, enabled the organization to expand its legal services work over the years and to train NGOs from all over Bangladesh regarding shalish. It would be unfair and inaccurate to credit MLAA alone with the growing use of shalish in Bangladesh. ASK has employed a variation of it productively in Dhaka, as have other organizations in other locales. But leaders in the legal services and human rights community describe the association as a pioneering institution with the most systematic approach to mediation.

What, then, is that approach? Typically learning of MLAA through word of mouth, clients contact the organization through its village-based mediation workers or through its town-based branch offices. Most clients are women involved in marriage-related conflicts. Low-income farmers with land-related disputes constitute the next largest group. Once a client approaches MLAA and provides relevant information, the association decides whether and how it can help. In most instances this results in MLAA organizing a shalish to which it invites both the client and the opposing party. Relatives and friends are also welcome to attend. A mediation worker facilitates the event to some degree.

Village-based mediation committee (MC) members play a larger role. These are respected community figures whom MLAA has recruited to participate whenever a shalish takes place, and whom the association trains regarding family law, land law, mediation skills, and related matters. Some may have participated in traditional forms of shalish, but others (particularly the growing ranks of female MC members) are new to the process.[3] The number of MC members in attendance depends on their availability.

The actual shalish is often a loud and passionate event in

which disputants, relatives, MC members, and even uninvited community members congregate to express their thoughts and feelings. Additional observers—adults and children alike—gather in the room's doorway and outside. More than one exchange of opinions may occur simultaneously. Calm discussions explode into bursts of shouting and even laughter or tears. All of this typically takes place in a crowded schoolroom or other public space, sweltering most of the year, often with the noise of other community activities filtering in from outside. The number of participants and observers may range from a few dozen to well over one hundred.

The shalish for a given dispute may stretch over several months and a number of sessions. These may be supplemented by discussions and negotiations between the sessions. The MLAA mediation worker documents in writing the details of the conflict and the settlement agreement. MLAA reports that disputes are successfully resolved in 80 percent of its shalish cases.

Despite the expanding and apparently effective use of shalish in Bangladesh, enthusiasm for it must be tempered by the reality of the societal context. With some exceptions, this is a male-dominated procedure in a male-dominated society. A woman who resorts to shalish rarely expects equal treatment, as much as she deserves it. She more typically asks that her husband stop beating her, for example, or that he take her back into their home, or that he provide some minimal maintenance for their children.

Despite its pioneering role, MLAA has not aggressively sought to build gender equity into shalish and its other operations. One possible weakness in Ford's and other donors' support for the association, and in this author's donor-sponsored evaluation of its work, was insufficient attention to this important issue. The challenge for MLAA is a difficult one: to promote gender equity and still maintain credibility among men. Pushing for equity too fast could undermine that credibility in organizing shalish sessions and jeopardize the association's long-term efforts to gradually transform community attitudes. Not pushing hard enough undermines the very goal of equitable dispute resolution. With the encouragement of TAF, MLAA now is moving to better address this tension.

While it is not the perfect tool, NGO-initiated shalish in Bangladesh represents a significant advance over other options. Traditional shalish[4] is typically marked by gender bias and legal ignorance. This includes ignorance of Islamic law and how its more equitable aspects have been incorporated into the national legal framework. Patronage ties with community leaders also can come into play. These easily can work against a person who is less well connected than her or his opponent. Moreover, village "touts" (individuals who capitalize on a bit of legal knowledge and secretly sell their influence) may manipulate the process.

Those who can scrape together the will and resources to go to court face a similarly daunting array of obstacles that include expense, delay, corruption, sexism, processes they cannot comprehend, and the lack of enforcement of judgments. And where the poor do nothing, they face continued abuse, or additional dowry demands by a woman's husband, or some other undesirable combination of circumstances. Finally, when these very bad alternatives run their course, or if they never do, a woman may find herself without home or without income. She and her children may go hungry. She may be forced into begging or prostitution.

Against this backdrop, what difference does NGO-initiated shalish make? NGOs have taken this accessible, comprehensible and free dispute resolution vehicle—effectively, the only option open to impoverished villagers—and have started the slow process of fixing the vehicle's biases. They have already employed shalish to the benefit of many thousands of Bangladeshis. A 1999 study conducted for TAF by a Dhaka-based firm turned up encouraging results regarding the work of former Ford grantees and other NGOs. By a four-to-one margin, women who have been through NGO-initiated mediation expressed satisfaction with the results.

Just as significantly, the NGOs back up this process with litigation where necessary. They have neither the resources nor the inclination to take every case to court, nor is that the preference of many clients. But selective use of this option waves a big stick in front of recalcitrant husbands, discouraging egregious conduct. MLAA uses local attorneys to take a case directly to court in instances of serious criminal offenses such as murder and rape. It may also do so if mediation does not reach resolution, or if a husband breaks his agreement. As TAF Representative Karen Casper emphasizes, "If you don't have the power or means to litigate, you don't have a way to persuade a party to honor an agreement."

The NGOs have introduced national law into otherwise ill-informed community deliberations, where bias and ignorance previously had shaped standards. This enables shalish participants to inject the law into contentious discussions, or bolsters arguments they are prepared to make anyway. It would overstate the case to claim that the legal discussions are very sophisticated. At one heated session the author attended, a female MC member exclaimed, "This is Bangladesh, not Saudi Arabia! We have our own laws!" Even when actual legal content is not discussed, mere reference to the law is a significant step forward from absolute ignorance. And sometimes the actual content of the laws does enter the fray.

As significant as the words themselves, the MC member's interjection was important because of the speaker's gender. MLAA and other NGOs are gradually integrating women into MCs, placing anti-domestic violence posters in shalish meeting places, and encouraging women to attend and to speak up. While by no means a scientific sampling, the more than a dozen MLAA and other NGO-initiated shalishes that the author attended during three 1993–1997 consulting assignments possibly reflected a trend. The first few sessions featured a spurned wife huddled alone or with perhaps one female relative in a room full of men loudly deciding her fate. The more recent ones had women attending and participating, some as MC members and some as interested (and even vocal) observers. This was not gender equity in action: the procedures remained male dominated. But women are starting to have a voice, and that voice tends to be more sympathetic to the wives involved in disputes.

Furthermore, in the case of the very unusual movement, Banchte Shekha, which has worked for many years to build women's economic, organizational, and educational empowerment in a relatively limited area of the country, shalish actually puts women on something closer to an equal footing with men.[5] Mediation differs in such a context because underlying community attitudes and relative power of women have shifted. Law is used here as part of an integrated strategy for establishing gender equity, one that recognizes the many extralegal forces at play. The movement's influence in some communities is such that its staff can act as mediators.

At least two overlapping lessons flow from these phenomena. One is that education, economic empowerment, and other basic development efforts are fundamental to advancing women's rights. Mediation and other legal services alone are not enough.

The matter should not come down to an "either/or" choice, however, for the other lesson is that legal services can complement mainstream development programs. That lesson is confirmed by a 1994 evaluation of a pilot project in which four family planning organizations used MLAA training to offer shalishes and other legal services in their communities. The project and the research were initiated by TAF, with U.S. Agency for International Development funding. The findings indicated that the integration of legal services and population control programs benefited both activities.[6] The potential value of such integration is suggested by a 1995 World Bank study, which documents domestic violence's damage to a variety of socioeconomic development priorities.[7] To the extent, then, that legal services help ameliorate problems such as domestic violence, they may promote societal development more broadly. An additional lesson that emerges from this discussion regards the need for further research in this field, in view of both the potential impact and the limitations of NGO-initiated shalish.

BLAST: Engaging the Mainstream Legal Community

Another respect in which MLAA proved important to the Ford law initiative was that it served as partial model for the creation of BLAST. Founded in 1993, BLAST quickly evolved into a nationwide network of offices engaged in litigation, mediation, and policy advocacy.

The Foundation saw potentially replicable strategies in how MLAA had both improved on the traditional shalish process and at the same time had engaged local lawyers in legal aid. Chiel was convinced that "to create a human rights culture in a country and make the 'social change' function of law more than a foreign idea, you must have a large array of lawyers involved." As of 1992, the core of legal services grantees could not provide the necessary critical mass of lawyers, and few new groups were emerging.

Fortunately, a widely respected Bar Council leader, Kamal Hossain, already had a vision for a nationwide legal aid program. His ideas both informed and matched the Foundation's evolving thinking regarding PILI. Over the course of a year of constructive but sometimes taxing discussions with the Foundation, the gap between vision and details was closed, and plans for the new organization were finalized. A crucial step was the recruitment of MLAA's Huq to also head BLAST. Another was the identification of Shahdeen Malik, a lawyer whose multifaceted background included several years in London, to effectively run the organization on a daily basis. Huq had the experience and savvy to provide valuable advice on how to set up a legal aid office, recruit lawyers to work with it part time for limited compensation, and to establish NGO-initiated shalish. Malik had the time and breadth of perspective to integrate Huq's detailed knowledge into Hossain's vision.

Ford's original PILI paper explained the assumption that motivated the Foundation to support Hossain's idea: if more mainstream attorneys are introduced to legal aid, they "will increasingly be willing to render assistance to indigent clients and will in the process be exposed to the broader issues of social justice and reform of the legal system." And even if the ethics and attitudes of many bar members precluded focusing on the Bar Council itself, Chiel was convinced that "there were some good [lawyers] . . . present throughout the country." Above and beyond the important services it would provide in offices throughout Bangladesh, BLAST could help build a community of activists by facilitating interaction among mainstream lawyers, legal services groups, and other NGOs.

Partly because of its Bar Council links, BLAST won quick acceptance in the legal community and established a nationwide network of offices. Will this translate into the bar as a whole becoming a strong force for reform? Perhaps. But the arrangement promises to at least make the legal profession more supportive of legal aid and human rights. Hossain points out that "getting a district bar association to [psychologically] 'own' a local BLAST" unit increases the unit's effectiveness. He also notes that "the possibility of Dhaka backup by established lawyers emboldens local lawyers" to take on tough cases against influential individuals.

Based on a recent consultancy for the Dutch development agency Novib, Margaret Groarke concludes that "BLAST is very respected because it has moved slowly but steadily. Frequently, the most tired side gives up [in protracted legal disputes], but BLAST doesn't, which is especially impressive because its attorneys get compensated on a per case basis. So people see them as honest, hardworking, and committed. Also, the connection to the Bar Council and to the upper echelons of the local bar has helped them tremendously."

In some respects, BLAST has exceeded initial expectations. The organization has expanded its network of offices from eleven to fifteen, becoming even more prominent as the nation's largest legal aid organization. In combination with ASK and MLAA, it also is conducting policy research and advocacy on proposals for a human rights commission and a national legal aid scheme. And with Novib's support (partly through Groarke's consultancy), it is addressing a gap in its initial operations by developing a gender policy that will enable it to better advance women's rights within and outside the organization.

Finally, BLAST has moved into public interest litigation, winning key Supreme Court decisions. One regards health and consumer rights—specifically, the practice of selling salt that lacks mandated iodine content. (Iodine deficiency causes goiters.) In another case, pertaining to deaths in police custody, BLAST took on the common but rarely challenged practice of prisoner abuse, and the legal pretexts under which it occurs. Yet a third case successfully challenged those sections of a 1997 law that required a show of hands, rather than secret balloting, for village council representatives. Given the pressure that open voting would invite from powerful community figures, the ruling is highly significant.

Law Clinics:
Investing in the Next Generation of Lawyers

Building up both an NGO core and a network of legal aid lawyers would begin to address current needs. But looking ahead, many Bangladeshis saw a need to invest in law students, the legal profession's future, for the nascent public interest law community to thrive. There also was a strong consensus among legal services lawyers and mainstream attorneys regarding the low quality of graduating law students' legal skills. These factors motivated creation of PILI's third branch: the introduction of clinical legal education programs at the nation's three major law schools, at Dhaka, Chittagong, and Rajshahi universities.

For these new law clinics to thrive, they needed good leadership with a demonstrated commitment to educational innovation. Mizanur Rahman, a law professor and an inspiring faculty advisor to the University of Dhaka law student group, was an ideal candidate to head the clinic there. At the University of Chittagong, Dean M. Shah Alam offered a progressive perspective on legal education. And at Rajshahi University, Law Department Chairman A.F.M. Mohsin's prior experience as a judge brought extensive trial expertise and good local bar connections to bear in establishing the program. Without such dedicated faculty at the three universities, Foundation support would have gone for naught.

Finding and funding the right talent was only a part of the process of launching the clinics. One of the greatest challenges was overcoming many key figures' understandable concerns that clinical legal education was a creature of resource-rich Western nations and that it could never succeed in Bangladesh. On a Ford-sponsored visit to the United States, Rahman indeed found nearly all American programs too complex for easy adaptation to Bangladesh. Exposure to such programs in neighboring countries, however, was far more fruitful. The Foundation supported visits by law faculty members to a pioneering clinical legal education program in Nepal, to India's National Law School, and to other sites in Sri Lanka.

Another key element in building clinical legal education was the recruitment of two successive American lawyers as advisors to the clinics. The reasoning here was that ongoing advice and training was necessary for a concept as new as clinical legal education. Already resident in Dhaka, Catherine Lincoln and then

Groarke (subsequently the Novib consultant) undertook a variety of tasks. They helped formulate new courses and introduced new teaching methods that emphasized practical training, and they demonstrated by example how these courses and methods could be employed.

The clinics aimed to upgrade Bangladeshi student skills while exposing them to legal aid and NGO work. This experience takes place at a crucially formative stage in the students' careers, when many mix idealism with surprising cynicism about their profession's ethics and orientation. As one observer put it, "NGO exposure can help put these students in touch with their country's problems, because many of them [coming from relatively privileged backgrounds] are removed from that reality." NGO links also can create a "pipeline effect," helping to convert student dedication into concrete knowledge and actions that broaden the community of legal activists. Some may commit to NGO or pro bono work after graduation; others might develop new perspectives on social justice. And as their role in the legal profession grows over the years, they could become powerful voices for reform.

As the clinical programs matured, so did the potential to link them to NGOs. Groarke helped assess how NGOs could use students, and acquainted these organizations with the considerable work involved in supervising interns. To avoid misunderstandings, she provided written guidelines to both the law schools and the NGOs regarding student placements. These preparations led to student internships that Groarke reports are starting to "work well for the NGOs as a recruiting mechanism" for attracting top law graduates to such organizations as BELA and BLAST. A number of students reportedly have built on their clinical experiences to conduct legal awareness sessions for impoverished Bangladeshis during their semester breaks, reflecting a possible interest in continuing to provide assistance after they become attorneys. Groarke speculates that whereas some law students otherwise might have sought involvement in the bitter (and even violent) political battles that periodically plague Bangladeshi campuses, they now have an outlet for more constructive engagement with societal issues.

Conclusion

Changes and Contributions

The long-term nature of development means that the larger effects of Ford-supported law work in Bangladesh will become clear only years from now. Nevertheless, some tentative impressions are starting to emerge regarding grantees' progress and impact, and the roles Ford played.

Consider the standard set by the 1994 PILI description cited earlier in this chapter: "If successful, this initiative should forge an increasingly broad-based community of like-minded activists committed to changing the existing legal structures and conventions." It would be a vast overstatement to give sole credit to Ford or its grantees for the growth of legal advocacy and legal awareness work in Bangladesh in recent years. Still, these grantees are part of a growing movement that involves mainstream development NGOs. The Legal Awareness Forum, comprising twenty-four organizations, includes several that only became engaged in this work in the late 1990s. What's more, some top law graduates are opting for full-time or part-time work with legal services NGOs. Shahdeen Malik of BLAST reports that "we're now hiring students from the upper 10 percent of their classes" for Dhaka-based positions. And leading young lawyers have maintained affiliations with ASK policy research projects, despite leaving the country to obtain advanced degrees in Britain.

Of equal importance, what was a set of relatively isolated entities five years ago has become "an increasingly broad-based community" demonstrating growing sophistication in fields ranging from mediation to public interest litigation to policy advocacy. A leading NGO figure, Khushi Kabir of the group Nijera Kori, feels that "what started as individual support for victims has moved into using cases to educate, to publicize, to pursue policy change." BELA's Farooque similarly observed that increased NGO interaction has helped once isolated legal services groups move "from a localized vision to a national vision. For example, now they're talking about the rights of female prisoners and proposed amendments to the jail code." And with the law clinics starting to link students with NGOs, there is the prospect that this community will keep growing.

Other evidence of this community's evolution is seen in grantees' growing connections with one another and outside groups. Only the most detailed diagram could depict the increasingly intricate web of cooperative connections among NGO lawyers, mainstream practitioners, law students, professors, journalists, and development NGOs' personnel. For example, ASK, BLAST, and MLAA are cooperating in a policy advocacy project. ASK has trained field-workers of the Grameen Bank (an internationally renowned NGO) on basic legal issues. As it does with other non-Dhaka cases, ASK refers Grameen-generated work to BLAST field offices. A Chittagong law student group, Rights Implementation for Social Emancipation, also has sent cases to the local BLAST office. The law clinics are arranging internships at former Ford grantees and other groups. ASK, BNWLA, and BELA work with media in various ways. And BLAST and BELA have worked together on public interest litigation.

Above and beyond providing funding, the Foundation occasionally facilitated some of this progress. For instance, participants report that Ford/TAF-sponsored meetings that arranged student internships (through the law clinics) at NGOs helped break down barriers between law schools and NGOs. The author has also observed a much more general development over the course of three consulting assignments in Bangladesh: legal services personnel spoke of each other in a more familiar and supportive manner in 1996 and 1997 than they had in 1993.

To some extent, the Foundation directly funded the community's growth. This is the case with the law clinics and BLAST's nationwide network. But, as ASK, BELA, and BLAST all report, Ford's support also led to other sources providing aid.

These are positive medium-term results. Yet, the sad realities of widespread poverty and gender inequity continue to permeate Bangladeshi society and will do so for many years to come. But Ford's former grantees have helped start a process through which the legal system is beginning to be used to positively impact specific populations and policies, and may effectively contribute to ameliorating injustices and promoting development over the long term.

Lessons and Insights

The same caveat that applies to assessing the impact of PILI's grantees applies to lessons that might flow from their work: in many respects, it is too soon to tell. Still, certain innovations that marked their work and the initiative overall might prove useful in Bangladesh or abroad. Some of these promising insights follow.

Legal Services Strategies

1. NGO adaptation of traditional community mediation (shalish) has arguably expanded access to justice perhaps more than Bangladeshi courts have. NGO-initiated shalish is far preferable to the unmodified traditional practices in which harsh, unfair judgments spring from local leaders' legal ignorance, indifference, corruption, or gender and class biases. The new shalish also offers strong advantages over the courts, which are often tainted by delay, high costs, and procedures incomprehensible to most nonlawyers. MLAA and certain other NGOs accordingly have emphasized mediation over the past decade.

2. The NGO approach to shalish has worked best when integrated with other ongoing activities. Bangladeshi NGOs do not simply arrange for mediation sessions to take place. By selecting, training, and informally monitoring mediators, they ameliorate biases that plague traditional mediation. And they do take cases to court for a minority of clients. The very threat of litigation creates a strong incentive for parties to reach and honor settlements. Going to court addresses client problems that are too severe for mediation to treat.

3. NGO-initiated shalish has been particularly effective where an NGO builds its mediation program on a base of deeper social change. Such is the case with Banchte Shekha. This women's movement conducts a range of activities that organize, educate, and economically empower women. The mediation sessions it coordinates place women and men on close to the same plane. This reflects the transformations Banchte Shekha has brought about in communities where it has operated for years. The duration

of Banchte Shekha's commitment (and that of its donors) also merits emphasis. The social change it spurs is based on intensive long-term work on a number of fronts.

4. Innovations in mediation took root in Bangladesh in ways that imported processes could not. MLAA and other groups based their mediation work on societal traditions, while seeking to change inequitable aspects of those traditions (most notably how they treat women).

5. Grantees have served women partly by defining human rights protection as starting within the household, emphasizing that women's rights are human rights, regardless of who perpetrates abuses. "Many of our worst problems are not just a matter of human rights with respect to the state," comments a former BNWLA leader now with a Western development organization. "Many issues are within the family."

6. Familiarizing jurists with progressive legal thinking and organizations arguably helped BELA obtain a landmark legal victory regarding standing to bring suit. It may not be a coincidence that this ruling followed a 1992 (Ford-funded) ASK/MLAA regional seminar that helped make Bangladeshi jurists more familiar with expanded notions of standing in India, and a series of fora to which BELA invited selected jurists.

7. The experience of MLAA on a local level and BLAST across the country suggests that engaging mainstream lawyers in legal services can serve multiple purposes, particularly when done by an NGO specifically devoted to legal services. Most immediately, it deepens the pool of attorneys available to help the poor. It also may generate professional support for law-oriented NGOs, which can strengthen those groups' impact. In the long run, it may contribute to building an important constituency for human rights and legal reform.

Clinical Legal Education

1. Placements with legal services groups offer Bangladeshi law students valuable opportunities to broaden their perspectives, integrate such services into their careers, and

join the community of legal activists. There are initial indications that such placements are affecting the career choices of some and encouraging pro bono work by others. Even where a clinical program does not link students with NGOs, its classroom instruction could acquaint them with development issues and the legal needs of low-income populations.

2. By addressing human rights and social justice concerns, law clinics and NGOs may help upgrade the quality of the legal profession in general. Dismay at the profession's low ethical and professional standards drove many top law graduates into teaching or business in the past. The clinics and expanding NGO opportunities improved legal training and encouraged high-caliber graduates to practice law.

3. Launching and refining a clinical legal education program is a laborious process. Clinical teaching differs markedly from the theoretical, lecture-oriented method that dominates legal education in many nations, and considerable up-front effort must be devoted to materials preparation and teacher training. University of Chittagong Law School Dean Alam emphasizes that "it is important not to be too ambitious."

Donor Approaches and Actions

1. PILI profited from being grounded in existing opportunities, interests, and needs. Although the Foundation's initial needs assessment of Bangladesh's legal system revealed significant weaknesses within such institutions as the judiciary and law enforcement, its assessment of interests at play within these institutions found that by and large they were not dedicated to reform. The Foundation's opportunities assessment, on the other hand, found that it could best contribute to impact on the nation's legal system by working with the nation's NGOs and law schools. Yet another consideration informing the focus of the initiative was the Foundation's longtime experience working with NGOs and laws schools in other countries.

2. Bangladeshi grantees' innovations in mediation suggest that often the best methods for building good practices can

involve supporting in-country organizations' operations. Where those organizations evince innovation and effectiveness on their own, a heavy investment of Western advice and training geared toward improving their operations may not be the best use of inevitably limited resources. What grantees often need most is not extensive foreign advice, but the funds to provide services and to "learn on the job" while doing so.

Looking Ahead

What issues confront the law clinics, BLAST, and other groups the Foundation supported? As in most countries, one challenge is financial: the extent to which BLAST and the other legal services groups can sustain their funding levels is uncertain. Still, it is a promising sign that other donors have entered the legal services arena, enabling BLAST, for example, to expand both the scale and nature of its operations.

Law clinics may face fewer financial hurdles than the law-related NGOs, since the clinics' long-term costs are low and interest apparently remains high. University of Chittagong's Alam says, "Institutional momentum is building up among teachers and students to demand continuation of the law clinic." A constituency has been created. This may hold particularly true at Chittagong, which thus far is the only law school to offer credit for law clinic enrollment. Market forces of a sort may influence the other two universities to maintain the clinics, since the clinics seem to provide students with skills that both students and law firms seek. Another factor will be the degree to which the universities retain high-quality personnel to supervise these programs.

Ford's former grantees face other challenges, and in two respects could become victims of their own success. First, a few may face the administrative task of managing larger operations and growing sums of donor funds. And to the extent that the government seeks to emulate the NGOs' mediation innovations, it could put in place a state-run system that might prove bureaucratic, politically partisan, and ineffective.

It is encouraging that more NGOs, including large, mainstream organizations, are engaged in law-oriented work. The existence of a twenty-four-member Legal Awareness Forum would not have been thought possible a decade ago. The degree of impact could hinge on whether this expansion is mainly confined to legal awareness work, or whether it increasingly includes other important functions such as litigation, mediation, and policy advocacy. With this in mind, donors and NGOs alike may want to probe questions that this paper only begins to answer. What concrete benefits flow from law-oriented work? Are good laws being implemented more? To what degrees are mediation, building legal awareness, and other legal services affecting people's lives positively? In what ways can this best be documented? One approach might be to assess whether communities where mediation and other services are being carried out demonstrate changes in legal knowledge, attitudes, actions, or material circumstances compared to others where such activities are absent.

There also is the question of how legal services can be best integrated with other development work. The PILI-supported groups could conceivably draw on their expertise to be resources to larger, mainstream development NGOs. The TAF-supported research and the encouraging Banchte Shekha experience cited in this report offer evidence that real benefits can flow from such integration.

This chapter has scratched the surface of some of these questions. Appropriate research, carried out by the country's social scientists in partnership with NGOs, could yield firmer answers.

Notes

1. Data International, *Women in Bangladesh: A Situation Analysis,* a report prepared for UNICEF/Dhaka (Dhaka: June 30, 1993), pp. 81–82.

2. Eirik G. Jansen, *Rural Bangladesh: Competition for Scarce Resources* (Dhaka: University Press Limited, 1986), p. 84.

3. Other NGOs have adopted variations on MLAA's approach. Some seek to advise and modify the perspectives of participants in traditional shalish. Others seek to set up parallel structures that do not involve traditional participants. Many take the hybrid approach of MLAA. Much hinges on the degree to which socioeconomic change, often spurred by development work, has paved the way for departures from tradition in a given community.

4. In its more extreme forms, as documented by Amnesty International in 1993 and 1994 reports, shalish has imposed brutal and even lethal punishment on women.

5. During PILI, TAF actually funded Banchte Shekha's legal services component, Ford its health program, and NORAD its construction of a major training center. But because these efforts related to each other, all three were engaged with Banchte Shekha's overall work.

6. Karen L. Casper and Sultana Kamal, *Evaluation Report: Community Legal Services Conducted by Family Planning NGOs,* a report prepared for The Asia Foundation (Dhaka: March 1995).

7. Lori L. Heise with Jacqueline Pitanguy and Adrienne Germain, *Violence Against Women: The Hidden Health Burden; World Bank Discussion Paper No. 255* (Washington, D.C.: The World Bank, 1994).

Appendix: People Interviewed for This Study

[Note: This list includes individuals interviewed by the author during his three consulting trips to Bangladesh during the 1990s and who contributed directly or indirectly to this Bangladesh case study. It does not comprehensively cover, however, the names of all persons, including clients of former Ford Foundation grantees, with whom he has conducted group interviews.]

Kafil Ahmed
Project Officer, OXFAM, Dhaka

Nawshad Ahmed
Program Officer, The Asia Foundation, Dhaka

Rafique Uddin Ahmed
Deputy Director, Centre for Development Services, Dhaka

Shafique Ahmed
Barrister-at-Law and Secretary-General, Bangladesh Law Teachers Association, Dhaka

Khurshid Alam
Director, Legal Action Unit, Ain O Salish Kendra, Dhaka

M. Shah Alam
Professor and Dean, Faculty of Law, University of Chittagong

Salma Ali
Vice President, National Women Lawyers Association, Dhaka

Ershadul Bari
Professor and Dean, Faculty of Law, University of Dhaka

Rabeya Begum
Project Director, Shariatpur Development Society, Shariatpur

Rashida Begun, Project Officer, OXFAM, Dhaka

Maren Brennesvik
Second Secretary (Development Affairs), Royal Norwegian
Embassy, Dhaka

Karen L. Casper
Representative, The Asia Foundation, Dhaka

David Chiel
Former Acting Representative, The Ford Foundation, Dhaka;
now, Assistant Representative, The Ford Foundation, Namibia

Omar Faruque Chowdhury
Executive Director, Centre for Development Services, Dhaka

Rezaul Karim Chowdhury
Coordinator, Bangladesh Legal Aid and Services Trust,
Chittagong

Mohiuddin Farooque (deceased)
Secretary-General, Bangladesh Environmental Lawyers Association, Dhaka

Fawzia Karim Feroze
President, Bangladesh National Women Lawyers Association,
Dhaka

Angela Gomes
Director, Banchte Sheka, Jessore

Jacinta Gonsalves
Population Program Officer, The Asia Foundation, Dhaka

Margaret Groarke
Consultant/Law Clinic Advisor, The Ford Foundation, Dhaka

Syeda Rizwana Hasan
Staff Lawyer, Bangladesh Environmental Lawyers Association,
Dhaka

Hameeda Hossain
Honorary Secretary, Ain O Salish Kendra, Dhaka

Kamal Hossain
Barrister-at-Law, Dhaka

Sara Hossain
Legal Affairs Officer, International Centre for the Legal Protection of Human Rights (INTERIGHTS), London

Fazlul Huq
Executive Director, Madiripur Legal Aid Association,
Madiripur

Wahida Huq
Senior Program Officer, The World Bank, Dhaka

M. Amir-Ul Islam
Barrister-at-Law, The Law Associates, Dhaka

Nazrul Islam
Senior Program Officer (Training), The Asia Foundation,
Dhaka

Md. Faizul Kabir
Barrister-at-Law, Dhaka

Khushi Kabir
Coordinator, Nijera Kori, Dhaka

Shahjahan Kabir
Program Advisor, The Asia Foundation, Dhaka

Borhan Uddin Khan
Assistant Professor, Faculty of Law, University of Dhaka

Reidar Kvam
Former Assistant Resident Representative, Norwegian Agency for Development Cooperation, Royal Norwegian Embassy, Dhaka

Catherine Lincoln
Consultant/Law Clinic Advisor, The Ford Foundation, Dhaka

Abdullahel Mahmud
Coordinator, Centre for Development Services, Dhaka

Shahdeen Malik
Advisor, Bangladesh Legal Aid and Services Trust, Dhaka

Fazlul Hoque Miah
Project Coordinator, Palli Shishu Foundation of Bangladesh, Dhaka

Alauddin Mollah
Programme Head, Social Mobilization and Development Program, Ganoshahajjo Sangstha, Dhaka

Tawfique Nawaz
Juris Counsel, law offices of Tawfique Nawaz and Associates, Dhaka

Fazilatun Nessa
Population Program Officer, The Asia Foundation, Dhaka

Ghazi Shafiqur Rahman
Executive Director, Palli Shishu Foundation of Bangladesh,
Dhaka

Mizanur Rahman
Senior Lecturer and Law Clinic Supervisor, Faculty of Law,
University of Dhaka

Mozibur Rahman
Chief Executive, Shariatpur Development Society, Shariatpur

Masud Karim Ripon
Finance Coordinator, Madaripur Legal Aid Association,
Madaripur

Rokeya Sattar
Staff member, Banchte Shekha, Jessore

Khan Md. Shahid
Chief Coordinator, Madaripur Legal Aid Association,
Madaripur

Salma Sobhan
Executive Director, Ain O Salish Kendra, Dhaka

Ayul Ali Talukder
Director, Palli Unnayan Kendra—A Centre for Rural Development, Madaripur

Neelan Tiruchelvam (deceased)
Director, Law and Society Trust, and Director, International
Centre for Ethnic Studies, Colombo, Sri Lanka

Tahera Yasmin
Country Representative, OXFAM of the UK and Ireland,
Dhaka

Group Interviews

Members of Law Review, a law student group at the University of Dhaka

Staff of the Madaripur Legal Aid Association, Bangladesh Environmental Law Association, Banchte Shekha, Ain O Salish Kendra, the Palli Shishu Foundation, and other NGOs

Members of Banchte Shekha

5

Contributing to Legal Reform in China

AUBREY McCUTCHEON

The Ford Foundation's law-related activities in China have evolved in the context of fundamental and wide-ranging changes in Chinese society—a society with a fifth of the world's people and some four thousand years of recorded history. One aspect of those changes has been China's endeavor to rebuild and improve its legal system. From the start of the "reform and opening" era, begun in earnest in December 1978 by the ruling Chinese Communist Party, China has worked to rebuild a body of formal law and the infrastructure of the legal system, such as courts and law faculties, among other components. Citizen mediation committees were also established to resolve minor disputes through informal means. But the legal reform process is far from complete, and the need for improvement of the formal legal system increases as the society deepens its economic, social, and political transitions. At the same time, the unmet need continues for a legal system that fully protects the civil rights and liberties of all citizens.

Through ongoing involvement since 1979, Ford's law grants have contributed to needs identified in collaboration with Chinese legal experts. But it is the work of those experts along with Ford's grantees that is the noteworthy contribution to legal reform.

The Foundation hoped to be a long-term partner in China's efforts to rebuild and reform its formal legal system by initiating contributions in the legal research and teaching community that it felt would play an increasingly important role over time. Its first law-related grants went to support legal education and scholarship, and to help rebuild law faculties. From 1988, when the Foundation first opened its Beijing office, law grantmaking grew to include support for training of judges and for legislative research and drafting. While continuing to evolve and sharpen their focus, these lines of work have been carried on into the 1990s. Since the early 1990s, scholars have been supported in their research on specific legal policy and law, the enhancement of citizens' rights, as well as exploration of law's role in society, and basic principles underlying a formalized legal system. From the mid-1990s, the Foundation has been able to assist an expanding Chinese legal community increasingly focused on judicial reform and the problem of implementation of laws. The latter is addressed in a line of Foundation programming that has come to be called "law-in-action." It supports legal services, the improved design and operations of legal institutions, and efforts to increase public awareness of new possibilities in the legal system.

After reviewing China's changing legal context, this study discusses the evolution and early approaches of the Foundation's law-related grantmaking there. It then explores two more recent and ongoing foci of work: judicial reform, including training of judges, and law-in-action. The conclusion briefly restates some of the most salient lessons and insights that emanate from the study.

China's Changing Legal Context

Chinese society is one not only of great size but also of tremendous accomplishments and complexity. These factors should be borne in mind when considering the challenges of its current transition. The transition in China's legal culture and system is addressing characteristics of its past fifty years of experience with Chinese socialism, as well as others that are much more deeply rooted. Millennial and powerful traditions emphasize the guidance of human behavior through internalized moral standards rather than external rules of law, and favor informal means of compromise over formal adjudication of disputes. In spite of more recent major changes, these traditions still maintain some influence today.

The Chinese legal system is now undergoing its third major transformation of the past century. The first began during the final years of China's last imperial dynasty as the society was increasingly impacted by foreign cultures. It was accelerated with the fall of the dynasty in 1911, the declaration of a Republic in 1912, and the subsequent coming to power of the Nationalist government. During this period, the government abrogated imperial laws and adopted laws based on the models of French, Japanese, and German civil codes.

A second legal transformation followed the revolution of 1949 and the establishment of the People's Republic of China (PRC). For a short period thereafter, the policy of the Chinese Communist Party (CCP) focused on replacing laws of the Nationalist government with selected aspects of the Soviet legal system. During this stage, a system of laws, legal services, and legal institutions—although of a new provenance—was maintained. It was followed, however, by an even deeper transformation that began with the Anti-Rightist Campaign in 1957 and continued through the Cultural Revolution of 1966–1976. The CCP initially sought to use law as a tool in its policy of class struggle. It later decided there was little need for law in the context of class struggle, and that in many cases law was an obstacle. As is now widely acknowledged by Chinese scholars and officials, between 1957 and 1976 law and legal institutions were despised, ignored, and then largely destroyed. Some lawyers were condemned as rightists and some were sentenced for labor reeducation. The Ministry of Justice, the procuracy,[1] and legal advisory offices were all closed. Legal education also ceased, and the courts, under the control of military commissions, virtually did not operate. For nearly twenty years a formal legal system ceased to function.

China's third and current legal transformation also corresponds with wide social, economic, and political changes, in this case the "reform and opening" era begun in 1978. As part of these changes, a formal legal system is being rebuilt. Legal education and the procuracy were reinstated in 1978 and the Ministry of Justice was reestablished in 1979. The role of the judiciary, and its caseload, have steadily increased, and efforts are under way to train judges and procurators. Legislation has also proliferated over the past two decades. Moreover, the PRC is now a signatory to most of the principal multilateral treaties for economic cooperation, as well as international covenants on women's rights; civil and political rights; and economic, social, and cultural rights.

Most experts agree that the current legal transformation was prompted by both economic and political concerns: the need to support domestic market reforms and encourage new foreign investment, and the desire to control the arbitrary misuse of power by government officials that characterized the Cultural Revolution. The absence of a formal legal system for nearly twenty years went hand in hand with rejection of fundamental principles of rights, governance, and the supremacy of law, and this will not be easy to rectify. These principles, not firmly established earlier, remain incompletely grounded, as do the implementation of new national laws, full provision of human rights, and the enforcement of court judgments.

The reestablishment of formal legal education was one of the first basic steps in the current reform effort. Professor Li Dun of the Chinese Academy of Social Sciences (CASS) notes that, in all of China, only some sixty qualified potential law professors were available in 1978. Professor Randle Edwards of Columbia Law School remarks that there were only two partially functioning law faculties at the time. In addition to the task of reviving and modernizing legal education, there was a great need to develop the legal profession. In response to the grave and immediate need for lawyers in the early 1980s, accreditation was conferred upon many people who had little practical experience or legal training. No national qualifying exam for lawyers existed before 1986, and criteria for granting qualifications also varied throughout the country. As a result, great disparities exist in the quality of lawyers, depending upon educational and occupational background and date of admission to practice.[2] Furthermore, the concept of lawyers as independent professionals rather than state legal workers was not recognized until the early 1990s.

China has reestablished a formal judicial system, with four levels of courts and over one hundred fifty thousand judges, but few believe the judiciary is yet a competent and professional institution. "Just how far China has come, and how far it still must go, in building a legal system that can serve the needs of a rapidly changing society is illustrated by the state of its judiciary," says Phyllis Chang, the Foundation's program officer in Beijing responsible for law programming. With the decision to rebuild the courts at the end of the 1970s, many demobilized and retired military personnel and other civil servants with no formal legal training were transferred to the judiciary. This exacerbated a skills problem that had developed much earlier, when judges were selected from among peasants, workers, and soldiers who were also without legal training. Many judges still lack training in law beyond a vocational degree certificate. Although greatly cut back, the practice of filling judicial posts with retired military staff continued throughout the 1990s in some lower courts in small towns and rural areas. In these lower courts, where most cases are heard, high numbers of judges have no formal postsecondary education in any academic field. To address this exigency, the government has pursued judicial training programs since the late 1980s.

Aside from the need for training of judges, the government has more recently recognized the necessity for more fundamental judicial reforms. Court procedures have recently undergone great change, but many experts and officials see a need for improvements in the way judges conceive their role and obligations within the new legal order. This will undoubtedly be hard to achieve in spite of China's changing legal context. Many judges do not view their role as different from that of any other state civil servant. The appeal process is often threatened by judges seeking guidance in their decisions from their superiors on higher courts. Furthermore, courts are weak in comparison to government agencies and CCP organs, making them vulnerable to outside pressures. Although Chinese law now provides citizens with the right to sue government agencies, such challenges are often thwarted by courts that are hesitant or unwilling to take on administrative organs. The problem of judicial corruption has also stirred public and official attention.

The current legal reform effort has been strengthened by a revived legal education and research community. This community plays an important role in training judges, introduces new ways of thinking about law in Chinese society, and informs government awareness and policies about both the implementation of laws and judicial reform. Since the end of the 1970s, there have been numerous areas in which government entities, CCP officials, and a cross section of Chinese legal academics have agreed on an agenda for research, development, and implementation of new laws and other related changes to the legal system. As in some other countries, in China the success of policy research, formulation, and promotion on sensitive policy topics can often be facilitated by low-key but sustained endeavors, without pressure to publish or publicize results.

In one important example of such governmental and academic synergy, discussions were held over many years among academics and policymakers about policy on the "rule of law." Should law be pursued as merely an instrument to achieve state policy goals, or rather as a value to be embodied by both the state and society? Put differently, this is the contest between the "supremacy of law" and only "running the country according to law" in order to maintain social stability and achieve economic development. China's history of past imperial rule and the use of law as a means of class struggle were considered in those debates, along with current legal reform efforts. Some scholars acknowledged the inevitable instrumental uses of law and legislation, but described the importance of permanent underlying principles designed to achieve a just and lasting legal order.[3] In late 1997, the CCP adopted "*yi fa zhi guo*" as its official policy objective. Some experts interpret this phrase, read with other official statements, to mean, "governing according to law," while others say it represents the concept of the rule of law. In either case, it is widely agreed, although there is still a considerable need for definition of the role law will play in Chinese society, China's legal transformation took an important new step.

One final aspect of China's changing context should be noted because of its increasing influence on the implementation of the new legal system and the delivery of legal services. As described by Anthony Saich, the Foundation's representative in China from 1994 to 1999, the wider transition taking place has resulted in a greater degree of autonomy for government-supported organizations, such as the All China Women's Federation, and the emergence of new social organizations that fulfill social welfare functions and liaise between state and society. Some of these new organizations conduct law-related activities, including, increasingly, the delivery of legal services.

A number of these law-related organizations are hosted by government academic institutions or rely on relationships with government leaders to facilitate their work. Others are created by the state or CCP, and are what would be known in other parts of the world as GONGOs—government-organized nongovernmental organizations. Still others are self-organized and managed. These new groups have proven instrumental in advancing the law reform agenda in China.

Ford's Law Program Evolution and Early Approaches

The Foundation's law program in China has evolved over twenty years from modest grantmaking for the exchange of Chinese and American law scholars to a full law and rights program based in Beijing. During its early years, the program's primary focus was on support for legal education and research. Prior to 1979, the Foundation was a major supporter of Chinese and other geographic area studies in the United States and several other countries. Support for Chinese studies was intended to enhance understanding of China in the United States and elsewhere in the world, and was motivated by a belief that too little knowledge existed outside of China to understand the dramatic changes taking place there or their wider international consequences. The Foundation also helped establish the National Committee on U.S.-China Relations and the Committee on Scholarly Communications with the People's Republic, and supported the East Asian Legal Studies program at Harvard Law School. The Andrew Mellon Foundation was another major supporter of such early work.

The Foundation's first direct support to Chinese institutions came after China's reform and opening began in December 1978. For the first two years, the emphasis was on promoting mutual access and understanding between the two societies. Beginning in

1981, with the availability of additional funding, Foundation support was concentrated in the fields of international relations, economics, and law, reflecting the salient features of China's reforms. Annual commitments grew during the 1980s, and in January 1988, the Foundation became the first private foreign foundation to open an office in China. Thereafter, grant programs were expanded to include rural poverty and resource management, reproductive health, and culture.

By that time Foundation staff had already gained several years of insight on the needs and priorities of China's rapidly changing legal system. Much of that insight was provided by CASS, the government-organized research institute that is one of the Foundation's earliest and most long-standing grantee partners in China. CASS also remains the Foundation's official sponsor, allowing it, as a foreign organization, to maintain offices in China. Other early grantee partnerships were established with the small and newly revived legal education community at several leading universities.

Some of the early considerations in the Foundation's law programming are recalled by Peter Geithner, who initiated the Foundation's law grantmaking in China and was later its first representative there. "As our grant budget grew we were able to expand from efforts at mutual understanding to actual programs. The question then was: what programs? We recognized from the start that we should take the long view, and legal education was chosen." Former Program Officer Mark Sidel, who served from 1988 to 1990, articulates a similar strategy concerning that initial choice: "We believed the growing legal research and teaching community would have a major multiplier effect on other future law programs."

A subsequent evolution in the program led to a more focused concern with rights and governance, from merely rebuilding a legal system to "providing Chinese with access to an expanded range of ways of thinking about and using law to protect rights and promote effective, responsive governance," says former Program Officer Jonathan Hecht, who served from 1990 to 1994. Chang, who joined Ford in Beijing in 1994, says programming has continued to support efforts to build a legal culture in which law applies to and is respected by both government and citizens, as well as to rebuild a national legal infrastructure—including legislation, trained lawyers, courts, and other legal institutions.

In the program's formative years, Foundation staff proceeded to deepen support for Chinese legal scholars. This resulted from a belief in the critical and long-term importance of the academic community, as well as recognition of the need for concentrated efforts in such a large country. The earliest and largest project of the law program to date has been the U.S.-China Committee for Legal Education Exchange (CLEEC), a project that ran from 1983 until 1995. The project, designed to build law faculties, generally focused on seven of the strongest faculties at universities and institutes of political science and law—a small but important subset of China's rapidly expanding law schools. CLEEC supported bilateral exchanges of legal scholars, enabled more than two hundred Chinese law students and professors to pursue foreign legal education and research, and broadened understanding about China in the U.S. legal community.

CLEEC built upon limited earlier support for visiting lectureships that took place in the few years before its creation. A 1982 conference cosponsored by CASS and a group of U.S. legal scholars, the first Sino-American legal conference since 1949, revealed interest in an ongoing program of exchanges that later became CLEEC. Translations and sharing of Chinese and English language law materials were soon added to CLEEC's activities. The Henry Luce Foundation later became a co-funder, supporting training of law librarians and providing library materials. The U.S. Information Agency helped fund summer workshops. CLEEC was the central focus of the law program until the Foundation's Beijing office opened in 1988.

CLEEC has been formative and instructive for Ford's entire China law program. While it is not a main focus of this study, a few of its results merit emphasis. From the start CLEEC selected its participants from a limited number of member schools and institutes. Geithner explains that this was to create a critical mass of faculty, help prevent their isolation upon return, and foster a mutually supportive intellectual environment, especially for new ideas, within those faculties. Looking back, this approach seems to have worked for those CLEEC alumni who returned to their law schools. But not all returned.

Just over 68 percent of CLEEC participants who went abroad returned to China; only about 49 percent returned and took up law teaching or research positions as planned. This seems disappointing; however, Hecht notes that the rate of return to China was in fact notably high compared to almost every other program of long-term overseas training for Chinese in law and other fields. Reviewing the experience, Foundation staff stress the importance of simultaneously addressing the institutional environments participants would return to as well as their training and research needs, in order to enhance returns to the targeted academic institutions.

Even with discerning selection processes, some factors will, of course, be largely beyond a donor's influence. For example, Edwards, the first American cochairperson of CLEEC, attributes the lower-than-hoped-for return rate partly to the increased marketability of Chinese lawyers with postgraduate degrees and partly to an unwillingness of young scholars to return to faculties with low seniority. Geithner suggests that the fluctuating political climate in China was another factor. For example, some students and scholars remained abroad in the years following the tragic Tiananmen Square events of June 1989, but the return rate picked up after about 1992 when the momentum of reforms increased again and those abroad saw better prospects for contributing to China's development by going home. Chang also points out that CLEEC participants who returned to China but not to law faculties brought other benefits that were not entirely anticipated. Its alumni have also become founding or senior members of important law firms and have contributed to in-service government training programs, bringing much-needed talent to the fledgling legal profession. Others have contributed to public education about the law. As will be seen below, still others made contributions to the development of important legislation.

Looking forward, Wang Liming, a CLEEC alumnus and now an associate law dean at the People's University of China, recommends a project that would secure short-term or visiting professorships for CLEEC alumni who have remained abroad or outside of the teaching profession. William Alford, director of the Center for East Asian Legal Studies at Harvard Law School and a founding member of the U.S. CLEEC Committee, recommends that any project similar to CLEEC give wider attention to areas outside of Beijing that may have a greater ability to experiment. He also suggests more directed exposure to training opportunities and models in public interest law. Nevertheless, while most CLEEC participants studied trade and international economic law, Alford explains that "even students of those fields deepened their understanding of the rule of law."

Many and varied factors have contributed to recent legal reform in China. Peter Harris, the Foundation's representative in China from 1990 to 1994, is therefore cautious about disaggregating the effects of CLEEC. What can certainly be concluded, he explains, is that the project enabled some of China's most important current and future legal actors to gain critical new insights. Professor He Jiahong of People's University in Beijing credits CLEEC with increasing his critical reasoning and inspiring subtle changes in his thinking about law. Professor and Senior Judge Wan E'xiang explains that his exposure to public interest law projects through CLEEC inspired his development of the Centre for the Protection of the Rights of the Socially Vulnerable (Wuhan Centre), which operates from Wuhan University. At Wuhan University, more than ten CLEEC alumni "are now the backbone of the University law faculty," says Wan.[4] CLEEC alumnus Professor Zhu Lanye of the East China Institute of Politics and Law in Shanghai says: "My experience overseas has affected my ideas about the concept of the rule of law, as well as my understanding of the legal system as a whole."[5]

Tremendous growth and diversity had been taking place in legal education in China while the CLEEC program was under way. Both undergraduate and postgraduate legal education was expanding, and some nondegree training programs existed for government officials. Enrollment in the growing variety of law courses had increased from some thirteen hundred in 1978 to nearly thirty-two thousand by the end of 1987. These developments confirmed the Foundation's original choice to focus grantmaking on the legal research and teaching community, but also pointed to a continued need for trained legal educators.

As the Foundation's Beijing office opened in 1988, Geithner explains, law programming expanded to include two new efforts—legislative research and drafting, and training of judges.

Opportunities were created for government officials and their academic advisors to study legislative approaches in a variety of countries with different legal systems, including Australia, France, Germany, India, Japan, Thailand, and the United States. The National Committee on U.S.-China Relations, based in New York, coordinated the U.S. study tours. Some limited training for legislative officials also began. The Supreme People's Court, the nation's highest tribunal, established a Senior Judges Training Centre to study the training approaches of other countries and to develop its own program. Such legislative training was more sensitive than the Foundation's past roles, especially for a foreign organization, but Geithner believes that the record of CLEEC's work made it possible. CLEEC created familiarity with and confidence in the Foundation that made others comfortable in approaching it for support. Furthermore, both the legal reform effort and the identification of its needs began with Chinese officials, he says. Wang Liming believes that the confidence and trust created by CLEEC still facilitates the Foundation's work today.

By 1991 the law program, while continuing to support legal education and research as well as judicial training, added similar work toward strengthening the procuracy. Less attention was given to legislative drafting, as the United Nations Development Programme (UNDP) now undertook a major effort in that field. Subsequent Foundation support for lawmaking focused on particular fields of law, such as administrative law and criminal procedure, which were seen as central to the rights and governance aspects of the legal system.

Beginning in 1992, the Foundation also supported research by organizations on legal topics related to human rights and constitutional and administrative law, hoping to broaden domestic dialogue in these areas. Hecht, the program officer at that time, describes this as an attempt, in the midst of other emerging initiatives, to refocus attention on basic principles of rights and governance, and on how law would be used in the new system. This too was a potentially sensitive endeavor. Again, gaining the trust of key and now long-standing local partners, as well as maintaining the flexibility to work with government agencies and their affiliated organizations, facilitated this effort.

For example, CASS, among others, had identified the need

for more research on human rights law and undertook to conduct comparative work in several countries. Similarly, another grantee, the Administrative Law Research Group (ALRG), which was composed of government officials and law professors appointed in the late 1980s by the Legislative Affairs Commission of the National People's Congress (China's Parliament), helped research and draft a framework for administrative law.

ALRG was at the forefront of efforts to enact path-breaking legislation such as the 1989 Administrative Litigation Act, which expanded liability for official misdeeds and individual standing to sue government agencies and officials. ALRG's subsequent research and drafting work laid the basis for the 1994 State Compensation Law, which clarified citizens' rights to receive compensation for improper government action, and the 1996 Administrative Penalties Law, which limited what had previously been largely unfettered discretion of agencies to impose sanctions such as fines and property confiscation. CASS's research undoubtedly contributed to China's decision to sign international covenants on civil and political rights, and on economic, social, and cultural rights. Many of the scholars with both CASS and ALRG had earlier conducted studies or research under the auspices of CLEEC, and could contribute that knowledge to their new work. Some thirty people from CASS alone had been CLEEC participants.

The 1989 Administrative Litigation Act in particular has helped lead to an important shift in the way Chinese citizens view and use the law. "In the past people wouldn't dare sue government for violation of their entitlements or rights; now they can sue and get compensation," says Jiang Ming'an, a professor from Peking University. Studies report that cases brought under the law jumped from about thirteen thousand in 1990 to about one hundred thousand in 1998. Some scholars caution, however, that while the Administrative Litigation Act is a milestone, it does contain limitations.

The Foundation has gone on to support a second generation of ALRG scholars. A suggestion made by Zhang Chunsheng, a member of ALRG and vice director of the Legislative Affairs Commission, is that the group could benefit from financial support to study the successes and mistakes of administrative law regimes of additional developing legal systems and countries.

ALRG attributes its overall successes in part to a structure that guarantees scholars regular access to key policymakers. Saich similarly notes that organizations with close government links often can play a more direct role in policy formulation while helping to generate significant policy innovation.

Foundation staff members contrast the results obtained from ALRG's research work with those from earlier training programs for legislative officials. While the earlier programs helped to meet China's immediate priorities by speeding and improving the drafting of discrete laws, they only incidentally built capacity within the legislative drafting organs of government. The ALRG model focuses instead on a single area of law and includes in-depth academic research. Consequently, it has enabled an incremental development of expertise and helped train graduate students and young professors as a future resource base. This has enhanced Chinese capacity to develop the field of administrative law generally, explains Hecht.

In 1993 the Foundation's law program made plans to build on the research agenda with a study on the implementation of a new women's rights law. For the first time, the program also sought to complement its training, law development, and research components with support for an embryonic legal services project—the Wuhan Centre. The added focus on service and implementation reflected concern that volumes of legislation were being enacted without sufficient attention to how or whether new laws were working in practice. Attempts to apply the law, it was hoped, would lead to further improvements in statutes and legal machinery.

Grants were also made for research toward revision of China's criminal procedure law, with the aim of strengthening protections for human rights. A group of reform-minded law professors supported by the Foundation and led by Chen Guangzhong, former president of the China University of Political Science and Law, was asked by the Legislative Affairs Commission to develop an initial draft of the revised law. The group, which did not include members from the commission, was organized differently from ALRG. But it utilized similar links to government in the development of law and policy. The revised criminal procedure law, finally enacted in 1996, includes provisions that strengthen rights of the accused, including the right to seek counsel at an earlier point after detention. It also includes restrictions on some types of detention and new procedures that make trials more adversarial in nature. Some also say that the law represents a first step toward establishing a presumption of innocence. However, as Chinese authorities acknowledge, implementation of the new law has been difficult due to entrenched police and prosecutorial practices.

The Foundation's experience with this group of academics illustrates how a donor can help a grantee grow through transitions by staying with it over time. Following the successful enactment of the 1996 law, Foundation staff encouraged the group to consider establishing an organization to continue its work on criminal justice reform. Later that same year, the group founded the Centre for Criminal Law and Justice based at the China University of Political Science and Law. The center currently monitors the revised criminal procedure law to identify implementation problems and devise possible solutions. To do this, it utilizes a small criminal defense clinic and recruits legislators and judges to serve on monitoring panels and tours. The same approach is being used for the development and implementation of criminal justice laws that meet United Nations standards.

Changes in China, coupled with a steadily increasing law program budget, have enabled the Foundation's grantmaking to grow and diversify. Chang notes, "This expanding universe of programming possibilities, however, also carries the danger of diluting the impact of [our] resources, particularly in a country as huge and diverse as China, where the population of one province can equal that of entire countries in which the Foundation is working." For this reason, while maintaining some smaller grantmaking areas, since 1995 the law program has focused on two primary areas: judicial reform, which includes training judges, and "law-in-action." Law-in-action is a phrase coined for the line of work that grew out of the program's emphasis on legal implementation and legal services. The discussion below will focus on these two areas of grantmaking.

Judicial Reform

It is widely believed that a stronger judiciary would contribute to sustaining China's movement toward broader openness in all aspects of society. In describing the purpose behind the judicial reform focus of the Foundation's law program, Chang explains that "China's next step toward the rule of law must be transformation of its judiciary." The Foundation's willingness to support long-term endeavors and its familiarity with key Chinese legal actors, as well as the program's longevity and credibility in China, made it a logical partner in judicial reform efforts. While the Foundation in 1999 remained the only foreign donor supporting work on broader judicial reform, the Canadian International Development Agency and UNDP have sponsored training of judges.

Ford's first work with the judiciary in China began with the opening of the Beijing office in 1988 and was limited to training judges. The primary grant was for a "training of trainers" project that involved fellowships for young judges to study abroad. Those judges were selected by the Senior Judges Training Centre, affiliated with the Supreme People's Court. The hope was that these young judges would join the center's teaching staff to train other judges. While the staff was indeed enriched by many of the returning judges, a significant number took up opportunities elsewhere—in the private sector, their original courts, or abroad. The retention problem is indicative of an ongoing challenge faced by other training programs, such as CLEEC, and confirms the need to address the institutional environment to which trainees will return.

Currently Ford's support for judicial reform efforts includes four lines of work believed to be critical to the judiciary's emergence as a professional and impartial institution. One supports reform experiments undertaken by Chinese courts. A second involves applied research to help analysts and policymakers better understand how courts and judges in China's large system actually function. Third, some support is given to development of judges' associations and organizations. Finally, support continues for judicial training programs, which now emphasize fostering professional values and legal skills, rather than teaching substantive law. Because this is the area in which Ford's law program has the most accumulated experience, it will be the primary focus of this section.

In the first line of work, supporting reform experiments in Chinese courts, efforts have been concentrated on reforms of trial procedure. Other grants have been made for exploration of reforms in judicial administration and to examine how judgments are written and structured. Recent grants have also supported exploration of more systemic reform such as judicial appointments, court finance, and the internal processes by which courts reach decisions.

Liang Baojian, president of the National Judges College, the successor to the Senior Judges Training Centre, shared insights gained from his experiences with efforts to reform trial procedure. While noting the need for "holistic reform of the judicial system," which he says includes financial management, skills development, and judicial nomination and appointment procedures, he stresses that trial reform is one key to improving public knowledge and trust. In his view, the old inquisitorial trial model in which the judge undertook the duties of inquiry, "was not efficient, was too long, and was not transparent to the public." Reforms over past years require adversarial procedures for most trials, public proceedings with some limitations, and the presentation of evidence and judgments in open court. Liang says the implementation of new reforms will require time, and will depend, in part, upon the legal consciousness, customs, and quality of judges. For that reason the college teaches skills but also stresses to judges the far-reaching meaning of reforms in terms of their status. Liang views trial procedure reforms nationwide as a means to "raise the status of courts."

The second area of Foundation support—applied research— has provided some insights into general advantages and disadvantages of different types of grantee partners. Research projects undertaken by the courts can further internal momentum toward reform and sometimes have greater possibilities for follow-up implementation. But court-based projects have generally not produced many written products; thus, dissemination of new knowledge and approaches is limited. Similar projects by academics generally do produce valuable articles, case studies, and other writings, but these tend to be consumed primarily by other academics. Special efforts should be taken to ensure that research findings and recommendations are brought to the attention of judges and key CCP leaders.

The Centre for Judicial Studies at Peking University, led by codirectors He Weifang and Zhu Suli, has conducted some revealing studies on conditions and difficulties faced by courts in China's rural areas. These are especially important, since, despite increasing urbanization, the vast majority of Chinese still live in the countryside. In one study, Professor Zhu interviewed over one hundred basic-level court judges, who possess very limited formal legal education, in order to understand the methods they use and rules or customs they follow. The study yielded insights on both rural courts and public attitudes. Judges, for example, noted the difficulty they face in getting people to testify against their neighbors in rural settings—unlike in urban areas, where witnesses more often face strangers in court, or at least can live more separately once a court proceeding is completed. The question widely faced by rural judges is how to secure testimony—through encouragement and social pressure, or by court order? The concern is that the use of court orders and increased enforcement will only discourage rural residents from greater use of law and the court system when it is truly necessary. In addition to revealing a difficulty faced by rural courts, this highlights the fact that judicial strengthening alone is not enough. Public legal education on both rights and responsibilities is also important.

The center's research also noted the discretion China's rural judges—and perhaps urban judges as well—so often use, as well as the skills and judicial values they would need to achieve equity and justice in such circumstances. Judges must often use their discretion to fill in the many areas in which China's laws are silent, undeveloped, or ambiguous. However, given the public's historic experience with the use of authority and law in China, the courts must be seen to use discretion both effectively and fairly, if China is to build a respected judiciary.

Established in 1995, the judicial training program at South Central University of Political Science and Law in Wuhan is one of several now supported by the Foundation. Three trainees, from the district and intermediate courts in Hubei Province, are representative of the judges the program serves. One was a former military officer of twelve years who retired in 1987 to become a judge. Another is a middle school graduate with job experience in personnel management. A third graduated from a teachers college, had taught for three years, and was transferred from a department of the CCP to the court four years ago. When asked about their needs, the first judge replied that he needed "a reeducation process in legal knowledge and some skills to write judgments." He added, "An officer commands a platoon while a judge must search for fairness—not just give commands." He had completed his second training course two years earlier. Expressing consensus, the trainees prefer academics as trainers over their colleagues on the bench because, they say, academics have greater exposure to new knowledge.

From their experience, the faculty members at South Central University recommend selecting trainees from the same area or court so as to create a community of cooperation, standards, and values among peers. One judge with new ideas cannot have a broad impact, they say. But alongside others, she or he can set influential examples and engender a new legal culture. This lesson is similar to that established by CLEEC in its work. Jiang Ming'an from Peking University makes a similar argument when speaking specifically about the new administrative law. He argues that training in the substance of the new law is important, but that instructors should also stress that government action can in fact be regulated, by pointing out other judges who have been willing and able to do so. But even in the absence of such a group, he says, "one better-trained judge can still function better within a flawed judiciary."

Use of training to instill the judicial values and independence suggested above is encouraged by all the grantees and other experts consulted. Judge Jiang Huiling of the Research Office of the Supreme People's Court agrees, but cautions that substantive education on the law remains critical to help ensure judges' independence from the influence of colleagues who might otherwise be consulted for guidance in specific cases. This is especially true in China's current context, and would seem to suggest a holistic curriculum that includes substantive law, judge-skills, and ethics. Such a curriculum is beginning to develop for broad dissemination in print form. Wang Liming of People's University of China believes an early Foundation grant, which supported a publication that taught judges the substance of law by compiling notable and unique cases from throughout the country, was very effective. The publication was especially helpful in a legal system where written judgments are often very brief or unreported. Training sessions can also provide holistic learning by including some elements of substantive law, and encouraging dialogue among judges and scholars regarding legal and policy areas in need of research and development. One South Central University training session involved a comparison of Chinese and Japanese laws to protect the environment, and discussion on the need for better Chinese policy on environmental impact assessments for development initiatives.

While the three trainees at South Central University agreed on a preference for legal academics as trainers, the question of who should train judges is still widely debated. Some argue that the use of academics is most beneficial because judges can seek advice on ambiguous laws and professors can learn how laws are being applied in the courts. Other trainees prefer judges because they feel more encouraged to raise vexing practical questions. This accords with the lessons from retired Senior Judge Zhou Daoluan's many years of experience at the national Senior Judges Training Centre. Zhou and others, however, recommend utilizing a combination of both academics and judges in order to capture complementary skills. The professors at South Central University say academics as trainers are needed because so many of China's judges have no legal education, and contact with law professors is unusual and greatly sought. Some academics work part time as judges and many maintain part-time law practices, so they are able to teach from both academic and practical experience. Also, academics have greater influence on the functioning of judges and courts in a civil law system where there is no doctrine of judicial precedent as a form of lawmaking.

Training programs are having some effect on the competency and attitudes of China's judges, but they also reveal the distance yet to be traveled. The Shanghai Judges Training Centre provides an example through a story shared by one of its trainees when he returned for a follow-up course. After his first training session, the judge maintained his stance in resisting repeated requests from a local official to delay enforcement of a judgment against a real estate developer in a matter brought by a creditor. (The court had earlier ordered the repayment of a loan and the local official anticipated that the judge would soon freeze the assets of the developer to compensate the creditor.)

There are undoubtedly many factors contributing to change in China's context but, observing this particular judge, the center believes his behavior was inspired through training. This example is not isolated. In another region of the country, South Central University staff and law students conduct follow-up interviews with trainees in order to improve teaching methodology, and to assess impact. Prior to a training course, one particular judge had described his duty as "to protect the rights and views of the government." In a follow-up interview he described his responsibility as a judge to be a neutral "arbiter between views of parties, even if the government is a party." South Central University staff find that when the government or CCP is involved in a case, some incoming trainees still question how to handle the case. Trainees discuss this matter, they say, and realize that local officials should not interfere in cases or enforcement. Trainees know that this has been written into both law and policy, and that the challenge now is to help local attitudes and behavior conform to the principle. While notable progress in this area is occurring with trainees, there is still a difference between theory, law, and policy on one hand—and law-in-action on the other.

Law-in-Action

The area of work known as law-in-action has built on the Foundation's 1993 work to support the delivery of legal services and to improve the implementation of laws in China. It now includes efforts to strengthen citizens' awareness of law as a means to justice, demonstrate how the legal system can be used to protect rights, give practical experience to lawyers and students, and strengthen the ability of the legal system to deliver justice. When CLEEC was founded in 1983, Edwards explains, it was much too early in the redevelopment of the legal system to hope to reach the explicit social justice goals now being pursued. Although law is still only a weak force in Chinese society, says Chang, there is now a workable basis to protect individual rights and pursue social justice through legal processes. That basis includes a body of laws and regulations, a functioning if underdeveloped judiciary, a rapidly growing corps of lawyers, an emerging respect for law, and a new awareness of the importance of implementation. The general activities pursued by law-in-action grantees include community legal services, test case litigation, community legal education, and local and international comparative research to devise solutions, new laws, or revisions. Since 1998, the Canadian International Development Agency, UNDP, and The Asia Foundation have also included legal services components in their grant programs.

One Foundation grantee is the China Centre for Legal Aid, which was established by the Ministry of Justice in 1996. The center is the state's official agency responsible for overseeing the development of a nationwide legal aid system. At the behest of the Ministry, local governments have established legal aid centers throughout China; over six hundred such centers existed as of July 1999. The center's deputy director, Gong Xiaobing, cites changes in the legal system that propelled the need for the new center. These were primarily the transition from an inquisitorial to an adversarial system, with the added burden it places on people who can't afford legal representation, and the 1996 revisions of the criminal procedure law.

In addition to its supervision of local legal aid centers, the Centre for Legal Aid documents practical problems faced in the implementation of China's civil and criminal laws, and conducts outside research to resolve disputes and on possible solutions to needs. This material is provided to the Ministry of Justice for consideration of law revisions and new operational rules for courts and other institutions within the legal infrastructure. It is too early to assess lessons from this aspect of the center's work. But so far, the center's work has been aided by a government requirement that each private lawyer handle at least one legal aid case for the center each year in order to qualify for renewal of an annual license to practice law. Publications on notable cases handled by the legal aid system have contributed to public legal education, and encouraged more help from private lawyers.

One of the center's notable successes came as the result of a recently strengthened law. In a 1998 criminal case the procurator sought the death penalty against an indigent defendant who maintained that the public security bureau had coerced his confession through torture. The defendant was too poor to hire a lawyer, but the newly revised criminal procedure law required defense counsel in all capital punishment cases. Before the law was revised, the defendant would have been forced to defend his own life in court. The center helped implement the revised law by assigning a defense lawyer through its private lawyer scheme, and the defendant was acquitted.

In the field of women's rights, two organizations established with Foundation support in 1995 and 1996 have quickly set new milestones in the use of law to close the gap between women's rights in law and women's rights in practice. Women's equal rights have been guaranteed in law since the first PRC constitution in 1954 and were reemphasized in a 1992 statute. Moreover, the place China was achieving in the wider international women's movement, and the role it played in hosting the 1995 Fourth United Nations World Conference on Women, further highlighted women's issues. As elsewhere in the world, however, discrimination and privilege die hard, and Chinese women still struggle to secure their rights and to gain equal status with men.

One grantee, the Qianxi County Rural Women's Legal Services Centre (Qianxi Women's Centre), was founded in late 1995 to test measures for addressing obstacles to realizing rights offered by the women's rights law. The center was established by current Director Wang Shuzhen, county head of the state-sponsored All China Women's Federation, with the assistance of Professor Chen Mingxia of CASS, who had led an earlier study on problems in implementing the law. The center is located in the county seat some 180 kilometers outside of Beijing and works with a network of seventeen substations, one in each township of this largely agricultural county. With paralegals and a few lawyers, it offers ongoing legal services and education on women's rights and related issues at weekly rural markets. It has also provided training for police officers and worked with the government to establish a special women's and children's division in the local county court. Through close cooperation with the county's Bureau of Justice, the center has trained state legal workers in townships who normally conduct informal dispute resolution to handle legal cases involving women's rights. The center's substations often operate from bureau facilities. Chen Mingxia believes the center's work and cases will be valuable sources of information for analysis of legal implementation problems.

The creation of the special division in the county court, the use of paralegals, and cooperation with the County Bureau of Justice have all effectively enhanced the center's work and implementation of the women's rights law. The center's contribution as a model for rural legal services for women is already clear, as is its likely contribution to some changed social attitudes. Beyond these insights, however, Chen Mingxia asserts that it is still too early in the center's history to assess the impact of its work toward broader implementation of reforms.

The arrangement between the Qianxi Women's Centre and the Bureau of Justice township offices is mutually beneficial. The center is grateful to local officials because it would not be able to afford placing paralegals in every township on its own. Meanwhile, poorly trained state workers have grown in awareness and skills with regard to women's rights. The center's staff members have also observed higher numbers of attendees and more sophisticated questions at their educational stalls and classrooms. They conclude that community education about women's rights may be affecting individual attitudes of both men and women more than it is actually encouraging the use of the legal system. They feel that knowledge of women's rights in Qianxi has had a deterrent and proactive effect to protect and promote those rights. Staff members also note that when cases do emerge, they are more often settled by mediation than litigation, but that mediation is now more often done in accordance with law. Mediation was always the preferred method due to tradition, the nature of some family law issues, and the potential effect on the courts of handling the vast caseload such a large population would produce. But increased awareness of rights and the new option to resort to legal services have added standards to the mediation process, which is often arbitrary or unfair to women.

Another new organization specializing in women's rights is the Centre for Women's Law Studies and Legal Services of Peking University (Peking Women's Centre). In comparison to the Qianxi Women's Centre, the Peking Women's Centre focuses more on research and litigation of selected cases that it believes are particularly important or representative of women's problems. The Peking Women's Centre's university base clearly facilitates the mix of legal services and research. In a recent example, a staff member's research helped lay the groundwork for the law creating the national legal aid system. The center's experiences using the legal machinery are a source of research data and other insights for academic staff. Some test cases try the routine application of women's rights laws. An example is a case filed on behalf of eighty women against a Beijing employer for failure to pay wages over two years. Other cases test the willingness and ability of courts to enforce judgments. "We won and the decisions only sit up there on the shelf," says Guo Jianmei, the center's executive director, expressing both dismay and resolve in light of such poor enforcement.

The cases and causes the center takes on reveal not only the status of women in society, but also the need for judicial strengthening and the problems of local malfeasance and official corruption. In the case of a schoolgirl raped by a powerful local school director, the center stirred media attention to force the reluctant local procurator to act. The media is used extensively and serves multiple purposes for the center. It plays a public education function; it is sometimes a tool used together with advocacy or litigation to influence public opinion; and it serves to publicize the center's work, thereby encouraging more women to come forward with their legal issues. Despite many remaining challenges, Guo and her staff assert that women and the media are paying closer attention to the effects of law on women, and women are more often turning to the legal system. Through the engagement of the university's respected law professors, Guo says, the conditions faced in many of these cases will get more government attention.

Foundation support was also behind the establishment of China's first nongovernmental legal aid center—the Wuhan Centre. Founded by CLEEC alumnus Wan in 1992, the Wuhan Centre pioneered the concept and practice of legal services in

China and has also been a model for university-based legal aid clinics and student voluntarism. Wuhan is a major city of about four million people, so this group faces many of the same issues as the Peking Women's Centre and has used similar tactics to confront them. One example is the regular use of the media. Its client groups and focus are wider, however. It handles legal needs on behalf of senior citizens, women, youth, and the disabled, and includes a unit that files administrative lawsuits against government agencies and officials. The Wuhan Centre has also further institutionalized the role of students. Ten law students are accepted each year to work there and several of its current lawyers began as student volunteers. In the near future, final-year students will be able to receive academic credit for working at the center.

The emergence of the Wuhan, Peking, and similar university legal aid organizations has raised new issues related to practical legal education, ways to supplement fledgling government legal aid, and future legal careers in public interest law. Traditional Chinese legal education emphasizes theoretical training with no practical component. The student only serves an apprenticeship immediately before formal admission to practice. At least one expert has suggested that graduates fulfilling apprenticeships for admission to the profession could bolster public interest legal service organizations at universities and elsewhere. While students can provide some client advice through the Wuhan and Peking centers, there are no regulations allowing supervised student appearances in court.

More faculties are considering the benefits of university legal aid clinics that award academic credits to participating students— to add a practical component to their education, and to supplement legal services. Some argue that citizens unwilling to use government legal aid offices for suits against the government would have an alternative in university organizations. Others assert that, as has been shown in some other countries, clinics will encourage students toward future careers in legal aid or public interest law.

Yang Xinxin, a graduate student intern at the Peking Women's Centre, shared an essay that describes what law-in-action work has meant for her, and the potential it might have for her future. Her reflections capture three of the Foundation's goals in its wider twenty-year China law program: "These experiences make me aware that there have been a lot of people struggling for the improvement of women's social status. . . . China's legal education system might realize benefits by integrating a legal aid program into its law schools and using it as the basis for training future legal professionals with a strong sensitivity to public interests. . . . From my experience, a clinical program like this gives students an opportunity to apply their skills in a practical situation and to strengthen their belief in law."

Conclusion

China's endeavor to improve its legal system, inspired by new policy choices in late 1978 and by the country's evolving needs, is taking place in the context of wide societal changes and increasing demands on the legal system. To meet the old and new challenges, this endeavor has been imbued with a talented new pool of Chinese legal minds over the past twenty years—and will gain in the future from students like Yang.

Early and continuous involvement since 1979 has enabled the Foundation's law program to contribute, in a limited way, to various aspects of this endeavor. Over time, the law program has supported needs in legal scholarship and teaching, legislative research and drafting skills, judicial reform, legal services, community legal education, and the implementation of new laws. These grantee activities have crossed diverse substantive fields within the law, and have been mutually reinforcing. This consistent and diverse involvement has also put the law program in a position to support a number of Chinese projects and individual activities that have been demonstrational for others.

The Foundation's experience as a donor in China indicates that the objectives of strengthening the judiciary and of law-in-action will require a long-term commitment—one that will involve successive generations in the legal profession and academe. In addition, many fundamental factors are converging to advance legal reforms in China. This makes it difficult to assess approaches and isolate contributions, and it is often inappropriate to attribute direct causation to a specific program, project, or approach. In most instances, it is more appropriate to identify a range of contributing factors, or perhaps proximate factors most closely related to the outcome or its timing.

The lessons and insights shared in this case study cannot cover every aspect of Ford's twenty years of law programming in China. They are further limited by the specific foci of this study and the newness of some activities. Nevertheless, for ease of reference, the most salient lessons and insights are summarized below.

Lessons and Insights

1. A grant program focused on the legal research and teaching community can have a multiplier and long-term impact on initiatives to strengthen or reform laws and legal institutions. In China, the CLEEC project had many effects. It reduced the isolation of legal scholars and laid a foundation for longer-term relationships and cooperation between Chinese and U.S. scholars and faculty. It also reached scholars that have subsequently contributed to legislative development, policy formulation, and judicial strengthening, and even nurtured relationships that enabled the Foundation's law grantmaking to expand into new and more sensitive fields. Perhaps CLEEC's most significant effect has been in introducing new ways of thinking about and using law in Chinese society.

2. The model employed by the ALRG for the development of new administrative law, that is, university-based scholars affiliated with a government entity, provided academics with consistent access to policymakers and allowed them to successfully vet and promote new ideas. A similar and effective model facilitated policy formulation by involving policymakers and practitioners in field research and monitoring. Scholars at the Centre for Criminal Law and Justice at the China University of Political Science and Law recruit legislators, government officials, judges, procurators, and others to observe firsthand the needs and research findings behind proposed policies.

3. By encouraging judicial independence and by instilling

basic judicial values such as impartiality and equity, judicial training programs can, in some contexts, have an impact beyond the specific skills they develop. This is especially important in the Chinese context, where current emphasis is on rebuilding the formal legal system, the generalized application of laws, and the formal adjudication of disputes.

4. Recruiting a critical mass of trainees within a region, court, or faculty has enhanced both judicial and law faculty training by building supportive environments that have encouraged trainees' use of newly acquired skills and ideas.

5. The impact of judicial training programs can be maximized when coupled with public education about the formal legal system. Such education is necessary to inform public expectations about, and foster greater respect for, the courts; encourage better adherence to court orders and moral examples; and overcome reluctance by citizens to participate in formal court processes.

6. Judicial training seminars that involve legal academics can increase dialogue that is mutually beneficial. Judges can gain knowledge and skills to interpret new or ambiguous laws, while scholars can learn more about the practical challenges courts face in actually applying the law. The dialogue is also able to help identify law and policy areas in need of further research and development. On the other hand, conferences just for judges can serve as fora to examine common practical challenges, to share knowledge and lessons, and to portray appropriate judicial approaches that strengthen other judges. Where written court judgments are brief or unreported, as in China, publications of notable case decisions can be useful judicial training tools.

7. There is an important role for China's growing network of governmental and nongovernmental legal aid offices in providing basic services, conducting public education, and documenting constraints to the implementation of laws. Much of the work of such offices is successfully conducted by paralegals, and the media is an increasingly

important tool for alerting the public to these new sources of aid and the potential use of new laws. The nongovernmental offices also pursue test cases and utilize the media as a tool along with litigation to influence public opinion and inspire compliance with laws. Continued success of these offices will depend largely on consistent support from the government and donors, and the continued opening of Chinese society. But efforts at legal services and efforts to strengthen the judiciary should also go hand in hand in China, since poor judicial enforcement is a widely perceived limitation to the use of public interest litigation to pursue social justice there.

8. By documenting constraints to the implementation of laws with experiences from their casework, some legal aid offices are only recently attempting to combine the roles of legal services and research, acting as a laboratory for the improvement of laws and the legal system in China. Working closely with the state—a strategy that has been used successfully over time by influential Chinese legal scholars—such offices tentatively show promise for influencing policymaking.

9. In the area of women's rights, legal activists found that community-based women's rights education, especially when combined with increased availability of legal aid, changed women's perceptions about using the law and the legal system to pursue their rights. Activists also noted that community rights education served to protect and promote women's rights, to some degree, by affecting social behavior and relations between men and women. Litigation on behalf of women has helped to focus media and government attention on barriers to achieving women's rights. Finally, many cases are still handled by informal mediation without resort to courts, especially in family matters. However, the increased awareness of rights and the availability of legal aid for court actions have resulted in mediations increasingly being conducted with reference to legal standards. This has improved the mediation process, which has often been arbitrary or unfair for women.

10. Initiatives by a few of China's law faculties to establish law clinics, combined with a spirit of student voluntarism, hold promise for their growth throughout China. The recent experiences of these faculties suggest that clinics in China can add a needed practical component to legal education, provide needed public legal services, and encourage students toward future legal aid or public interest work.

11. One way to help promote public interest legal services in China might be to allow law graduates to serve their required apprenticeships at law-faculty-based clinics as well as other legal aid organizations before being admitted to the bar. Such service could also help popularize public interest law practice. Likewise, a new Chinese method for bolstering legal aid by requiring some pro bono work from every private practitioner and tying the requirement to annual renewal of licenses might be worth monitoring for possible adaptation to other countries.

Notes

The author expresses special thanks to Mr. Yu Xingzhong for invaluable assistance as interpreter and China law advisor during this study.

1. The Chinese procuracy is an extremely powerful and important organ responsible for prosecutions as well as supervising and investigating the police, prisons, and abuses by government officials. It also has unique powers to supervise judicial behavior and file suits to overturn court decisions it believes are erroneous. For a full description of the role and powers of the procuracy, see Albert Chen, *An Introduction to the Legal System of the People's Republic of China* (Butterworths Asia, 1994), pp. 124–127.

2. Ibid., pp. 131–132.

3. See, e.g., Yu Xingzhong, "Legal Pragmatism in the People's Republic of China," *Journal of Chinese Law* 29, no. 3 (1989): 49–51.

4. "Powerful Attorneys: Chinese Educators on Legal Training and Law in China," *China Exchange News* 22, no. 4 (Winter 1994): 4.

5. Ibid., p. 2.

Appendix: Persons Interviewed or Consulted

William Alford
Professor and Director, East Asian Legal Studies, Harvard
University Law School, Cambridge, MA

Jan Carol Berris
Vice President, National Committee on U.S.-China Relations,
Inc., New York

Alain Bissonnette
Judicial Training Project, Canadian International Development
Agency, Beijing

Phyllis Chang
Program Officer, The Ford Foundation, Beijing

Chen Guangzhong
Professor and Director, Centre for Criminal Law and Justice,
China University of Political Science and Law, Beijing

Chen Mingxia
Professor, Institute of Law, Chinese Academy of Social Sciences,
Beijing

Chen Xiaojun
Professor, South Central University of Political Science and Law,
Wuhan

Chen Zuanguo
Judge and Vice Director, Shanghai Judge Training Centre,
Shanghai

Randle Edwards
Professor and Director, Center for Chinese Legal Studies,
Columbia University School of Law, New York

Sofia Ericsson
First Secretary (Development Cooperation), Embassy of Sweden,
Beijing

Fang Shi-rong
Professor, South Central University of Political Science and Law,
Wuhan

Stephen Forbes
Second Secretary (Cultural), Cultural and Education Section,
British Embassy, Beijing

Peter Geithner
Former Representative, The Ford Foundation, Beijing

Yannick Glemarec
Deputy Resident Representative, United Nations Development
Programme, Beijing

Gong Xiaobing
Deputy Director, China Centre for Legal Aid, Ministry of Justice,
Beijing

Gu Changhao
Deputy Director, Legal Affairs Office, Shanghai Municipal
People's Government, Shanghai

Guo Daohui
Professor, Institute of Law, Chinese Academy of Social Sciences,
Beijing

Guo Jianmei
Associate Professor and Executive Director, Centre for Women's
Law Studies and Legal Services, Peking University, Beijing

Peter Harris
Former Representative, The Ford Foundation, Beijing

He Jiahong
Professor, People's University of China School of Law, Beijing

He Weifang
Associate Professor and Codirector, Centre for Judicial Studies,
Peking University Department of Law, Beijing

He Weiwen
Administrative Legal Affairs Institute, Shanghai Municipality,
Shanghai

Jonathan Hecht
Former Program Officer, The Ford Foundation, Beijing

Jiang Huiling
Judge, Research Office, Supreme People's Court, Beijing

Jiang Ming'an
Professor, Peking University Department of Law, Beijing

Jiang Ping
Professor and former President, China University of Political
Science and Law, Beijing

Jianlin Bian
Professor, Centre for Criminal Law and Justice, China University
of Political Science and Law, Beijing

Debra Kam
Program Associate, National Committee on U.S.-China Relations,
Inc., New York

Kong Haifei
Judge, Shanghai

Lei Xian
Professor and President, National Prosecutors College, Beijing

Li Buyun
Professor and Director, Centre for Research of Human Rights,
Chinese Academy of Social Sciences, Beijing

Li Dun
Professor, Chinese Academy of Social Sciences, Beijing

Li Hanchang
Associate Professor, South Central University of Political Science and Law, Wuhan

Li Hongyun
Peking University Department of Law, Beijing

Li Lin
Professor, Institute of Law, Chinese Academy of Social Sciences, Beijing

Liang Baojian
President, National Judges College, Beijing

Liu Donghua
Lawyer, Centre for Women's Law Studies and Legal Services, Peking University, Beijing

Liu Hainian
Professor and Director, Institute of Law, Chinese Academy of Social Sciences, Beijing

Liu Junning
Coeditor, Res Publica Journal, Beijing

Liu Ping
Chief, Department of Supervising Administration of Law, General Legal Affairs Office, Shanghai Municipal People's Government, Shanghai

Liu Zhongding
Judge and Vice President, Shanghai Yangpu District Court, Shanghai

Qi Wenyuan
Professor and Director, Law Department, South Central University of Political Science and Law, Wuhan

Anthony Saich
Former Representative, The Ford Foundation, Beijing

Shi Lei
Lecturer and Vice Director, Centre for the Protection of the Rights of the Socially Vulnerable, Wuhan University Law School, Wuhan

Mark Sidel
Former Program Officer, The Ford Foundation, Beijing

Franklin A. Thomas
Former President, The Ford Foundation, New York

Wan E'xiang
Senior Judge and founder of the Centre for the Protection of the Rights of the Socially Vulnerable, Wuhan University Law School, Wuhan

Wang He-min
Head, Exchange and Cooperation Office, National Judges College, Beijing

Wang Jiafu
Professor, Institute of Law, Chinese Academy of Social Sciences, Beijing

Wang Liming
Professor and Associate Dean, People's University of China School of Law, Beijing

Wang Shuzhen
Director, Qianxi County Rural Women's Legal Services Centre, Qianxi, Hebei

Wang Yan
Coeditor, Res Publica Journal, Beijing

Woo Leechan
First Secretary, United States Embassy, Beijing

Wu Handong
Professor and President, South Central University of Political
Science and Law, Wuhan

Wu Wei
Professor and Assistant Director, Centre for Criminal Law and
Justice, China University of Political Science and Law, Beijing

Xie Tianfang
Director, Legal Affairs Office, Shanghai Municipal People's
Government, Shanghai

Xin Chunying
Professor and Deputy Director, Institute of Law, Chinese
Academy of Social Sciences, Beijing

Xu Yufen
Deputy Secretary General, Shanghai Women Judges Association,
Shanghai

Vincent Yang
Director, China Program, International Centre for Criminal Law
Reform and Criminal Justice Policy, University of British
Columbia, Vancouver

Yang Xinxin
Graduate student intern, Centre for Women's Law Studies and
Legal Services, Peking University, Beijing

Yu Xingzhong
Lecturer-on-Law and Research Fellow, Harvard Law School,
Cambridge, MA

Yue Liling
Associate Professor, China University of Political Science and
Law, Beijing

Zhang Chunsheng
Vice Director, Legislative Affairs Commission of the National
People's Congress, Beijing

Zhang Zhiming
Professor, Institute of Law, Chinese Academy of Social Sciences, Beijing

Zhou Daoluan
Judge and former Director, Senior Judges Training Centre, Beijing

Zhu Jingwen
Professor, People's University of China School of Law, Beijing

Zhu Lanye
Professor, East China Institute of Politics and Law, Shanghai

Zhu Qichao
Professor, Centre for Women's Law Studies and Legal Services, Peking University, Beijing

Zhu Suli
Professor and Codirector, Centre for Judicial Studies, Peking University Department of Law, Beijing

Groups Interviewed or Consulted

Members of the Institute of Law, Chinese Academy of Social Sciences, Beijing

Staff and clients of the Centre for the Protection of the Rights of the Socially Vulnerable, Wuhan University Law School, Wuhan

Staff, clients, and student interns of the Centre for Women's Law Studies and Legal Services, Peking University, Beijing

Staff of the Qianxi County Rural Women's Legal Services Centre, Qianxi, Hebei

Trainees of the Judges Training Program, South Central University of Political Science and Law, Wuhan

Trainees of the Shanghai Judge Training Centre, Shanghai

6

Participatory Justice in the Philippines

STEPHEN GOLUB

When the popular movement known as "people power" toppled
Philippine dictator Ferdinand Marcos in 1986, it triggered an
equally arduous struggle: to gradually attach civil society sinews
to the revived democracy's skeletal institutional structures. That
struggle to bolster government accountability and effectiveness
has included work to reform elements of a historically unjust
legal system, and to increase Filipinos' access to it. This chapter
describes how some Ford Foundation grantees have sought such
goals by bolstering Filipinos' active participation in the pursuit of
justice, development, and better governance.

Alternative law groups (ALGs), as these grantees and similar
Philippine NGOs call themselves, mainly seek social, economic,
and environmental progress for disadvantaged populations. The
"alternative" in their name flows from the several ways in which
their perspectives and operations differ from private legal practice
and traditional legal aid in the Philippines. These differences are
detailed later in this chapter.

The first ALGs were founded in the early 1980s and began
receiving Ford Foundation support in 1986. Ford's New York City
headquarters previously had been in contact with Philippine
human rights groups through various international programs, and
in 1985 it had reopened a full-fledged office in Manila (having
reduced its presence there to a liaison status in 1982). For the next
decade, the Foundation had a program officer in the Philippines

working on human rights and governance issues full time, and support for ALGs became a key strategy for addressing a wide range of social problems.

ALGs address such issues as illegal logging, violence against women, agrarian reform,[1] housing for the urban poor, and indigenous people's rights. Most ALGs are headed by attorneys, and all include lawyers on their staffs. They have contributed to scores of post-Marcos legal reforms while also addressing an enduring Philippine problem—the implementation of laws on the ground. They typically work in partnership with other nongovernmental organizations and with disadvantaged communities. Sometimes they play leading roles; more often, supporting ones.

While ALGs have never been the exclusive focus of the Foundation's human rights and governance grantmaking in the Philippines, this chapter concentrates on them for three reasons. First, they have had considerable impact in a number of important areas. Second, their work has overlapped with other Ford grantmaking dealing with natural resources, women's reproductive health, and strengthening local philanthropy. Finally, their experience may hold useful lessons for development work in the Philippines and beyond. A related facet of this chapter is how Ford's support for ALGs, initially under a human rights rubric, justifiably continued even as the Foundation ended its human rights funding, per se, in the Philippines, and shifted resources to civil society and governance work. Support for ALGs survived because they were seen to occupy a nexus of issue areas that span program boundaries.

Former Foundation Program Officer Terrence George funded more than a dozen ALGs during his 1989–1995 Philippines tenure because these groups address a range of human rights and development concerns, and not just abuses committed by the government. Many of these issues play out at the local level, and there have been growing opportunities to work with elected officials and decentralized executive agencies. Hence, George's successor, Gary Hawes, supports selected ALGs through Ford's local governance program. That program seeks greater civic participation in governance, especially by underrepresented sectors.

At the time of this study, the Foundation was funding eight ALGs in the following areas:

- Indigenous people's rights and environmental issues:
  Legal Rights and Natural Resources Center
  Developmental Legal Aid Center (DLAC)
  Environmental Legal Aid Center (ELAC)
  Tanggol Kalikasan (TK)
- Agrarian reform:
  Tungo sa Kaunlaran ng Kanayunan at Repormang
    Panasakahan (Kaisahan)
  Balay Mindanaw Foundation, Inc. (BMFI)
  Sentro ng Alternatibong Lingap Panlegal (Saligan)
- Women's rights:
  Women's Legal Bureau (WLB)

While this study describes the work of Foundation-funded ALGs, not all of that work is Ford funded. Some activities draw on other donors' assistance. Ford does not, for example, support legislative lobbying. The ALGs' efforts cut across Ford programming categories in ways that illuminate the interface between law and other fields. This chapter explains the context, evolution, and impact of ALG work and of Ford support for it, and concludes with a summation of possible lessons that flow from this experience.

Alternative Law Groups:
Context and Characteristics

ALGs are organizations that promote Philippine development by enhancing popular participation in lawmaking, policy development, and other government actions. They are staffed mainly by lawyers, law students, other development professionals, or paralegals (laypersons to whom an ALG provides basic legal training). They are relatively small; even the largest, Saligan, has fewer than twenty attorneys. Most are based in Manila, though some have affiliated offices and lawyers elsewhere in the country. At this writing, the ALG network included twenty-one separate organizations.

Much ALG work is collaborative. Partners include low-income communities and individuals, other NGOs, and grassroots associations (which in the Philippines and this chapter are referred to as people's organizations, or POs).[2] ALGs depart from private practice and traditional legal aid by seeing clients as partners in development, and seeking to empower them to develop their own legal and political strategies. Their activities embrace both conventional and unorthodox legal work. They may litigate; appear before quasi-judicial proceedings, such as labor and agrarian reform tribunals; negotiate with corporate leaders regarding environmental and labor issues; and provide legal assistance and guidance regarding strikes and protest activities. They may also secure government services for partners; organize communities; train paralegals; pursue efforts to affect jurisprudence; conduct research; produce scholarly articles and publications; advise advocacy groups; and work on legal and regulatory reform.

While sharing some goals and strategies, ALGs vary in other respects. In fact, as former Tanggol Kalikasan head Hector Soliman notes, much of their dynamism "comes from the fact that they have evolved independently of each other." Their network is by no means monolithic in terms of its members' perspectives and operations. Some are more adversarial than others in relating to government. Some smaller ALGs based outside Manila do not become involved in national policy advocacy at all. Not all litigate, and many do so only as a last resort. Not all carry out paralegal work. For the many that do, their paralegal operations are driven substantially by the needs of their partner communities. These partnerships also affect the ALGs' orientations toward various issues. An ALG that focuses on indigenous people's rights, for example, does not necessarily agree with a women's rights ALG on the degree to which indigenous law should govern family relations.

The roots of the ALGs reach deep into Philippine legal culture and political history. They have evolved in a political and legal environment dominated by closed circles of patronage and power. A number of writers have noted the oligarchic nature of the Philippine polity. University of Wisconsin Professor Paul Hutchcroft sees the nation's post–World War II dictatorship and democracy as sharing an enduring pattern of patrimonialism, in which public office serves as a vehicle for personal profit.[3] Hutchcroft's analysis of the national government and elites applies to local politics as well. Similarly, University of the Philippines Professor Alex Magno laments the "weak state" that "has failed to evolve the bureaucratic capacity to make good rules and enforce them uniformly and well," and in which policy formulation and implementation is captive to narrow, vested interests. Even a 1988 Philippine Senate report highlights the pervasive nature of an "extreme personalism [that] leads to the graft and corruption evident in Philippine society."[4]

In a related vein, University of the Philippines law professor Alfredo Tadiar has maintained that "the most dominant single characteristic of Philippine society is the pervasive influence of close personal relations upon almost any conceivable human interaction."[5] His assertion has important analytical implications; in some ways, the Philippine legal system is best understood not as a set of institutions and processes, but as a network of personal connections affecting and often dictating its operations. The government enforces many laws only to the extent that private parties press for such action, whether overtly, informally, or corruptly.

Given these circumstances, how do Filipinos gain access to justice and government services? For those with sufficient resources, it often is via personal connections: family, friends, landlords, moneylenders, politicians, or other local power brokers. Where these sources of influence are not available or do not suffice, bribery is an alternative. Describing an exceptional situation in which Filipinos refused to pay for government services that should be free, a newspaper columnist illustrates the rule: "A long time ago, [Manila's Chinese-Filipino community] established their own fire brigade because they simply couldn't trust the fire department to come to their aid. They figured that the amount they would have to bribe the firemen to put out the blaze could be better used buying their own fire fighting equipment and establishing their own volunteer fire brigades."[6]

A crucial problem for most Filipinos is that they lack the legal knowledge, financial resources, or personal connections to extract services from the government, enforce their rights, or influence policies that affect them. They may sometimes have the option of turning to a local power broker, but this creates *utang na loob* (a debt of gratitude) that binds them to that individual in ways that can later influence their political or personal conduct.

At the same time that the Philippine legal and governmental systems reflect underlying societal realities, lawyers are taught to take an unquestioning and very formalistic view of their roles. Kaisahan's Magistrado Mendoza recalls professors instructing him that "the law is harsh, but it is the law." By virtue of subsequent work with farmers, he says, "I've learned that being a lawyer is not merely following the narrow letter of the law, [but] that the court can also be persuaded, and that I can still do something that addresses the needs of marginalized sectors."

ALGs' activities, then, can be seen as an effort to make client populations more legally and economically independent. They aim to inject fairness, accountability, and predictability into a legal system that is often abused or ignored by elite interests. More broadly, ALGs seek to democratize access to state-allocated resources and policymaking processes.

Ford Foundation Programming Approaches

This section traces the evolution since 1985 of both ALGs and the Foundation's support for them. It very briefly explores the Foundation's civil and political rights grantmaking in the early post-Marcos years, describes the Foundation's gradual shift to an emphasis on supporting ALGs' social and economic rights efforts in the early 1990s, and finally looks at support for them under Ford's local governance program from 1995 to date.

When the Foundation's Philippines program officer, John Humphreys, took up his human rights/governance post in 1985, political violence plagued the country. Even after Marcos was driven from power in February 1986, politically inspired killings, torture, and other violations persisted under the democratic administration of President Corazon Aquino (1986–1992). Fueled by the government's war against a communist insurgency and by coup attempts that undermined civilian control of the military, the abuses abated only after both threats diminished toward the end of her term. Initially, the human rights portion of Humphreys' portfolio accordingly was weighted toward civil and political rights concerns.

At the same time, Humphreys began supporting a few ALGs, as well as other activities mainly concerned with social and economic rights. This approach dovetailed with the broadening thrust of NGO work in the post-Marcos years. Having defeated the dictatorship, many progressive individuals and organizations turned their attention to other endeavors. Constraints affecting what Ford could fund in the civil and political rights fields also affected the Foundation's program. Some Philippine groups would not accept money from a U.S.-based organization, even a private one such as Ford, or would only do so to a limited degree.

The Free Legal Assistance Group (FLAG) was an early grantee that, while focusing mainly on individual civil and political rights, reflected founder José Diokno's "developmental legal aid" philosophy and strategy. This emphasizes that lawyers should attack injustice in ways that address underlying issues and reach beyond individual cases. FLAG gave rise to a law student group, the University of the Philippines Paralegal Volunteer Organization (UPPVO), which became an incubator for many budding attorneys who went on to found and staff ALGs. It provided their first exposure to the developmental legal aid philosophy, to interaction with disadvantaged populations, and to lawyers concerned with social justice issues. Several UPPVO alumni worked as volunteer or part-time FLAG lawyers before (and even after) joining ALGs.

Similar experiences at the country's other leading law school, the Ateneo de Manila College of Law, inspired other attorneys who went on to launch or join other ALGs. Here the formative influences were Ateneo-based development institutes concerned with labor, agrarian reform, and other sectoral concerns, and later the Ateneo Human Rights Center, itself an ALG, whose internship programs the Foundation began supporting in the late 1980s. The UPPVO and Ateneo experiences suggest that exposing law students to social justice issues can crucially affect their future career choices.[7]

In the 1990s, various factors shifted the balance of Ford's human rights programming toward social and economic rights, and toward ALGs. One was that politically inspired human rights violations diminished early in the decade, as the communist insurgency faded and the country's overall situation stabilized. Police brutality and other nonpolitical abuses remained common, but they did not add up to nearly as severe a problem as did the violations of the Marcos and early Aquino years.

A central consideration for the Foundation's human rights grantmaking was that democracy's revival had done little to cure the enduring social and economic inequities that reached back centuries, traversing colonialism, dictatorship, and democracy. These inequities perpetuated a concentration of wealth and influence in a relatively small segment of the population, allowed the ongoing draining of state resources by those in power, and made the rule of law an illusion for the legal system.

Another influence was the work of Frances Korten, the head of Ford's office in the Philippines from 1988 to 1992, on agrarian reform in lowland areas and on land tenure and environmental issues in upland regions. That work stressed grassroots participation, good governance, and sustainable development for low-income farmers. Through co-funding, informal coordination, and grantee impact, these efforts, along with the Foundation's women's reproductive health program, reinforced Ford's human rights grantmaking. A 1991 Foundation document illustrated the mutually beneficial interface: "An upland farmer pressing for land security, an environmental activist facing threats from loggers, and a women's health activist working to remove discriminatory laws all require the legal and political skills necessary to assert their rights and to strike down unjust laws and practices."

Ford's human rights funding supported ALGs to help such persons develop those skills and to provide related backup services. ALGs, noted George, "were able to link up with community-based NGOs and POs, so they could understand community-based issues. The ALGs stayed overnight in villages. They took the all-night buses to get there." They also tramped through malarial jungles, sweated through sweltering community consultations, and otherwise went places and took on tasks beyond the interest of many governmental personnel or traditional lawyers.

Ford also collaborated with other donors, especially with The Asia Foundation (TAF), by co-funding grantees and informally cooperating. In a number of cases, one foundation helped an ALG get started and the other supplemented that initial support when the group could usefully absorb additional resources. The foundations together covered the bulk of ALG staff salaries and expenses throughout the first half of the 1990s, paving the way for other donors to play greater roles toward the end of the decade.

Interaction with TAF also aided George's thinking regarding a programmatic road not taken: work with the judiciary. It was clear to him that the greatest legal problems facing Filipinos "were of a social justice nature and were not necessarily handled by the courts, which in any event were backlogged, expensive, and hard to access." He knew of TAF's decade-long attempts to address those backlogs through training, international exchanges, and consultancies involving the judiciary. He was also aware that, despite the good intentions of some judicial leaders, that effort had foundered due to the impact on the court system of corruption, patronage, and other undue influences. For both TAF and Ford, ALGs offered a more productive, alternative route to legal reform.

Indeed, ALGs were among the most promising organizations seeking Ford support. Some of the ALG lawyers were top graduates of the nation's leading law schools. They persuasively articulated both their goals and their willingness to experiment with new strategies. The fact that many hailed from elite institutions did not necessarily make them elitist. Many had cut their professional teeth on fieldwork with disadvantaged populations, and their community orientation suggested that they would remain rooted in grassroots realities.

Still, the first ALG grants were experimental investments. George explains that "what [Ford and TAF] were doing was seeding the field, seeing what would happen, and then working to consolidate the field and to facilitate contact among ALGs."

Much of this "seeding" took the form of core or institutional support for salaries, office expenses, in-country travel, and the like. As opposed to project funding for narrowly defined activities, core support gave the NGOs flexibility in setting and adjusting priorities and strategies. It was far from a blank check, however. Ford engaged ALGs in prolonged discussions over extended periods before making initial grants.

WLB Executive Director Evalyn Ursua praises the institutional support approach: "Along the way, we encountered a lot of developments or needs we hadn't predicted. Ford gave us a lot of room to define our agenda." Antonio La Viña, cofounder of the Legal Rights and Natural Resources Center, similarly recalls that "in our first year or two, the most important thing was to establish credibility, doing a lot of fieldwork and lots of legal assistance for communities in a nonstrategic way."

"Seeing what would happen," as George put it, required patience: many ALGs' early fieldwork did not yield quick results. Furthermore, a low-key approach on the part of the Foundation proved advisable. The Foundation is open about its programs, and is well regarded by Filipinos who know its work. But given the history of United States involvement in the Philippines, funding by a U.S.-based organization can be a sensitive matter.

"Seeding the field" meant more than core funding. It also included support to establish new ALGs beyond Metro Manila (MM), and funding for existing groups to set up branch offices or affiliates in the provinces. Looking toward the next generation of legal services lawyers, grants provided opportunities for law students to gain exposure to ALG work. The university-based Ateneo Human Rights Center set up a clinical legal aid program and helped non-MM law schools to do the same. Funding to both the schools and the ALGs themselves supported internships for students from at least eleven law colleges across the country. Some of these took the form of yearlong postgraduate placements. The result of these combined efforts and similar independent initiatives was a pipeline effect: the majority of current ALG attorneys came to these organizations by way of various internships.

Ford, TAF, and the ALGs themselves have sought to facilitate ALG interaction in various ways. Perhaps the most successful vehicle was a series of annual ALG conferences, starting in 1990, that for the first time brought these organizations together and introduced some of their members to each other. The gatherings' greatest value might have been informal networking. The conferences helped break down a traditional rivalry between some Ateneo University and University of the Philippines graduates; bolstered personal connections; facilitated subsequent cooperation; and fostered solidarity among attorneys who mainly operated outside the legal profession's mainstream.

Other attempts at creative programming met with more mixed results. George feels that he "pushed hard, perhaps too hard," in funding a secretariat for the ALG network. And not all of the ALGs, branch offices, or law school programs flourished. At various times, the Foundation also funded an ALG database, a study of paralegal training, and a review of these NGOs' work by a former ALG attorney. The impact of these initiatives is unclear. On the whole, efforts to build a formal ALG network structure proved less effective than facilitating informal interaction and collaboration.

Innovation entails risk. Ford's programmatic disappointments were an almost inevitable by-product of investing in experimental ideas and organizations that proved fruitful. Some of these successful efforts are described later in this chapter.

In 1995, incoming Program Officer Hawes was given a funding portfolio focused solely on local governance, without the former human rights component. Why the change? First, Ford had already plowed some fertile ground in the local governance field. Of at least equal importance, the enactment of the 1991 Local Government Code devolved significant taxation, expenditure, planning, and service functions to local levels. Finally, in some provinces a new generation of local government leaders was becoming more open to cooperating with civil society elements.

While the end of grantmaking under a human rights rubric entailed a reduction in the number of ALGs Ford supported—to eight from more than a dozen during the early 1990s—it by no means ended the Foundation's support for human rights work. Civic participation, which ALGs directly aid by strengthening the capacities of partner populations to protect their rights themselves, was already at the core of Ford's local governance program. A focus on local governance was thus a natural outgrowth of the Foundation's support for law-related work.

The ALGs continued to focus on human rights, civic participation, and local governance, regardless of the rubric under which they were funded.[8] But a subtle shift in their Ford-funded efforts was represented by ELAC. "Under the Ford grant, we're still doing community education and advocacy," explains Executive Director Grizelda Mayo-Anda, "but expanding into new [geographic] chapters, community-based resource management, and expanding relationships with local government." As with other ALGs, Ford support enables ELAC personnel to participate in short courses and workshops on development management, local governance, and resource economics.

Though the transition from Ford's human rights grantmaking to its local governance program was smooth, it clearly involved trade-offs. The Foundation decided to forgo opportunities to support ALG and other NGO operations that do not pertain to local governance. In addition, the six ALGs funded by local governance grantmaking no longer have as much leeway to utilize their Ford support as they see fit, since it must pertain to this targeted set of activities. There were sacrifices, then, in not continuing the previous human rights programming and building on its accomplishments.

Alternative Law Groups in Action

In their efforts to advance human rights, strengthen democratic processes, and bolster government accountability, ALGs have served as both allies and critics of government. They have assisted legal and regulatory reform, and provided policy advice, while at the same time seeking to improve implementation of laws by applying pressure from outside the system. The following sections highlight some of those efforts.

Policy Advice and Regulatory Reform

Most of the major 1990s legislation addressing the needs and priorities of disadvantaged Filipinos was accomplished with ALG involvement, either in response to legislators' requests for information or by helping to build legal expertise of other NGOs and POs. The result has been new laws, many of them landmark in nature, pertaining to such issues as rape, sexual harassment, indigenous peoples' rights, natural resources, agrarian reform, and urban housing. While lobbying efforts are not supported by the Ford Foundation, grantees were able to supply critical research and analyses that enabled activists and legislators to develop progressive new laws and policies.

The Legal Rights and Natural Resources Center, for example, provided Congress with budgetary analysis that led the Department of Environment and Natural Resources (DENR) to partly cover the cost of delineating indigenous peoples' ancestral domains. This was a potentially important step toward recognizing and enforcing their historical land rights.

ALG attorneys' legal analyses and credentials carry weight in a lawyer-heavy Congress. Their expertise especially enables them to assist legislative aides. According to Marvic Leonen, executive director of the center, "The aides have to come out with a product," in the form of draft legislation, so they may solicit outside input. The ALGs stand ready to help.

ALGs have also affected scores of executive agency policies. Most notably, they have contributed to rules, regulations, and administrative orders promulgated by such institutions as DENR, the Department of Agrarian Reform (DAR), and the Office of the President.

The ALG Tanggol Kalikasan has been instrumental in the development of environmental regulations. Its work with a number of government agencies has contributed to natural resources conservation in officially protected areas, and community and local government participation in the environmental impact assessment process. It has also helped design better regulations regarding lumber exports; protections for fishing communities against commercial fishing boats' encroachment; prohibitions on the once common practice of catching dolphins; and stronger penalties for fisheries law violations. Praised by some government officials, Tanggol Kalikasan backs its regulatory reform efforts with scientific research when possible.

On another front, Saligan helped draft Urban Development and Housing Act regulations that advance the urban poor's residential rights and opportunities. It also contributed to a presidential order legitimizing the businesses of registered street vendors. Work in both of these sectors complements scholarship (such as Hernando de Soto's *The Other Path*) that concludes that development can benefit from granting legal recognition to the urban poor's residences and businesses. Such research also suggests that this legal recognition diminishes extortion and other corrupt activities by government personnel.

Kaisahan and other ALGs have had a tremendous impact on agrarian reform policies. For example, Kaisahan contributed to the development of an administrative order setting equitable standards for the land rent that farmers pay landlords. Similarly, the Legal Rights and Natural Resources Center and Tanggapang Panligal ng Katutubong Pilipino (Panlipi) contributed to regulations regarding indigenous peoples' land rights and related environmental issues. And, according to Ermelita V. Valdeavilla, head of the official National Commission on the Role of Filipino Women, "We wouldn't know how to survive without the kind of partnership we have with Women's Legal Bureau. They do a great job of helping us think through and crystallize our positions on legal issues." These positions affect not only this governmental body itself, but also executive agencies across the board.

ALG policy work also extends to the local level. Saligan and Sentro ng Batas Pantao, for example, were involved with drafting regulations pertaining to the Local Government Code. With Ford support, Saligan also helps local governments adapt to the opportunities presented by the code. It contributed to the Naga City government institutionalizing the role of a People's Council (for which Saligan is the secretariat), which provides an official channel for NGO and PO input into running the city.

Such impact plays out differently elsewhere, and often hinges on the local presence of ALG attorneys. ELAC's membership on the Palawan Province Council for Sustainable Development has probably contributed to stronger provincial environmental policies in some respects and at least prevented backsliding in others. In the Palawan provincial capital of Puerto Princesa, ELAC has provided information and analysis useful in fashioning regulations regarding illegal fishing.

Key themes run through these ALGs' regulatory reform and policy work. These groups sometimes are de facto policy advisors to officials who value their grassroots experience and legal expertise. Yet, when acting alone, ALGs may find that their arguments regarding contentious issues sometimes carry only limited weight. In the many instances where politics permeate the policy fray, ALGs are most effective when they belong to advocacy coalitions.

In reviewing these policy successes, Gerardo Bulatao, formerly a Department of Agrarian Reform official and currently an Institute of Politics and Governance (IPG) consultant, emphasizes the personal element in advocacy. In contrast to the hostile "pressure politics" of the Marcos era, he sees value in advocates getting to know key decisionmakers or their aides personally. This lesson applies worldwide, but is particularly salient in the Philippines, where *pakikisama* (smooth interpersonal relations) is often more important than institutional structures.

How, though, to establish such contacts? As IPG Executive Director Marie Victa Labajo emphasizes, "Informal, casual gatherings can be very important for establishing good interpersonal relations." In the experience of Tanggol Kalikasan head Ted Bonpin, it also helps to attend and even speak at the same conferences as government officials. Bulatao adds that to make contact "in the Philippine context, with people you don't know, look for a mutual friend, relative, or contact." He also stresses the importance of identifying the key players in policy formulation—sometimes aides to important officials, rather than the officials themselves.

None of this is to suggest that personal contact, even when coupled with legal expertise and coalitions' political influence, can necessarily trump patronage, corruption, and other undue influences that often sway Philippine government operations. But neither should it be underestimated. Personal connections are a part of the fabric of Philippine society. By cultivating this aspect of Philippine life, ALGs and their allies are simply playing on the same field that elite interests have historically exploited.

ALG personnel have not been confined to "the outside looking in" on policymaking. Particularly under the 1992–1998 administration of President Fidel Ramos, some moved into government and drew on their NGO experience to benefit official practices. Antonio La Viña, of the Legal Rights and Natural Resources Center, served at the Department of Environment and Natural Resources. He enlisted ten ALG attorneys to join him there. Two other ALG leaders, Bulatao and Hector Soliman, went on to fill top slots at the Department of Agrarian Reform. While there, they directly affected a host of policies, and facilitated input by Kaisahan, Saligan, and their coalition allies into those policies. Now a presidential assistant, Donna Gasgonia formerly headed Panlipi, a premier ALG concerned with indigenous peoples' rights.

There are several other respects in which ALG personnel have applied their experience in other settings. As U.S. Agency for International Development (USAID) consultants, Panlipi leaders helped formulate a key DENR policy that strengthened indigenous peoples' land rights. Other attorneys also have moved on to influential consulting or staff positions, some with international organizations, to contribute to a ripple effect of ALG policy impact.

Legal Implementation, Good Governance and Accountability: Converting Reforms into Reality

In the Philippines, as in many countries, reforming laws is but half the battle—ALGs work just as vigorously to see that laws are implemented. Sometimes this is a matter of educating Filipinos regarding the law and helping them to take advantage of it. But implementation often overlaps with getting government officials to do their jobs and holding them accountable when they do not. ALG implementation strategies are shaped by the ways in which local officials respond to community priorities. ALGs help communities to work effectively with progressive elected leaders, nudge traditional politicians toward more development oriented initiatives, and challenge corrupt officials' misconduct.

The lack of implementation has long diminished the meaning of democratic protections in the Philippines, and eroded public faith in the legal process. The state's failure to enforce laws is a central reason why many rights go unrealized, why many Filipinos remain mired in poverty, and why many resources are drained away illicitly. Ford Philippines Representative Suzanne Siskel explains, "Ignorance and flouting of the law are very important causes of inequity and hardship" for disadvantaged groups. The ALGs are "reinforcing the goals of progressive legislation and policy, and bringing this to the local level by enabling [local governments], civic groups, communities, et cetera, to understand and, at least sometimes, to realize the benefits of good policy and legislation."

The issue of implementation is intimidating in its scale. ALGs can attack these problems only selectively. But strategies such as paralegal development, community organizing, litigation, and media outreach can create a ripple effect, and perhaps provide a basis for replication elsewhere in the country. They also provide ALGs and their allies with insights that shape new policies which, in turn, sometimes lend themselves to easier enforcement.

Paralegal development is a central implementation strategy. It begins with ALG consultations with communities to identify the legal issues that most concern them. Such consultations may lead to a series of paralegal training sessions, followed by ongoing contact between ALGs and paralegals as new situations arise. Paralegals also often have access to ALG legal assistance in pursuing cases through court or administrative mechanisms, where necessary. And given that Philippine institutional operations often hinge on personal relationships, paralegals' ongoing involvement with official proceedings helps them build useful links with personnel in relevant government offices.

A prominent example of Foundation-supported paralegal development is the work jointly carried out by Saligan, Kaisahan, and BMFI. They have trained almost five hundred paralegals who guide their fellow farmers' land reform applications through DAR processes. This involves gathering data and affidavits regarding such matters as crop yields and land occupancy, and, if landlords contest the applications, representing farmers at DAR quasi-judicial hearings. The paralegals handle most applications themselves, though ALG attorneys provide legal representation if disputes reach court.

Another instance of effective paralegal development is WLB's partnering with a PO to address violence against women in a community in the Metro Manila area. General training for males and females alike has been complemented by more specialized education for a core of five paralegals. The three the author interviewed in late 1997 provided written documentation indicating substantial success in handling approximately two hundred cases dating from late 1995. The disputes most commonly involved wife beating and child support. Regarding the former, the paralegals typically explained the law to the police; persuaded them not to ignore the wife and instead to prepare the requisite report that can help deter subsequent spousal misconduct; enlisted male "allies" to counsel the husband and explain the criminal nature of his actions; and drafted a written agreement under which the husband promised to change his conduct. Where such interventions fail, WLB can and does take perpetrators to court. The threat of prosecution is a major stick to back up the paralegals' attempts at persuasion.

ELAC has helped paralegals and fishing communities control outsiders' illicit fishing techniques in Palawan Province, which had caused local catches to plummet. Armed with knowledge that the practices are illegal and that they have a right to intervene, the fishermen intercepted the outsiders. Catches have reportedly climbed since.

ALGs focus most paralegal training on domestic laws and processes of greatest interest to partner organizations, as opposed to international or constitutional law. Depending on the community, the focus can be fisheries or forests (as with ELAC and Tanggol Kalikasan), domestic violence (WLB), or agrarian reform (Saligan, Kaisahan, and BMFI). Many also provide training in how to prepare affidavits and gather evidence. Leonen, of the Legal Rights and Natural Resources Center, points out that imparting legal skills useful in the local context is important. "A lot of communities would rather learn about how to make an affidavit than weightier international human rights issues," he says. WLB's Ursua agrees that "international law generally is less important," unless "there's not domestic legislation to fall back on, as with trafficking of women."

A cohesive PO is another crucial component in building effective paralegal services. This is a reason why the Foundation supports BMFI to carry out community organizing as well as paralegal development, and why some ALGs will not engage in paralegal development where the partner PO is weak. Of course, law can be a tool in organizing: Tanggol Kalikasan has helped launch POs geared toward battling illegal logging and fishing practices by educating communities about those practices. Still, the general ALG experience is that legal knowledge, in and of itself, does not build strong organizations.

A strong PO can bring countervailing pressure to bear on officials who otherwise might be biased or simply unresponsive. Sometimes the combination of organization and legal knowledge can create such pressure even where actual power is lacking. This is because of the *palakasan* ("pull") system that permeates the society. A police officer, provincial bureaucrat, or local elected official may avoid taking the risk of crossing a PO whose cohesiveness and relative legal sophistication make it seem connected to more powerful personages.

As a complement to mobilizing paralegals to serve as frontline facilitators, some ALGs use community organizing, followed by community-wide nonformal legal education, as another means to increase citizens' participation in government, promote accountability, and ensure implementation of progressive laws. With funding from the Foundation's local governance program, ALGs have helped familiarize Filipinos with their rights and responsibilities under the Local Government Code, and have increased their input into local government and planning processes. Citizens learn, for instance, that the code grants NGOs and POs seats on local government councils, and they become familiar with how to get this provision implemented.

Kaisahan works with POs to build their capacities to set community priorities and to work with local governments to allocate funds for those priorities. Hawes points out, "Even *trapos* [traditional politicians] are interested in reelection. They're willing to listen to constituents when constituents tell them what they want. So if people want immunizations and clean water systems instead of waiting sheds [shaded shelters at public transportation stops, often emblazoned with public officials' names before elections], often politicians will provide them." Of course, such projects hinge on the availability of resources. But strengthening citizen understanding of and participation in local government enables POs and NGOs to monitor and help maximize effective use of public revenues. This addresses a historical lack of knowledge that allows funds to be siphoned off from government coffers through insider contracts, substandard project work, or outright theft. Kaisahan training also encourages community members to think about not just their rights, but about their responsibilities as citizens and even about how they can contribute resources (such as volunteer time) to their priority projects.

Where politicians are not responsive, nonformal legal education could have indirect electoral impact. Such education, along with Saligan training regarding electoral laws (including poll watching), may have helped prompt dozens of farmer leaders to seek and win local office in the provinces of Bataan and Bukidnon.

As with paralegal training, ALGs' other operations adapt to community-specific conditions. Litigation, while typically a last resort, is another important strategy for many ALGs as they seek to combat gender violence, advance agrarian reform, or even protect allies who are hauled into court. Tanggol Kalikasan has defended partner populations and DENR personnel against harassing lawsuits brought by environmental law violators. Another example of ALG adaptation is found in Palawan's capital, Puerto Princesa, where the progressive mayor has sometimes called on ELAC for legal advice and analysis. Such assistance helped him persuade the Secretary of Justice to bar the establishment of an environmentally threatening sugar mill in a watershed area. ELAC also helped the mayor obtain a favorable Supreme Court decision upholding the city's confiscation of a boat that illegally used cyanide for fishing. The mayor has in turn worked with ELAC to combat illegal fishing practices.

The flexibility and diversity of ALG strategies has allowed these groups to take many new directions in pursuing legal implementation. WLB, for example, serves as a secretariat for a new national network of lawyers focusing on stemming violence against women. It also is working with the Philippine Judicial Academy to construct a curriculum for judges, prosecutors, and other government personnel regarding laws pertaining to gender violence. The ramifications of this development could reach beyond this single issue to provide a model for other ALGs and their partners to fashion government training curricula in many other fields. There is some evidence, for example, that enforcement has been improved by involving such civil society forces in educating judges and prosecutors about the Urban Development and Housing Act.[9]

Given the continuing corruption in Philippine public life, not all ALG work involves cooperation with government officials. Where alerted to graft by their partner groups, ALGs sometimes can attack this problem. Armed with legal knowledge by Tanggol

Kalikasan, a PO in Rizal Province persuaded the provincial council to overturn an apparently corruption-induced municipal government decision favoring a firm that violated environmental laws. ELAC and its paralegals have aided the successful prosecution of municipal officials involved with illegal logging and fishing in Palawan. Coupled with media coverage, this led to at least one corrupt mayor's defeat in the subsequent election.

Such use of the media to publicize problems is another strategy used by ALGs. When officials in the province of Cebu passed a zoning ordinance designed specifically to allow a cement plant proponent to evade land use regulations, ELAC organized a site visit and press conference, and helped journalists arrange interviews with community members. Ensuing publicity contributed to the local government revoking the ordinance. The Legal Rights and Natural Resources Center assigns specific staff to press relations duties. Many times, media attention and public education are heightened by the diverse, complementary activities carried out by ALGs and their allies, ranging from court cases to demonstrations and hunger strikes.

An important lesson rises from ALGs' various efforts at law reform, paralegal development, community organizing, nonformal legal education, litigation, and media outreach. It concerns integration of these strategies: they often work best when they work closely together. What ALGs learn from grassroots experience, for instance, is often converted into policy proposals. And where they are successful in policy advocacy, they naturally seek to implement resulting reforms on the ground.

Having noted many positive features of ALGs' implementation work, two concerns crop up. The first is not unique to ALGs, although it applies to the Foundation's funding of them. As IPG's Bulatao puts it, there is "the big gap between the Ford Foundation's NGO grants and the research the Foundation supports. In the end, you want some feedback on what good your money did." While Ford and other donors have long supported university-based research in the Philippines and elsewhere, they have put very limited or no resources into academic studies of the impact of the very projects they fund. By and large, research institutes have not examined ALGs' and other NGOs' legal implementation work to discern, for instance, the dynamics behind and effects of local legal victories, the best paralegal development methods, or how nonformal legal education affects target audiences' knowledge and actions. Such studies could contribute to improving NGOs' operations and impact in the future.

Another potential difficulty for some ALGs regards what could be called their "unit of analysis." Tanggol Kalikasan's Bonpin correctly describes ALGs as "serving the community, not the individual." This is a great strength of their work. On the other hand, the relevant community may, under some circumstances, be larger than the one an ALG has chosen to serve. Halting a government or private sector project may benefit a partner PO, but harm a larger population. In a related vein, TAF's former assistant representative in the Philippines, Karin Gollin, praises ALGs generally, but wonders whether they sometimes should emphasize negotiation more. She perceives the value of some litigation to the extent that certain ALGs undertake it, but at least in the environmental sphere sees "lots of banging of heads against brick walls and not getting what they want." Some ALGs may be starting to adopt more flexible positions. Rather than fighting a power plant project, ELAC and its coalition recently negotiated an agreement that commits the National Power Corporation to adhere to environmental standards, study any impact on the surrounding sea, and mitigate any ill effects. In Ms. Gollin's view, Tanggol Kalikasan also is notably moving toward more mediation and negotiation in its work.

Conclusion

How have the ALGs, their partner communities and organizations, and the Foundation contributed to Philippine social progress? What are some of the lessons and promising ideas that have emerged over the years? What challenges do they face today? This section offers brief responses to those broad questions.

Changes and Contributions

ALGs have contributed to scores of administrative rules and regulations that, when implemented, benefit farmers, fishing communities, indigenous peoples, the urban poor, disadvantaged women, and other populations across the country. When requested by Congress and local governments, they also have lent their legal expertise to governmental consideration of many pieces of legislation. At the same time, that expertise has strengthened the advocacy capacities of their NGO and PO coalition partners. Even today, one foreign diplomat familiar with the Philippine Congress's generally conservative composition expresses amazement at the legislature's enactment of progressive laws, typically with NGO input.

Despite the many ALG contributions to policy formulation, there should be no illusions regarding the ongoing, widespread lack of implementation. But in view of their limited resources, these relatively small NGOs have proven very cost-effective at helping their partners raise Philippine law from rhetoric to reality.

Ford's contribution to the ALGs' work has been manifold. Most fundamentally, the Foundation has taken an attitude that could colloquially be expressed as, "If it ain't broke, don't fix it." Many ALGs are sophisticated organizations that the Foundation has funded, for the most part, in a flexible manner that has let them chart their own courses. In addition, by sometimes providing potentially risky initial grants to launch new organizations, Ford opened doors for other donors to provide subsequent support. It also encouraged and funded some of these groups to slightly adjust their programs to match emerging opportunities and needs in Philippine society, most notably regarding local governance. Finally, its facilitation of interaction among ALGs has helped these groups to become more than the sum of their parts, to constitute a public interest law movement that continues to evolve and attract other donor support after more than a decade.

Lessons and Insights

Law Reform and Implementation
1. By becoming known to policymakers through workshops, conferences, and informal channels, an adept NGO can draw on its grassroots experience and legal expertise to play an important advisory role regarding legislation and

regulations, as requested. Legislative and executive agency officials often call on ALG lawyers to provide such advice.

2. In the Philippines, executive agencies, Congress, local governments, and multilateral agencies make most of the key decisions affecting the disadvantaged majority's rights and development. These bodies also have proven more amenable than the courts to addressing ALG partner populations' needs. The ALGs therefore have focused most of their policy-oriented work on these institutions, rather than the judiciary.

3. Nonlegal elements can be crucial for effective legal advocacy. ALGs often belong to coalitions that employ political pressure and persuasion to effect policy reform and implementation, drawing on tools that range from community organizing to scientific and budgetary data.

4. ALG paralegal development efforts include both formal training and ongoing professional support. Saligan, Kaisahan, WLB, and other ALGs develop effective paralegals by connecting them with lawyers who can answer questions as they arise. Learning through experience is crucial.

5. Paralegals are cost-effective, particularly when lawyers provide backup services. Paralegals trained by WLB and other grantees have handled problems related to gender violence and agrarian reform that otherwise would have gone without remedies, or that would have consumed lawyers' much costlier time. Attorneys still are necessary, however; their availability to occasionally take recalcitrant parties to court constitutes a valuable "stick" for paralegals.

6. These paralegals' work is often most effective when they concentrate their efforts on a community's most pressing needs. Kaisahan's and Saligan's partner paralegals, for example, focus on shepherding land reform applications through bureaucratic processes. The training for this includes learning how to negotiate, prepare affidavits, and maintain written records.

7. Organization is power. Though paralegal effectiveness might seem based solely on the premise that "knowledge is

power," another theme also emerges from ALG experience: knowledge most effectively translates into action when wielded by an organization. A well-organized group is often more likely than an individual to be able to make its voice heard by the press, a sympathetic mayor, the police, a prosecutor, a judge, an executive agency official, or even a corrupt politician concerned about the group's votes.

8. ALGs have operated effectively by taking an integrated approach to their work. They and their partners often blend community mobilization, litigation, administrative advocacy, use of media, and other actions. The mix of strategies naturally varies, depending on the issue and community involved.

9. Under the right circumstances, ALGs may play valuable roles in training government personnel. They know about concrete problems in the ways laws are implemented, and can prioritize key issues, rather than attempt to cover entire legal fields with ineffective generalities. One example is WLB's curriculum development for judges and prosecutors regarding violence against women.

Donor Programming Approaches

1. Flexible, permeable donor program categories reflect reality. ALGs have been supported under various Ford categories, meeting different objectives: human rights, local governance, natural resources, and reproductive health. ELAC, for example, helps protect the human rights of fishing and indigenous community members; strengthens the capacities of civil society organizations to advance their interests on their own; helps them manage natural resources; and aids local governments in relating to these groups and in handling other issues. Donor programming categories can help focus resources, thinking, and expertise. But this is perhaps best done when they allow and even encourage the inevitable crossover that marks many grantees' work.

2. Programming should reflect local realities. The Foundation's local governance grantmaking has tried to adapt to

those realities by, in addition to focusing on local governments, addressing the important roles of civil society and
decentralized executive agencies, and featuring contributions by legal services NGOs. Many Philippine legal and
governance issues boil down to a common focus: community control over local resources, be they aquatic, agrarian,
upland, or even urban land. Executive agencies make many
decisions regarding these resources. Thus, Saligan,
Kaisahan, and BMFI address vital local governance concerns through their work with the Department of Agrarian
Reform.

3. Long-term support for effective grantees is justified and
advisable. A key factor is not how long the donor has supported a grantee, but whether the grantee continues to have
significant impact. During more than a decade of Ford support, the Legal Rights and Natural Resources Center has
become a leader regarding indigenous peoples' rights and
upland development issues. Yet the center and other ALG
grantees started with promising but inexperienced leaders
who spent their first few years cutting their professional
teeth. Had the Foundation been impatient or shifted programming priorities after a few years, ALGs' impact might
have been stifled.

4. Funding the ALGs' core costs enabled them to experiment,
evolve, learn through experience, and respond to unanticipated opportunities and obstacles. Even as the shift to a
local governance focus has precluded Ford support for certain activities, the support has remained flexible enough to
give the ALGs considerable leeway in their work.

5. A broadly defined view of a legal system sometimes can
make for the most effective donor work in the legal field.
The support of Ford and other donors for ALGs has helped
them strengthen elements of the Philippine legal system.
By working through government agencies more than the
courts, ALGs have affected scores of policies and processes that have practical relevance for their partner populations. It also is possible that ALGs have helped bring a
modest amount of additional accountability to the judici-

ary, by pursuing redress there and strengthening their partners' understanding of its operations.

6. Donor support for law school clinics can help incubate public interest law movements. Most ALG attorneys entered the field through exposure provided by law school programs, and through internships organized by individual ALGs. Law school clinics often need funding to get off the ground. Their direction can be influenced by the specific activities, such as NGO placements, that donors support.

7. Applied research merits greater emphasis in grantmaking. Ford and other donors might be wise to support such research to assess the work of ALGs. Conducted in cooperation with grantees, such research could document impact, illuminate the dynamics underlying that impact, and crystallize lessons for future use by grantees and donors alike.

Looking Ahead

Where do the ALGs go from here? The answer depends on the organizations themselves. Still, a few common challenges emerge.

One relates to the 1998 election of President Joseph Estrada. Some ALGs no longer have the level of contacts and access in the current administration that they enjoyed under its predecessor, particularly in DENR. They may need to build new relationships or develop new strategies.

Another challenge facing all NGOs is that of financial sustainability, particularly exploring opportunities to generate funding from Philippine sources. Ford, TAF, and USAID are supporting initiatives to strengthen NGO fundraising in general and ALG capacities in particular. Yet in-country resources can come with demanding strings attached, particularly given the strongly personal nature of Philippine society. And even in the United States and Western Europe, most NGOs are by no means self-supporting. So while ALGs cannot afford to ignore this issue, the challenge also confronts donors. They may need to initiate more long-term mechanisms (such as endowments) that help solid grantees remain in business.

There is also the matter of personnel sustainability: some ALG staff move on to private sector and government jobs paying better salaries. Fortunately, these jobs often keep them engaged in development issues while meeting their financial needs. Moreover, their replacements at the ALGs generally have maintained the organizations' dynamism. Striking a balance among staff compensation, competence, and dedication is an ongoing challenge.

In coming years, ALGs' accomplishments, expertise, and grassroots orientation may weigh in favor of their seeking to increase their impact in two ways. First, through "mainstreaming": making greater contact with the established bar, the judiciary, and elected officials through presentations, legal publications, and personal links. Second, they could become resources for the international development community. To a limited extent, they already are taking such steps, particularly regarding judicial engagement. But enthusiasm for greater influence must be tempered by the potential for any successful NGO to stretch itself too thin (or for a donor to push it to do so).

A final challenge regards strategic flexibility. ALGs and their personnel have evolved in ways that provide for varied approaches to problems. Population growth, globalization, and a host of other trends present obstacles and opportunities that will force these groups and their partners to keep rethinking their individual and collective goals and devising new strategies that can potentially extend their effectiveness to areas now unforeseen. There seems little doubt, however, that ALGs will evince the requisite flexibility and will continue to crucially contribute to the inevitably long-term endeavor of strengthening human rights, development, and democracy in the Philippines.

Notes

1. Agrarian reform includes land reform, the change in farmer-landlord land tenure arrangements to the benefit of the farmers, typically so that they have greater control over the land (which can include outright ownership), and/or greater shares of crop proceeds. Agrarian reform is a more all-embracing term, however, in that it also includes

various technical or financial support services geared to assist farmers and to ensure the tenurial changes' success.

2. In a literal sense, POs are NGOs, so a brief delineation is in order. POs generally are self-help entities whose (generally low-income) members hail from a single sector (tenant farmers, urban poor, etc.), and most directly benefit from development activities. [In some other countries, similar groups are referred to as community-based organizations (CBOs).] They typically are not compensated for their PO work. In this context, NGOs are service organizations that work with POs in pursuit of development goals. They sometimes are not sector specific in their operations and membership. Their staffs tend to be better educated and more affluent than PO members. NGO personnel often are compensated for their work. As an example of the distinction, community organizers and agricultural technologists from an NGO might assist farmers belonging to a PO on livelihood projects.

3. Paul D. Hutchcroft, "Oligarchs and Cronies in the Philippine State: The Politics of Patrimonial Plunder," *World Politics* 43, no. 3 (April 1991): 415–450.

4. Senate of the Philippines, Committee on the Education, Arts and Culture and the Committee on Social Justice, Welfare and Development, *A Moral Recovery Program: Building a People—Building a Nation,* Report submitted by Senator Leticia Ramos Shahani, 9 May 1988, p. 16.

5. Alfredo F. Tadiar, "The Administration of Criminal Justice in the Philippines: Some Aspects for a Comparative Study with That of the United States," *Philippine Law Journal* 47, no. 4 (September 1972): 548.

6. Boo Chanco, "A Police Bereft of People's Trust," *The Manila Chronicle,* 20 January 1993, p. 5.

7. In fact, several ALG attorneys today teach law school courses, where their instruction can shape students' perspectives on the profession, perhaps drawing some into ALG service.

8. Two of the six ALG grantees are not involved with local governance. They are leaders in their respective fields: the Women's Legal Bureau defends women's rights (particularly the right to be free from violence); and the Legal Rights and Natural Resources Center promotes indigenous peoples' rights and environmental law. WLB's funding comes from Ford's reproductive health program (though it originated under the rubric of Ford's human rights program), and the center receives support from the Foundation's Philippines, Indonesia, and India offices to serve as secretariat for the NGO Working Group on the Asian Development Bank.

9. Anna Marie Karaos, Marlene Gatpatan, and Robert Holtz,

Making a Difference: NGO and PO Policy Influence in Urban Land Reform Advocacy; Pulso Monograph No. 15 (Manila: Institute on Church and Social Issues, 1995), p. 100.

Appendix: People Interviewed for This Study

[Note: This list includes individuals the author interviewed both during his 1999 trip to the Philippines for this study and several other persons he interviewed during previous consulting and research trips there. It does not comprehensively cover, however, all of the persons with whom the author has discussed law-oriented work in the Philippines over the years, including many members of people's organizations assisted by ALGs and persons with whom he has conducted group interviews.]

Alberto C. Agra
Policy and Legal Consultant, Governance and Local Democracy Project, Makati, MM

Joselito C. Alisuag
Chair, Executive Committee, Haribon Palawan, Puerto Princesa, Palawan

Audie C. Arnado
Executive Director, Center for Paralegal Education and Training, Cebu City, Cebu

Nesorio G. Awat
Legal Area Manager for Palawan, Tanggapand Panligal ng Katutubong Pilipino, Puerto Princesa, Palawan

Normita V. Batula
Coordinator, Legal Affairs Unit, Tungo sa Kaunlaran ng Kanayunan at Repormang Panasakahan, Quezon City, MM

Ernesto D. Bautista
Assistant Resident Representative, United Nations Development Programme, Makati, MM

Ted Bonpin
Attorney, Tanggol Kalikasan, Haribon Foundation for the
Conservation of Natural Resources, Quezon City, MM

Gerardo J. Bulatao
Senior Consultant, Institute of Politics and Governance, Quezon
City, MM; and former Undersecretary, Department of Agrarian
Reform, Quezon City, MM

José Canivel
Visayas Coordinator, Environmental Legal Assistance Center,
Inc., Puerto Princesa, Palawan

Karina Constantino-David
Executive Director, Harnessing Self-Reliant Initiatives and
Knowledge, Inc., Quezon City, MM

Sheila S. Coronel
Executive Director, Philippine Center for Investigative
Journalism, Quezon City, MM

Ma. Vicenta P. de Guzman
Executive Director, Tanggapand Panligal ng Katutubong Pilipino,
Quezon City, MM

Eduado de los Angeles
Partner, Romulo Mabanta Buenaventura Sayoc & de Los Angeles,
Makati, MM

Rebecca Nadine D. Dichoso
Committee Secretary, Committee on National Cultural
Communities, House of Representatives, Quezon City, MM

Ma. Socorro Diokno
Secretary-General, Free Legal Assistance Group, Quezon City,
MM

Daniel Edralin
Chairperson, Alliance of Progressive Labor, Quezon City, MM

Raquel Edralin-Tiglao
Executive Director, Women's Crisis Center, Quezon City, MM

Jaime Faustino
Director, Venture for Fund Raising, Pasig, MM

Vincent Edward R. Festin
Attorney, Sentro ng Alternatibong Lingap Panlegal, Quezon City, MM

Victoria P. Garchitorena
Executive Director, Ayala Foundation, Inc., Makati, MM

Donna Z. Gasgonia
Presidential Assistant, Office of the President, Manila, MM; and former Executive Director, Tanggapand Panligal ng Katutubong Pilipino, Quezon City, MM

Terrence George
Former Program Officer, The Ford Foundation, Makati, MM

Karin Gollin
Former Assistant Representative, The Asia Foundation, Makati, MM

Gary Hawes
Program Officer, The Ford Foundation, Makati, MM

Anna Marie A. Karaos
Research Associate, Institute on Church and Social Issues, Ateneo de Manila University, Quezon City, MM

Antonio G.M. La Viña
Former Undersecretary for Legal and Legislative Affairs and Attached Agencies Department of Environment and Natural Resources, Quezon City, MM; and former Director for Research and Policy Development, Legal Rights and Natural Resources Center, Inc., Quezon City, MM

Marie Victa Labajo
Executive Director, Institute of Politics and Governance, Quezon City, MM

Nick Langton
Representative, The Asia Foundation, Makati, MM

Ida J. La'o
Executive Director, Development Legal Assistance Center, Inc., Quezon City, MM

Marvic M.V.F. Leonen
Executive Director, Legal Rights and Natural Resources Center, Inc., Quezon City, MM

Ma. Paz Luna
Former Program Director, Tanggol Kalikasan, Quezon City, MM

Icasiana Luzong-deGala
Attorney, Sentro ng Alternatibong Lingap Panlegal, Quezon City, MM

Inocencio Magallanes
Vice Chair, Executive Committee, Haribon Palawan, Puerto Princesa, Palawan

Ed Tami Mansayagan
Secretary-General, National Confederation of Indigenous Peoples of the Philippines, Quezon City, MM

Grizelda Mayo-Anda
Executive Director, Environmental Legal Assistance Center, Inc., Puerto Princesa, Palawan

Carlos P. Medina, Jr.
Executive Director, Ateneo Human Rights Center, Ateneo de Manila College of Law, Makati, MM

Armand H. Mejia
Lawyer, Tanggol Kalikasan, Quezon City, MM

Magistrado A. Mendoza, Jr.
Coordinator, Legal Affairs Unit, Tungo sa Kaunlaran ng
Kanayunan at Repormang Panasakahan, Quezon City, MM

Carol Mercado
Program Officer, The Asia Foundation, Makati, MM

Beth Pua-Villamor
Associate Executive Director, Legal Rights and Natural
Resources Center, Inc., Quezon City, MM

Eduardo E. Queblatin
Environmental Management Specialist, Governance and Local
Democracy Project, Makati, MM

Rodolfo Ferdinand N. Quicho, Jr.
Program Director, Tanggol Kalikasan, Quezon City, MM

Mary Racelis
Former Country Representative/Assistant Regional Representative, The Ford Foundation, Makati, MM

Glenda Ramirez
Coordinator, Internship and Legal Aid Program, Ateneo Human
Rights Center, Ateneo de Manila College of Law, Makati, MM

Joel Rocamora
Executive Director, Institute for Popular Democracy, Quezon
City, MM

Ronaldo Romey-Gutierrez
Lawyer, Tanggol Kalikasan, Quezon City, MM

Carolina S. Ruiz
Coordinator, Feminist Legal Services and Development Program,
Women's Legal Bureau, Quezon City, MM

Antonio L. Salvador
Executive Director, Sentro ng Alternatibong Lingap Panlegal,
Quezon City, MM

Rodrigo Saucelo
Acting Tourism Officer, Office of the Mayor, Puerto Princesa, Palawan

Philip B. Schwehm
Deputy Chief of Party, Governance and Local Democracy Project, Makati, MM

Howie Severino
Environment Desk Coordinator, Philippine Center for Investigative Journalism, Quezon City, MM

Suzanne E. Siskel
Representative, The Ford Foundation, Makati, MM

Hector D. Soliman
Former Undersecretary for Field Operations and Support Services, Department of Agrarian Reform, Quezon City, MM, and former Program Director, Tanggol Kalikasan, Quezon City, MM

Alfredo F. Tadiar
Professor, University of Philippines College of Law and Project Director, Reproductive Health, Rights, and Ethics Center for Research and Training, Quezon City, MM

Evalyn G. Ursua
Executive Director, Women's Legal Bureau, Inc., Quezon City, MM

Ermelita V. Valdeavilla
Executive Director, National Commission on the Role of Filipino Women, Quezon City, MM

Tomasito S. Villarin
Executive Director, Kaisahan, Quezon City, MM

Marites Danguilan Vitug
Journalist, Cainta, Rizal

Frederick A. Ylaya
City Councilor, Puerto Princesa, Palawan

7

Eastern Europe: Funding Strategies for Public Interest Law in Transitional Societies

AUBREY MCCUTCHEON

When the Ford Foundation sponsored the 1991 "Symposium on Public Interest Law Around the World," convened by the U.S.-based National Association for the Advancement of Colored People Legal Defense and Educational Fund, the paucity of participants from countries of Eastern and Central Europe was conspicuous. After monumental social and political changes in the region, those same countries would now be well represented at any comparable gathering. Through the creativity and commitment of individuals from the region, and the support of a handful of donors, public interest law (PIL) in Eastern and Central Europe has taken great strides. Ford's PIL grantmaking program today supports more than a dozen groups in Eastern and Central Europe (hereinafter referred to as "Eastern Europe"). The Foundation and its grantee partners in the region have gained important experience and insights regarding donor strategies for building PIL within societies in transition. Those lessons are the focus of this chapter.

The Eastern Europe PIL program is young; it officially began only in 1995–1996, and is evolving as the region's transition continues and as organizations emerge and mature. In addition to providing organizational support, the funding program is specifically designed to develop PIL as a new field of law work in Eastern Europe, to promote a regional community of PIL organizations, and to facilitate their networking with similar organizations elsewhere in the world. The activities of PIL grantee partners today are diverse, and include impact litigation, basic legal services, clinical legal education, and community legal literacy programs. Using international and domestic law, they address issues ranging from ethnic discrimination to environmental protection. The program and its partners have laid foundations for wider acceptance of PIL, engendered or strengthened specific PIL practices, and encouraged the creation of a newly defined community of organizations and individuals involved in PIL throughout the region.

This chapter examines the Foundation's PIL work in the Czech Republic, Hungary, Poland, and Slovakia. It describes this program's background and growth in the context of the changes taking place in those countries, ongoing human rights and social justice concerns, and the Foundation's broader regional priorities. It sets out selected programming approaches gained from the experiences of grantees, donors, and other partners, and notes some of the opportunities and constraints that influenced program choices at different stages.

The case study is based on interviews conducted in late 1998 with organizations in the four countries of focus, and individuals elsewhere who are familiar with PIL and donor activities in Eastern Europe. Many of the lessons discussed here are newly derived from recent experience in those countries. Others are more familiar, but are valuable in reconfirming experiences of law-related grantmaking programs, as well as other types of donor programs, in other countries.

Evolution of the Public
Interest Law Grantmaking Program

The Ford Foundation's efforts to promote the consolidation of democratic institutions in Eastern Europe after the end of communism led to the conclusion in 1995 that a focused PIL grantmaking program was both needed and possible. Joseph Schull, then the Foundation's deputy director for Ford's Russia and Eastern Europe program, says that many believed that PIL could provide a framework for beneficially engaging the human rights community with new constituencies in these societies on an ongoing basis. As he recalls, "PIL appeared to be a vehicle for moving the human rights agenda from an abstract ethical plane to a more practical legal level." Schull says a long-term goal of the program was to develop PIL as an effective civil society activity in the region—so that governments, the private legal profession, and the non-governmental sector would be encouraged to advance legal protections and solutions for their societies.

Program staff planned a long-term institution-building approach that could support grantee organizations as they evolved and became more independent, and could encourage grantee sustainability. The Foundation was fortunate to have active donor partners with many shared objectives. While employing slightly different terminology to describe their legal program activity, the Open Society Institute (OSI) and its affiliates and the German Marshall Fund are two primary and important contributors to PIL in Eastern Europe.

As Eastern Europe's young democracies developed, a legacy of public mistrust of legal systems, courts, and other institutions remained from an undemocratic past. This was a major influence in the decision to pursue a PIL program. Irena Grudzinska Gross, the Foundation's program officer for Eastern Europe, explains that under previous regimes in the region, law was primarily an instrument of the state; citizens and civil society organizations rarely pursued causes or grievances through the legal system. While some government subsidies were theoretically available, legal services did not always exist in reality. In criminal matters, for example, defense attorneys were reputed to be ill prepared at trial, if they showed up at all. Only the privileged could afford to pay for their own lawyers, and the poor generally saw the courts as a place to be avoided. Legal experts were concerned that ongoing law reform in the region, without mechanisms for implementation and expanding public access to justice, would be ineffectual and might actually deepen public mistrust of the legal system. Professor Leah Wortham of Catholic University Law School in Washington, D.C., who has worked in the region to establish a clinical legal education program there, restates the challenge by asking, "How do you create respect for the rule of law where the honorable thing to do, in some countries, was to avoid the law?"

There were other program opportunities and choices emerging in Eastern Europe at that time. Changes began taking place in the late 1980s, and although conditions in individual countries varied, many political, legal, economic, and social effects of the transition were common across them. There was marked, yet embryonic, growth in civil society entities and activities. Democratization of political systems was under way and new constitutions were being debated or adopted. Both substantive and procedural laws were being changed. The judiciary was undergoing reform and restructuring, including changes in its powers vis-à-vis other branches of government. A newfound respect for human rights was also emerging, and international human rights norms increasingly affected domestic laws.

The broader legal reform process occurring at the level of state institutions was attracting attention from a wide variety of public and private donors. For example, the countries in which the Foundation worked were soon to be admitted to the Council of Europe; thus, the European Convention on Human Rights would eventually become applicable in their domestic legal contexts. National courts could then apply the protections of the Convention in judgments, and parties could invoke it in cases. Both the European Union and the Council of Europe were devoting substantial resources to assist countries of the region to prepare for this process. The U.S. government and some private donors were also providing support for legislative redrafting efforts, constitutional and judicial reform, and public administration reform.

As staff evaluated Ford's potential contributions, they sought to match its particular strengths with areas of need, while avoiding efforts that would add little to foreign government aid coming into the region at that time. In particular cases, support was provided for legislative reform efforts, as with a 1992 grant to the Hungarian Ministry of Justice for an international consultation on the reform of the Hungarian criminal procedure code. However, strategic choices among PIL's desired and potential impacts convinced the Foundation to act primarily as a supporter of NGOs and public-private partnerships. Government agencies were perceived as large, bureaucratic, and difficult to engage, especially because officials tended to change too often to develop genuine long-term relationships or to expect significant impact. "[O]ur zone of greatest competence was in the nonstate sector," Schull says. But refining strategic choices seemed prudent even among those grant opportunities that were related to both law reform and NGO development. Schull provides this example: "We generally stayed away from projects related to developing the legal and legislative framework for nonprofit activity . . . there was enough funding available from other sources for generalized NGO support activities to enable us to focus selectively on institutions related to our substantive interests."

A principal focus of the Foundation's funding activities for Eastern Europe prior to the late 1980s was freedom of expression. Its support for international academic and artistic exchanges, publications, and conferences helped the Foundation build relationships with the human rights community—relationships that would serve as a natural base from which to construct a new funding program. Successful human rights groups and activists once part of underground dissident movements slowly moved to provide PIL services, among other program activities. Edwin Rekosh, director of the Public Interest Law Initiative in Transitional Societies, a Ford grantee housed at Columbia University Law School in New York City, explains that human rights organizations began to professionalize, differentiate, and build niches, but they continued to use protest tactics of the former era and were slow to use law and courts. "The role of the lawyer was seen as technician or state functionary," says Rekosh. It took some time to "reconceive the role of the lawyer, and the lawyer as part of the NGO. The Foundation helped by showing the role of lawyers in more activist legal settings."

Although legal and political reforms were widespread in the region as the new funding program was being conceived, many Eastern European countries throughout the 1990s continued to experience conditions that concerned human rights activists. Minority rights and nationality issues common to many countries in the region were reasserted in the wake of the reforms. Several minority groups struggled for their human rights, but the Roma stood out as the most deprived ethnic group throughout Europe. Long victims of discrimination from many quarters, the people known by the derogatory term "gypsies" experienced a rise in racist violence after the fall of communism. Other regionwide problems included domestic violence, police misconduct, and inefficient judicial processes.

These and other concerns were manifested to varying degrees in the four countries considered in this chapter. In the Czech Republic, continuing problems with the judicial system served to heighten distrust of courts. Administrative courts increasingly issued judgments without hearings and the length of judicial proceedings was generally felt to be intolerable. Deficiencies in the Czech citizenship law, which resulted from the peaceful division of Czechoslovakia in 1993, led to the expulsion of hundreds of Slovaks, including many Roma, and the separation of Slovak families along nationality lines.

In Slovakia, political uncertainties raised fears among NGOs about issues of free expression and press freedom. A law in 1996 limited the use of minority languages in government offices and the media. This most significantly affects Slovakia's Hungarian minority, which comprises 11.5 percent of the population. The Supreme Court found the 1996 law to be unconstitutional, but controversy around interpretation and adherence to the ruling has continued. Slovakia's failure to adopt a minority language law also drew criticism from the European Union, the Organization for Security and Cooperation in Europe, and the Council of Europe in 1997.

In Hungary, police misconduct was pervasive, and few victims had the confidence to file complaints. Due process was often denied, with the state often refusing to provide criminal defense counsel. The right to privacy for patients and recovering drug addicts remained a major issue until the passage of a new law in 1998. Children's psychiatric institutions were cited for poor supervision and violating children's rights.

In Poland, police abuse was likewise an issue. In 1997, the Polish Constitutional Court severely limited a woman's right to abortion. Journalists complained of a need for stronger laws on access to information, and civil rights activists cited legal measures restricting the constitutional right to privacy. The rights of refugees and aliens were insufficiently protected. Several cases regarding slow judicial proceedings were submitted to the European Commission on Human Rights in 1997.

As the 1990s proceeded, opportunities for PIL work in Eastern Europe became clearer. The Foundation had numerous program opportunities and choices, but also faced formidable obstacles to achieving the impacts sought through a PIL grant program. Indeed, many challenges continue today. As pointed out by Dimitrina Petrova of the European Roma Rights Center (ERRC), "public interest law" is hard to translate and understand in any local language of the region. "In the past, the 'public interest' was seen to be pursued by the state procurator, not by lawyers pursuing social change. The creative work of lawyers was limited," she says. The term is often confused to mean simply the field of public law, as distinct from private law. Others have confused the concept with the role of the lawyer defending the state against citizen claims. There were also practical limitations to the development of PIL in these countries; the right to counsel in criminal procedures was not fully and consistently provided, virtually no legal aid mechanisms existed for the indigent in civil matters, and very few lawyers themselves had any training or experience in PIL strategies.[1]

The ability of the Foundation to navigate these program opportunities and obstacles was aided by the intense investment of staff time in the early 1990s, which resulted in learning from and building relationships with local grantees and other local partner organizations and individuals during the region's transition. With the new funding opportunities presented by the transition to postcommunist societies, the development of indigenous civil society organizations and direct relationships with local grantee partners, rather than Western-based intermediaries, became a priority. The local knowledge and contacts derived made more strategic grantmaking possible from 1994 onward.

In the early 1990s, the Foundation had supported efforts by grantees in the region to build the freedom of expression and other human rights aspects of their work. At the time, this was not consciously directed at the development of a future PIL program. For example, Helsinki Committees in Poland and the Czech Republic—human rights groups that conducted monitoring, public advocacy, and education—were supported to conduct program planning processes. Among other programs, in 1994 the Foundation helped the two groups to develop litigation and legal counseling units, respectively. In 1995 the Foundation commissioned a consultant to report on the prospects for clinical legal education at several universities in the Czech Republic and Slovakia.

Recognizing that more systematic, broad-based PIL strategies were needed to shore up nascent legal reforms and restore public faith in legal remedies, Foundation staff outlined a PIL initiative in 1995 that included five funding strategies, targeting support for: (1) exemplary NGOs in fields such as human rights, environmental advocacy, women's rights, and consumer advocacy whose work included a substantial component of legal services, impact litigation, legislative monitoring, and legal education; (2) networking and exchanges of experience among these and other groups to strengthen the emerging field of PIL; (3) building stronger relationships among PIL NGOs, bar associations, and law schools; (4) innovative legal education programs promoting a more practical and public interest orientation among legal educators and law students; and (5) communication and educational efforts addressing diverse publics as well as policymakers to enhance recognition of PIL as a means of enlarging public access to justice. The overarching goal of the initiative was to support the development and dissemination of good practices in strategic litigation, legal services, clinical education, and legal literacy training, and to provide mechanisms for broader reflection and sharing of experiences among PIL practitioners in the region.

There was still some concern among Foundation staff that the approaches and vocabulary of PIL were too alien to firmly take root in Eastern Europe. To test possibilities further and to facilitate the initiative, the Polish Helsinki Committee was enlisted in 1995 to convene a small meeting of lawyers, judges, and human rights activists. Those participants affirmed PIL as a relevant framework for advocacy in the region and discussed strategies for addressing obstacles to further development of their work. The meeting was followed by symposia in the United Kingdom in 1996 and in South Africa in 1997, which brought together lawyers, educators, donors, and activists from Eastern Europe and Russia, as well as countries with longer experience in PIL. By all accounts, the gatherings were a stimulus for PIL activities in the region. Participants indicate that the symposia also strengthened a fledgling network of legal and advocacy groups, in part through the overlap of attendees, which was helpful in building relationships among both individuals and organizations. The use of external venues for the symposia facilitated contributions from PIL activists from outside the region with long experience in a variety of legal fields, and expanded the future resources available to Eastern European groups. The latter symposium led to the creation of the Public Interest Law Initiative in Transitional Societies at Columbia University to provide published resources and networking services to the expanding PIL community in the region.

The PIL symposia were models of collaborative work—not only for the organizations in attendance, but for grantmakers as well. The Budapest-based Constitutional and Legislative Policy Institute (COLPI), an affiliate of OSI, cosponsored the two symposia. Staff from Ford and COLPI indicated that the ongoing collaboration helped them refine their approaches and allowed them to learn from each other's experiences in the region. For PIL groups, the grantmakers' collaboration led to expanded resources and valuable contacts. For example, the joint meetings were able to utilize experts and successful models known to each of the donors. Subsequent co-funding of some PIL projects has increased sustainability of groups that had previously depended on a single major donor. Schull warns that important opportunities can be missed for both donors and grantees if donor collaboration is deferred until co-funding decisions are being considered. Early and ongoing collaboration can inform strategies and help donors to clarify their respective funding roles.

The PIL activities of Eastern European grantees eventually grew to include impact litigation, basic legal services, clinical legal education, and community legal literacy programs. Throughout the evolution of the program much has been learned about PIL programming itself. Other insights on a variety of related topics, from staff experiences, PIL groups, and other partners, are shared below.

Selected Donor Programming Approaches

Context and Adaptation

One of the most important lessons that emerged from Ford's PIL program in Eastern Europe was the need for sensitivity to context, as well as for care and flexibility in transplanting concepts and methods. This is an age-old caution, but it remains alive and was repeated often by donor and grantee staff alike. It was clearly raised not just as an admonition to foreign donors but also as a self-caution, as NGO staffers in Eastern Europe discussed the potentials and pitfalls of transplanting approaches from their neighboring countries, as well as from urban to rural settings. Awareness of outside approaches to PIL is highly desirable, but flexibility is required to allow for adaptation to new settings. These adaptations should take place with sensitivity not only to different legal, political, and economic situations, but also to cultural contexts, which can be either barriers or facilitators in the development of PIL.

Sometimes this sensitivity is a simple matter of terminology. The Czech Helsinki Committee provides a striking example in its adaptation of a U.S.-originated public education program, which offers basic legal information in an easily accessible form. The program is known in the United States and elsewhere as "Street Law," a term that in the Czech language would be popularly understood to mean the "law of the jungle"—clearly not the program's intent. While the Czechs readily utilize the Street Law concept, as do many countries in the region, they have adapted its title and some of its methods to suit their environment.

Professor Stefan Krieger of the Hofstra University Law School says that sensitivity to a local context should include recognition of past local efforts and successes—both as a matter of respect and as a foundation for adapting and guiding future initiatives. He also stresses the importance of considering the cultures of the private legal profession and of law faculties when developing any donor strategy. Krieger suggests that with a contextual analysis that includes these elements, a donor might better customize programming strategies to countries that are similarly situated.

When one university in the region launched its law clinic with partial support from the Foundation, the focus of its work was largely on commercial law. Ford Program Officer Irena Gross remembers that this was in response to the experiential context and culture of both the faculty and the wider legal profession at the time. While the founders sought both the pedagogical and the PIL benefits of a law clinic, they feared that a clinic with PIL objectives would be premature at best, and would possibly even be opposed within the law faculty. Over time, the clinic has evolved to include PIL work. The lesson for donors and universities is that flexibility, patience, and a willingness to experiment are often necessary for the successful adaptation of a PIL model.

This is not to suggest that flexibility be without boundaries. Recognition and respect for grantees' experience and local contexts should not cause a donor to sacrifice its own program objectives or the lessons from its own experience. Foundation staff learned that this is especially important when introducing new concepts and approaches of PIL. Donors must maintain a clear sense of their own objectives and constructively discuss an organization's plans to adapt a PIL approach to the local context. In cases where it is not possible to develop a desired program while remaining respectful of the local context, either due to a possible cultural clash or simply a lack of appropriate local organizations or resources, it is more appropriate to abstain rather than to insist upon an ill-fitted project that is perhaps only remotely related to the donor's program objectives. The same caveat should apply to grantee organizations. PIL programming (like all grantmaking) is inherently a conversation of *two* parties, in which each should remain authentic to its own purposes and self-understanding.

Strengthening Civil Society

Gross, who inherited the Foundation's young PIL program in early 1998, observes that in the context of the region's broad societal transitions, building PIL groups has also served to strengthen the wider body of civil society. While PIL programming is designed primarily to pursue social and economic justice including human rights, program choices can also help open space for other civil society organs to operate. This may happen in many ways, through law reform achievements, court cases or, as in the case of the Centre for Legal Advice in Warsaw, by advising and assisting other NGOs with their legal needs. PIL's impact may also be seen in a subtler strengthening of civil society that results from the promotion of active citizenship, and greater public involvement in social and economic causes, which is inherently a part of PIL's educational work.

Martin Palous of the Czech Helsinki Committee stresses the importance of this broader objective in societies undergoing wide-ranging transition. Noting that the protection of human rights requires vigilance in any society, he points out that transitional societies, such as those in Eastern Europe, may experience ebbs and flows in the respect accorded to human rights and in the development of an independent civil society. He argues that the "politics of transition" do not end with the achievement of democracy or the formal enshrining of human rights laws, but continue through the formation of civil society and further through its independence, maturation, and globalization. As a PIL organization, the Czech Helsinki Committee sees itself as part of a globalizing civil society that seeks to address threats to social and economic justice worldwide.

Proactive and Reactive Programming

The Foundation's Eastern Europe PIL program combined both proactive and reactive donor approaches, depending on the circumstances. In the beginning of Ford's PIL programming in the region, Schull says, grants were largely for technical assistance purposes. The general situation, needs, and actors were in such rapid transition that it was difficult to be proactive—at least in a systematic way. Staff learned that the best efforts of the Foundation were in quick and flexible responses that brokered high-quality technical assistance tailored to the needs and requests of grantee groups. This was also a reflection of the staff's own level of experience during the first years after 1989, which made reactive programming seem prudent.

At a later stage, however, as staff felt more confident in their understanding of the region's needs as well as the available institutional partners and resources upon which to draw, Schull began to view a proactive approach as both appropriate and necessary. "It is not presumptuous in some cases to broker, or convene groups to discuss new ideas. A donor should not always assume a passive role," he says. "In some cases donors control too much, but in others a proactive role is necessary to get beyond where grantees are, or simply to provoke them to examine their own views."

By taking a proactive role in convening symposia of PIL practitioners from both within and outside Eastern Europe, Ford helped introduce terms and concepts that were unfamiliar in the region. Discussions on impact litigation, test case litigation, and university legal aid clinics, for example, provided a counterpoint for legal activists to examine and understand their own current and potential practices more deeply.

Danuta Przywara of the Polish Helsinki Committee encourages donor staff to take a proactive stance in discussing project implementation with grantees. She believes that this provides "an opportunity to get a different way of thinking on implementation and approaches: the clash of perspectives is very instructive." Edward O'Brien, executive director of the Washington, D.C.–based Street Law Inc., stresses that donors can be more proactive by, for example, ensuring that the conferences they fund encourage "multinational presentations and participatory methods of teaching." O'Brien believes conferences can thus help to break down stereotypes and erode prejudices and chauvinism.

Monica Platek of the Polish Association of Legal Education says that in the embryonic stage of a field or program such as PIL, donors should be proactive to ensure that grantee groups gain skills in project planning, budgeting, and proposal writing. Further, she believes donors should actively encourage grantee efforts toward the development of second-tier leadership, both to widen networks and to nurture future NGO leaders.

Two specific experiences with proactive approaches in the Foundation's PIL program are worth comparing. In the first, Foundation staff decided to fund the establishment of a legal resource center, having consulted with local experts to confirm the need for such an organization. An enthusiastic host organization was identified, and extensive discussions were held in an attempt to establish a shared vision for the project. After two years in operation, however, the Foundation concluded that the effort had failed, and ended its support. According to Schull, "[O]ur mistake was to believe that a project could be entrusted to an organization that did not understand or own it fully. In retrospect, we should have understood that the protracted planning process, and the need for continuous involvement by Foundation staff to move it forward, was merely a symptom of the project's inappropriateness."

The Foundation's partnership with the Hungarian Civil Liberties Union (HCLU) has been far more successful. Ford contacted HCLU because of its experience in promoting individual civil liberties. While such work was new to Hungary and the group's model derived from foreign organizations, it had already been appropriated by these local legal activists. Foundation staff encouraged the HCLU to focus on high-impact cases, in addition to individual legal services. Staff also took the lead in urging that the group's budget include line items for organizational development and fundraising expenses. Today, HCLU's work focuses largely on patients' rights, privacy rights, and freedom of information. Its activities include impact cases, individual legal services, education of policymakers, and public education.

The HCLU's emphasis on high-impact cases has led to some notable successes. In 1997 HCLU brought suit against a hospital for the inhumane treatment of a psychiatric patient who had been subject to electric shock treatment and was denied family visits. At that time, there was no legal standard on the treatment of psychiatric patients. The suit asked for damages and for a declaration that such treatment was in violation of the patient's rights. The court adopted HCLU's arguments using both civil law and the new human rights provisions of the 1989 Hungarian Constitution. This was among the earliest uses of Hungary's new human rights laws. Furthermore, the case gained much press attention and was used as a tool to educate the public and Parliament. Later, HCLU educational materials were reviewed by members of Parliament before passage of the new 1998 Health Act, which incorporates patients' rights such as informed consent as a precondition to medical or psychiatric treatment, confidentiality of medical records, and the right to refuse life-sustaining treatment.

Strengthening the Legal Profession

Another aspect of the PIL program has been to introduce PIL concepts and strategies to other activists and lawyers. It is hoped that this will increase the legal resources available to groups as well as nurture a PIL ethos within the profession. For Jan

Hrubala, a young judge and vice president of the Association of Slovak Judges, the 1996 PIL program symposium was a turning point. Following the symposium, he left his promising judicial career to establish and work with the Centre for Environment and Public Advocacy (CEPA) in the Slovak Republic. He explained at the subsequent 1997 symposium that he had left the bench to persuade others that many issues come before the courts unnecessarily, while other problems that never reach court merit greater advocacy. His former fellow judges first looked askance at his activities, Hrubala said, but attitudes were gradually changing and he hoped that students would be attracted to this kind of work.[2]

The increased presence of PIL activity and organizations has helped draw the attention of private practitioners in Poland to the problem of public mistrust of the legal system. Wojciech Hermelinski, a private attorney and vice dean of the Warsaw Bar Council, states, "More private lawyers now even accept indigent clients and apply to courts for exemptions of fees based upon Article Six of the European Convention on Human Rights." Article Six establishes the right to fair trial, and the right to free criminal defense for the indigent in countries of the Council of Europe. The fee Hermelinski refers to is a required minimum attorney's fee established by the bar to prevent competition between attorneys. He notes, however, that the influence of fledgling PIL groups in Poland is still weak, and he believes a successful donor strategy must involve lawyers in private practice, as well as judges and prosecutors. In his view, the training of judges on the European Convention, made possible by funds provided by the Council of Europe, has enabled and encouraged more lower court judges throughout the country to rely on the Convention in their judgments.

In Hungary, the Legal Defence Bureau for National and Ethnic Minorities (NEKI) describes the effect of PIL activities on private lawyers who had been skeptical of their potential impact in small public interest or human rights cases. According to NEKI, private practitioners now display greater willingness to take on such cases as they observe some of NEKI's successes and gain confidence in its tactics and strategies. Director Imre Furmann explained that in the past NEKI actively and with difficulty sought help from private lawyers, but now many lawyers come forward to offer their assistance. CEPA has observed a similar interest develop in Slovakia, according to Hrubala.

Interest by students and public communities in PIL also appears to have had an effect on private practitioners, according to staff at Krakow's Jagiellonian University Law Clinic, which sends law students into Poland's courts to assist lawyers. The clinic's staff has noticed that the students' presence adds scrutiny, which has improved the level of service that lawyers offer indigent clients. Street Law Inc. has found that lawyers who teach community legal literacy in Eastern Europe programs go into communities and learn important lessons about public perceptions of law in society.

A small or closed legal profession, especially in the context of many new alternative economic opportunities, diminishes the number of lawyers serving public interest causes and organizations. Catholic University law professor Wortham points out, "A growing economy may not trickle down to deliver more . . . legal services for those in need." She recommends that in developing strategies, donors consider the routes by which people enter the legal profession and provide support for international comparative research on the relationship between access to the profession and access to justice in various countries. Other strategies to increase the practice of PIL, she suggests, might include professional exchanges among lawyers' associations and policymakers from diverse countries focusing on the numerous benefits of an open profession and potential reforms toward that end. Comparative research might also include the various methods countries use to encourage or require pro bono and other public service law work.

One way the PIL program has sought to strengthen the profession is through legal education that offers substantive and procedural instruction, instills public service values, and provides opportunities for practical experience. NGO partners were encouraged to offer internships to law students and graduates, and to solicit pro bono work from recent graduates now in private firms. While law students' perspectives were broadened by such experiences, these efforts could not reach enough law students or young lawyers with the right skills and at their most formative stage. The most direct link between formal legal education and PIL appeared to be the university-based law clinic. Experience elsewhere shows that clinics can provide practical skills that improve legal education, encourage PIL careers, supplement other legal services, nurture values in the legal profession, and increase public understanding of the legal system.

The Warsaw Bar Council's Hermelinski believes a multi-pronged programming strategy best supports these goals. Policy and regulatory reforms are needed in some countries to allow supervised student appearances in court. Public education work is needed to promote attitudinal changes in society and make PIL careers desirable to students. Without these additional components, Hermelinski points out, any grant program for clinics in the region may fall short of its full potential.

Others interviewed shared suggestions to foster the clinics' various objectives. Hofstra law professor Krieger believes that integrating community-based organizations and other civil society groups into the operations of the clinic from the start would extend the PIL impact of clinics beyond their educational purpose. This, he says, would bring students and instructors into contact with "people who see and experience the patterns of abuse and disadvantage that the clinic is meant to address." In Poland and Hungary, Ford-funded clinics and NGOs have established some forms of cooperation. The clinic at the University of Warsaw intended to serve clients referred by two women's groups, as well as the Polish Helsinki Committee. In Budapest, the Hungarian Helsinki Committee has a formal relationship with a clinic where it is responsible for case selection. According to Ferenc Koszeg, executive director of the Hungarian Helsinki Committee, this contributes to the pedagogical value of the clinic by ensuring that students are addressing important human rights and constitutional issues.

Professor Eleonora Zielinska of the University of Warsaw believes the use of NGOs for case recruitment or selection is a good strategy for clinics. For one, she is convinced that contact between students and NGOs is important to creating good PIL lawyers. She cautions, however, that all involved need to be extremely clear as to who controls case strategy. Given the nature of PIL litigation, and the multiple tactics it uses, there may be conflicts between the short-term interest of the clinic's client and the longer-term interests of larger causes. A conscious and carefully considered balance between these interests should be pursued.

Platek urges universities and donors to encourage more links between community legal literacy efforts and law clinics. Community literacy programs can identify clients for clinics and clinics can propose target communities and topics for instruction.

Donors can also do more to help clinics successfully integrate with law faculties in the region. COLPI, for instance, has convened a meeting of law school deans to inform them of the benefits clinics have achieved elsewhere. Such efforts would facilitate sustainability and access to the resources and talents of universities. This is particularly important in Eastern Europe where, as Gross notes, some faculties have been resistant to the concept of clinical legal education, believing that practical application is an inappropriate role for a student.

Wortham suggests that donors can assist this goal by, wherever possible, supporting clinic founders that have professional status within the host faculty. "Establishing a clinic by recruiting outside staff usually makes bad programming sense," she says. She cites as an example the early days of the clinical education movement in the United States. Societal circumstances were ripe and student interest was high, but law schools recruited practitioners who found it difficult to gain full acceptance within law faculties. This problem was somewhat alleviated when academic credit for participation in clinics was offered. "Look for enthusiasm within the faculty," she advises donors. "Don't worry if the administration is lukewarm or students enthusiastic. What drives most law schools is faculty interests."

Wortham also urges that donors ensure that clinical instructors are integrated into the normal salary structure of the law faculty. They should not be allowed to work on a voluntary basis or for less compensation than other law teachers do, she says. That would not institutionalize the clinic and its benefits, but would only capture the opportunity presented by a committed staff. To ensure success, Wortham adds, a donor should fund a clinic well, even if it is the sole initial donor, and provide clinical instructors salaries that are comparable to other law faculty.

Exchange programs and site visits, other staples of PIL donor programming, should be planned carefully, say staff at Jagiellonian and Warsaw universities. Such opportunities should be of sufficient length to ensure clinicians' actual acquisition of new methods or skills. Placements need not always be at foreign institutions, although this can often be beneficial. Where possible, donors should utilize examples of clinics that operate within similar legal, socioeconomic, and educational environments. The most established or prestigious clinics are not always the most instructive examples even in the same country. Offering them as learning models might unintentionally discourage fledgling efforts or underresourced universities. Finally, when foreign experts are used for short-term training purposes, they will likely reach more clinicians if donors bring them to the target country or region rather than sending small numbers of trainees abroad.

It is also inspirational, according to Zielinska, for fledgling clinics to see themselves as part of a new regional movement. Common problems then seem less insurmountable; common research can be undertaken and solutions fashioned. An example is the added momentum that the push for student practice regulations has sustained in Eastern Europe. Clinics in the region are now working together to develop model rules of student practice to be proposed for adoption in each country. A regional association of university clinics might be helpful to this young clinical movement in much the same way that the Helsinki Committee network continues to encourage the human rights movements in individual countries of the region.

Sharing Best Practice and Models

Several PIL groups suggested that donors should consciously seek to develop a few promising local organizations as models for later emulation in the region. To do this successfully, donors would adopt a long-term approach to organization building and be willing to maintain support through inevitable staff changes and fluctuating periods of success and failure.

The use of any foreign model can also be a long-term and evolving process, and such efforts have met with mixed success. In some instances this process has occurred relatively smoothly and quickly. The Helsinki Committees that have been replicated in different countries of the region are one example. HCLU, which patterned itself on the American Civil Liberties Union, is another. Borislav Petranov of the London-based INTERIGHTS observes, however, that international groups have been viewed in many ways: as mentors, imposers, agenda setters, and cofounders, just to name a few. As a result it normally takes a long time to develop sound international relationships, he says. "Sometimes there is an overdemand on international organizations as models and a lower-intensity, longer-term presence is needed."

Staff exchanges or placements, conferences, and subgrants have all been successfully used by various groups in the region as methods for conveying and replicating best practice. OSI and Ford have had success in the past few years incubating smaller human rights NGOs in Poland by funding a small grants program implemented by the Polish Helsinki Committee. Both donors have also supported the replication of the work of the European Roma Rights Center (ERRC) across national borders by allowing subgrants to be fashioned and awarded by that regional group.

The use of foreign experts to transmit experience should be done with care, cautions Platek. More than one interviewee felt that many foreign experts did not display the personal sensitivity, modesty, or deference necessary to be effective. Careful choice and preparation of outside experts is essential, so that the substance of what they have to share can be appreciated.

Sustainability and Organizational Capacity Building of Grantees

The different types of sustainability and capacity-building challenges facing PIL groups in Eastern Europe are exemplified by the experience of NEKI in Hungary. Although not its area of expertise, NEKI found itself giving essential managerial and administrative advice to Kesaj, a smaller group based in neighboring Slovakia. Both NEKI and Kesaj are devoted to addressing the plight of the Roma. Kesaj, originally established as a cultural theater for Romani people, expanded to provide legal services. Although its managerial capacity had begun to improve, Kesaj was forced to close due to a lack of funds, exacerbated by a new Slovakian law on philanthropy. According to NEKI, the new law made the organization subject to heavy taxes and a minimum budget requirement. NEKI's management assistance to Kesaj, and its observation that similar needs were widespread, led it to conclude emerging PIL NGOs would benefit from professional consulting services in management and administration. NEKI further points out that in order to build PIL as an institution in the region, NGOs and their donors must address three separate challenges to organizational and institutional development: internal management and administration capacity, indigenous philanthropy, and government policies.

Both NGOs and donors interviewed spoke of the need to diversify sources of financial support toward greater sustainability of PIL groups in Eastern Europe. Some referred to more diverse foreign sources while others mentioned fostering indigenous philanthropy from individuals and the emerging private sector. Still others suggested government subsidies and income-generating activities by NGOs. Both PIL groups and donors alike assert that diversified fundraising needs to be a more prominent aspect of an institution's development strategy. On the donor's part, this might involve greater collaboration within its own staff or with other donor agencies that have experience in income-generating projects and indigenous philanthropy.

The development of second-tier leadership is another critical need. Many PIL groups in the region are still managed by their founders and have yet to develop skilled leaders-in-waiting. A loss of leadership could have a devastating effect on those organizations. To mitigate or prevent this, a donor's programming approach might wisely include early efforts to develop and retain a second tier of leaders. This is particularly important in transitional societies characterized by the fluid movement of personnel between civil society organizations, government, and a growing private sector.

Staff of more than one group asserted that a funding strategy that made smaller grants but longer-term commitments would better serve the sustainability of their organizations. They indicated that ceilings on grant awards would relieve the felt pressure to scale up activities and spending as a measure of success. Premature expansion, they worry, could damage long-term effectiveness. In contrast, extended funding commitments would enable long-range program planning and promote staff stability. Donors and grantees could then build staff training and other organizational development activities into budgets.

This approach is worth consideration by donors when they have identified a PIL grantee partner that they seek to scale up over a period of years. It could also be used as a strategy for encouraging a grantee's consistent attention to securing diversified funding. It might be prudent, however, to couple this programming approach with other strategies such as regular assessments or evaluations to ensure the effectiveness of the PIL group throughout the period of the long commitment. It was also suggested that endowment grants, which can foster simultaneously stability and experimentation, be used more flexibly and creatively as a tool for sustaining a new field such as PIL. Yet endowments are clearly not right for every grantee, especially those without proven track records.

The Czech and Polish Helsinki Committees and Foundation staff each described the usefulness of planning grants to increase sustainability and capacity. Initial planning grants were awarded in the early 1990s as these human rights groups were evolving from underground dissident movements to organizations with more direct involvement with their country's changing legal systems. The grants allowed them to assess conditions, identify clear missions, and research and formulate strategic plans. In the process, the Foundation learned more about the legal, political, and cultural environment these groups were working in, and was able to assess programming opportunities and limitations. The grants enabled the committees to pursue processes of institutional review and restructuring while maintaining core activities. Danuta Przywara of the Polish Helsinki Committee says that the initial planning grant enabled them "to think carefully about new goals and methods and . . . to plan and consult specialists without suspending other activities." Jana Chrzova of the Czech Helsinki Committee emphasizes that the opportunity for strategic planning was especially important at a time of some public doubt about the continued need for human rights NGOs in the new democracy. The planning period also helped the Czech Helsinki Committee to define a complementary role with respect to the Slovak Helsinki Committee after the breakup of Czechoslovakia.

More recently, after approximately five years in both cases, Foundation staff made subsequent planning grants to the committees to support a second phase of strategic long-term planning. These grants enabled each group to review its role within a now wider PIL and human rights community. While experts stress how important planning grants can be to helping organizations sustain difficult periods or transitions, they also emphasize that planning should not be used as a substitute for project delivery or be mandated by a donor when it is not merited by special circumstances.

Last, both grantees and Foundation staff suggest that more attention should be given to performance assessment as a means of capacity building for PIL organizations in Eastern Europe. Grantee groups suggest assessments as a way to gain practical lessons that can be fed into their future decisionmaking and work. Foundation staff express the need to couple their current performance monitoring with other forms of assessment that include more qualitative and quantitative data on the impact of the new program, the network, and specific groups. Some interviewees emphasized that more formal assessments might be premature for fledgling groups in the new PIL community, especially in the midst of rapidly changing and unpredictable contexts. Others stressed the positive role that studies on societal impact and project performance can play. Participatory forms of assessment that involve PIL staff, clients, donors, and other stakeholders were suggested in light of some of these concerns.

Networks or Coordinating Structures

Another strategy employed by the PIL program is the use of a network support service. The New York City–based Public Interest Law Initiative in Transitional Societies (the Initiative) has delivered useful follow-up assistance to PIL groups that collaborated at the two symposia, as well as to the emerging network of PIL groups in Central and Eastern Europe and the former Soviet Union. Initiative Director Rekosh describes the organization as a short-term, external catalyst for the PIL network. Its activities include seminars, publications, electronic communications, and technical assistance. One 1998 seminar examined state-supported indigent defense and legal services programs. Another seminar was focused on university-based law clinics. Seminars add substantively to the groups' work, reinforce their mutual reliance, and provide opportunities to learn from each other's experiences. Initiative publications, disseminated to policymakers and the private legal profession, as well as PIL groups, attempt to identify new possibilities for activists and to provide a forum for debate. It offers news bulletins on developments in the field, documents, resource lists, job postings, and other materials on its website and by e-mail. The electronic network is also used to survey activities and needs. The Initiative invites requests for technical assistance and helps groups connect with appropriate resources.

By all accounts, the Foundation's programming approach to PIL in Eastern Europe, including the Initiative network support, has been extremely important in promoting the network's cohesiveness, especially its regional aspect. Groups within the network emphasize different factors that they believe are responsible for this success. For example, some credit the history of cooperation at the earlier symposia. They doubt that network support could be used successfully without some similar grounding. Many people agree that the Initiative's independence from any particular organization enables it to keep the needs of the network paramount, and to avoid being dominated by any one group's needs, expertise, or interests.

Some interviewees believe it would be more practical and effective to locate such an entity within the region it serves. They believe this would allow more direct contact between the structure and PIL groups, greater access to its offices and services, and more engagement in the issues groups face and their changing needs. Others interviewed believe an outside locus increases awareness of and access to external resources for use in the region. More than one interviewee emphasized that the effectiveness of such an entity depends less on where it is than on how it is run, and on the quality of its relationships with the groups it is designed to serve.

Cross-Sectoral Programming and Grantmaking

By employing a grantmaking strategy wider than PIL—one that crosses sectors but targets a disadvantaged population group—the Foundation has been able to magnify the effects of separate grants. For example three grantees, ERRC, NEKI, and Autonomia, all work with Hungary's Roma minority, which constitutes 5 percent of Hungary's population. Roma suffer severe social and economic hardship, including prejudice, poverty, and discrimination and an unemployment rate of nearly 90 percent in some communities. The three grantees contribute to Roma social and economic empowerment in different ways. Autonomia, the Hungarian Foundation for Self-Reliance, while not a part of PIL, provides Roma with grants and loans for self-help initiatives to build economic and social autonomy. ERRC and NEKI provide legal services and use the law to pursue Roma rights.

The experiences of two specific communities convey this lesson vividly. In late 1997, a racially motivated murder of a Roma fisherman took place in the community of Tunyogmatolcs in northeastern Hungary. The murder followed racial abuse and verbal insults. The first official response was to not prosecute the case, claiming lack of evidence. NEKI, which is partially supported by ERRC, provided legal advice to the victim's family in their successful effort to secure prosecution, and a conviction ensued. The deceased had been the principal income earner in his household. During and after the trial, Autonomia helped the family to maintain their income through a microenterprise project. Autonomia also supported others in the same community. Anna Csongor of Autonomia explains that it was important and instructive throughout the community that Roma found two vehicles for support, and that their interests could be pursued in both the new legal and economic systems.

Recsk is another community in which Autonomia works in northeastern Hungary. Csongor believes the economic empowerment that grew from Autonomia's earlier work there resulted in increased social confidence and an assertion of human rights. When a school official directed racial slurs at children, a parent sought NEKI's legal help. In this instance, NEKI combined a public education campaign with out-of-court negotiations and a complaint to the Ministry of Education to bring an end to the racial abuse. Autonomia believes its ongoing work toward economic empowerment could be furthered by PIL efforts to fight discrimination in employment and financial lending.

Conclusion

The PIL network in Eastern Europe continues to expand. A few of the PIL groups supported by the Foundation also went on to conduct their own grant programs, a development that allows the Foundation to indirectly support additional smaller groups and to reach more remote areas.

But PIL's accomplishments cannot be measured by the number of its organizations. The true potential of PIL—a young network and Foundation program, dating only to the mid-1990s—and its social impact in Eastern Europe have yet to be realized. The program and its partners have laid new foundations for the acceptance and practice of PIL. A new legal community has been strengthened, one that uses law and legal institutions to pursue social and economic justice for the disadvantaged. Former Ford Foundation Deputy Director Schull recognizes the significance of PIL, and the important role of the Foundation and other donors with which it has collaborated. "I think that we struck a vein and brought together a field in its early stage of development," he says, "when its members can most benefit from the networking and professional exchange that the Foundation is well placed to support."

In its few years, the program has provided the Foundation and its grantee partners many early, yet valuable, insights. Since the main body of this chapter sets out a variety of donor programming approaches, only a few of the most salient ones are summarized here.

Lessons and Insights

1. The PIL grantmaking program in Eastern Europe confirms a common caution heard about other donor programs and settings: sensitivity to context is important when transplanting concepts and methods both between and within countries. Donor flexibility is advisable to allow fine-tuning and adaptation of PIL methods to the different settings of Eastern Europe. At the same time, Foundation staff have learned that it is equally important, given the newness of PIL approaches in the region, to maintain a clear sense of donor program objectives.

2. The experience of Ford and COLPI with PIL in Eastern Europe reaffirms how beneficial donor collaboration can be for both donors and grantees. Such cooperation has expanded the pool of experts and other resources available to PIL groups and helped inform donor strategies.

3. The Foundation's proactive approach has contributed to the success of the Eastern Europe PIL program. Reactive programming approaches, however, have also been productively used, especially in the early stages of grantmaking.

4. The goals of university-based law clinics can be furthered by multipronged programming strategies, such as public policy work that pursues regulations allowing supervised student appearances in court, and public education work to promote careers in PIL. Cooperation between clinics and other civil society organizations can also be integrated into the operations of clinics to ensure that they more effectively address PIL objectives. Donors can help clinics integrate more effectively with law faculties, thereby increasing opportunities for sustainability through access to university resources. Strategies for doing this include supporting individuals already within faculty structures, where possible, and putting clinical instructor salaries on par with other law faculty salaries.

5. PIL organizations in Eastern Europe could be enhanced by greater attention to building capacity in management and administration. In some cases, professional services will be needed in strategic and long-term planning, project management, and project assessment for PIL NGOs. Furthermore, the experiences of organizations confirm that there are limits to this type of internal organizational development in isolation. The need for indigenous philanthropy and government policies on the broader NGO sector demand attention as well. It may require greater collaboration within and between donor agencies. Some grantees recommend smaller grants but longer commitments by donors. Planning grants proved to be useful programming tools to assist sustainability of the Czech and Polish Helsinki Committees as they matured from dissident and underground human rights groups after 1989.

6. The PIL meeting and two international PIL symposia proved very useful, according to participants. They carried added programming significance because of the newness of the PIL field; and the common challenges faced by countries in the region, such as negative public attitudes toward the legal system and the previous isolation of the participants. The non-U.S. venues and presence of so many non-American resource persons enhanced the gatherings further in confirming that PIL is not just a U.S. concept, and that it is being successfully used by other societies undergoing transitions. As a follow-on structure evolving from the symposia, the Initiative provides both continuity and ongoing services to the newly emerged PIL network, and thereby enhances the benefits of the two symposia.

7. Cross-sectoral grantmaking encourages synergy between legal services and economic development sectors, as illustrated by the three grantee groups in Hungary working on issues related to the Roma population. This suggests a potential to similarly use PIL to enhance other nonlegal efforts with additional constituencies.

Notes

1. See Dimitrina Petrova, "Political and Legal Limitations to the Development of Public Interest Law in Post-Communist Societies," *Parker School Journal of East European Law* 3 (1996): 541–567.

2. Public Interest Law Initiative in Transitional Societies (1997), *Symposium on Public Interest Law in Eastern Europe and Russia, A Symposium Report*, p. 11. New York: Columbia University.

Appendix: People Interviewed for This Study

Karoly Bard
Research Director, Constitutional and Legislative Policy Institute, Budapest

Pavel Bilek
Deputy Director, Czech Helsinki Committee, Prague

Bebs Chorak
Deputy Director, Street Law Inc., Washington, D.C.

Jana Chrzova
Executive Director, Czech Helsinki Committee, Prague

Anna Csongor
Executive Director, Hungarian Foundation for Self-Reliance
(Autonomia), Budapest

Lilla Farkas
Legal Expert, Legal Defence Bureau for National and Ethnic
Minorities (NEKI), Budapest

Imre Furmann
Director, Legal Defence Bureau for National and Ethnic
Minorities (NEKI), Budapest

Irena Grudzinska Gross
Program Officer for Eastern Europe, The Ford Foundation, New
York

Wojciech Hermelinski
Attorney and Vice Dean, Warsaw Bar Council, Warsaw

Jan Hrubala
Centre for Environment and Public Advocacy, Ponicka Huta,
Slovakia

Ferenc Koszeg
Executive Director, Hungarian Helsinki Committee, Budapest

Richard C. Kraemer
Development Officer, Jagiellonian University Law Clinic,
Krakow, Poland

Stefan Krieger
Professor, Hofstra University Law School, Hempstead, NY

Robert Kushen
Deputy Director, Open Society Institute, New York

Ewa Letowska
Member, Polish Helsinki Committee, Warsaw

Halina Niec
Professor, Jagiellonian University Law Clinic, Krakow, Poland

Zaza Nomaradze
Deputy Director, Constitutional and Legislative Policy Institute, Budapest

Edward O'Brien
Executive Director, Street Law Inc., Washington, D.C.

Martin Palous
Chairperson, Czech Helsinki Committee, Prague

Borislav Petranov
Legal Officer, International Centre for the Legal Protection of Human Rights (INTERIGHTS), London

Dimitrina Petrova
Executive Director, European Roma Rights Center, Budapest

Margo Picken
Former Program Officer for Human Rights, The Ford Foundation, New York

Monica Platek
Executive Director, Polish Association of Legal Education, Warsaw

Danuta Przywara
Secretary of the Executive Committee, Polish Helsinki Committee, Warsaw

Edwin Rekosh
Director, Public Interest Law Initiative in Transitional Societies
(PILI), Columbia University Law School, New York

Joseph Schull
Former Deputy Director for Russia and Eastern Europe, The Ford
Foundation, New York

Gabriela Schwarz
International Program Director, Street Law Inc., Washington,
D.C.

Maria Szewczyk
Director and Professor, Jagiellonian University Law Clinic,
Krakow, Poland

Franklin A. Thomas
Former President, The Ford Foundation, New York

Gabor Attila Toth
Project Director, Hungarian Civil Liberties Union, Budapest

Veronika Ujvari
Project Manager, Hungarian Civil Liberties Union, Budapest

Eva Viszlo
Office Manager, Legal Defence Bureau for National and Ethnic
Minorities (NEKI), Budapest

Filip Wejman
Student Assistant, Jagiellonian University Law Clinic, Krakow,
Poland

Leah Wortham
Associate Professor, Catholic University Law School,
Washington, D.C.

Monika Zacny
Student Assistant, Jagiellonian University Law Clinic, Krakow,
Poland

Eleonora Zielinska
Professor, University Center of Legal Aid, University of Warsaw
Faculty of Law, Warsaw

Group Interviews

Staff of the Hungarian Helsinki Committee, Budapest

Students of the Jagiellonian University Law Clinic, Krakow, Poland

PART 2

Thematic Perspectives

8

University Legal Aid Clinics: A Growing International Presence with Manifold Benefits

AUBREY MCCUTCHEON

In many different countries, university legal aid clinics facilitate the use of law in the pursuit of broad social justice goals. In some contexts university clinics have relatively long histories, while in others they have existed only a few years. As would be expected, such clinics take different forms, and they continue to develop with the changing social and political landscape. This chapter describes how Foundation-supported legal aid clinics are being used throughout the developing world. It discusses what clinics can offer to social justice agendas, and why legal practitioners, educators, and donors might consider launching and supporting them. Finally, it gives some insights that could help such university programs get off to a good start and assist them in pursuing social justice goals over time.

A variety of definitions may apply to university legal aid (or law) clinics. The focus of this discussion is primarily on university-based or affiliated clinics that involve law students in providing actual client service, rather than those that offer students only simulations and practical exercises. Most of the clinics discussed here also include classroom and lecture components, and some award student and teaching credits. Those described explicitly serve disadvantaged sectors of their societies with the aims of improving people's lives, securing justice, and advancing civil, political, economic, social, or cultural rights. In different settings these efforts have been initiated with different components and foci. Most notably, successful clinics often begin modestly, with great simplicity, under difficult circumstances and without significant resources.

The first legal aid clinic at a U.S. university was spawned by student volunteers seeking to provide free legal advice around the end of the nineteenth century. The growth of clinical programs was motivated by their practical educational value during the decades of the 1920s and 1930s. From the 1960s onward, they grew steadily and increasingly served the needed additional function of expanding legal services for America's poor and underprivileged. The Ford Foundation was instrumental in that expanded purpose, and clinics in the United States continue to make essential contributions, now supported largely by university budgets. This chapter, however, will focus on clinics outside the United States.

It should also be mentioned that some university clinics exist to provide training and client service toward a variety of other goals. For example, the World Bank–affiliated Russian Foundation for Legal Reform has supported university clinics in commercial law and small business law, examples of which can also be found around the world. The Ford Foundation's own experience, however, is largely with clinics that pursue social justice goals which connect with broader Foundation grantmaking programs in furthering public interest law, access to justice, and human rights. This discussion reflects that experience.

A Growing Multinational Presence

One of the greatest obstacles to the creation of new clinics is the assumption that clinical legal education and clinical services are entities of only the developed world. In fact, the benefits of university legal aid clinics have been realized over time in some difficult political and economic circumstances, and in countries with diverse legal systems. In some countries, fledgling clinics were started as recently as the 1990s.

When Bangladeshi law faculty members greeted the clinic approach with initial doubt, the Foundation arranged for them to visit a pioneering clinical legal education program in Nepal. There, they saw that such a program could function effectively without major long-term foreign funding and in a society similar to Bangladesh in some important respects. The Foundation also funded Bangladeshis to visit and study a clinic in Sri Lanka and a ten-year-old clinic at the National Law School (NLS) of India University in Bangalore. At NLS they saw students contributing to a range of services, typically without academic credit. These included client counseling, mediation, litigation preparation, community legal literacy instruction, paralegal training, and empirical research toward law reform.

Clinics have survived extraordinarily difficult political and economic circumstances, even in regions where overt human rights activities are no longer possible. A clinic at Sudan's University of Khartoum was begun in 1984 and continued into 1998. While its work had been limited, it was a focal point for both staff and students interested in law and social justice. It provided supplemental lectures on law practice and offered legal services mainly for university staff and students.

University legal aid clinics have grown to be a fundamental part of the legal infrastructure in South Africa. They first appeared in the early 1970s during the height of apartheid, when law was pervasively used as an instrument of oppression and segregation. By the early 1980s, most of South Africa's twenty-one law faculties had established clinics, and by the mid-1990s, the Foundation was supporting eight of those, mostly at traditionally nonwhite universities that suffer the legacy of apartheid policies. Since 1994, the government's legal aid entity has set up twenty additional clinics based at universities but using law graduates under apprenticeships. Similarly, in a number of South American nations, clinics have provided individual legal services since the late 1960s and early 1970s. At the end of 1996, after transitions to democracy and civilian rule, eight university-based clinics in Argentina, Chile, and Peru joined to form a new network. The network, coordinated by Chile's Diego Portales University Law School, was also created to develop broader approaches to public interest law in cooperation with other NGOs.

During the 1990s, Ford-supported clinics have emerged in other transitional societies. In China, they are helping to implement legal reforms by enabling disadvantaged groups to exercise their rights. Clinics are also utilizing new administrative laws that provide a greater measure of government accountability to the public, and are taking advantage of the new degree of autonomy allowed for government-supported social organizations. Likewise, fledgling clinics have emerged at universities in the Czech Republic, Hungary, Poland, and Russia. These too are operating in difficult circumstances of changing laws and legal procedures, as well as in contexts of long-standing legal nihilism among the public and extremely theoretical and conservative approaches to legal education.

Observers are generally optimistic about the potential of these new clinics. However, despite their abilities to surmount difficult challenges so far, greater success in some cases may depend upon further political or educational reforms. Clinical programs can influence the latter, but many law schools around the world are dominated by tradition and theoretical methods of teaching. Dean M. Shah Alam of Bangladesh's University of Chittagong law faculty notes that launching and refining a legal aid clinic is a laborious process.

Professor Leah Wortham of Washington, D.C.'s Catholic University Law Clinic assisted the Jagiellonian University clinic in Poland. Her observations when reflecting on that experience hold optimism for new clinics elsewhere in the world as well. "Clinical education there can build on the successes and mistakes of thirty years or so of development in other countries," she says. "Advances in communication with phone, travel speed, and electronic communication make it much easier for lawyers, teachers, and law students to work with counterparts in other countries and draw on research sources." Communications technology can help make the experience of other programs available to new clinic participants. Within a country as large as Russia, for example, the creation of an electronic network by the St. Petersburg Institute of Law, including course materials and details of training seminars and meetings, will allow faculty in the dozen or so new clinical programs to access information and interact with each other.

Clinics' Manifold Benefits

Practical legal education for students and free legal services for disadvantaged people are the most common, and among the most important, benefits of university legal aid clinics. But they are not the only ones. Clinics are used to pursue a range of potential social justice benefits in developing countries. While outcomes differ by clinic, country, and context, the examples below illustrate five of the most compelling potential benefits of clinics, including improving legal education, supplementing other indigent legal services, generating broader social impact, encouraging future work in public interest law, and enhancing access to the profession.

Improving Legal Education

The most commonly known educational benefits of clinics are the practical "lawyering" skills students gain through working directly with clients on specific problems. In addition, the experience can help students to better understand and apply legal theory, as well as to explore weaknesses in legal systems or procedures.

In clinics around the world, students gain experience interviewing clients, gathering facts, drafting pleadings and wills, negotiating contracts, examining witnesses in court, presenting oral arguments, and planning case strategy. In some legal systems, would-be lawyers are exposed to such practical matters during a postgraduate apprenticeship before being certified for law practice. Such apprenticeships differ in length and in quality, and the emphasis varies widely depending upon the supervising lawyer. Clinics help students connect the specific subjects taught in the law school curriculum to actual experience, which in many instances also involves public interest law and work with the disadvantaged. One South American practitioner notes that teachers' involvement in clinics can also positively impact their teaching abilities in the classroom. V. Nagaraj, director of the clinic at NLS, notes that the educational benefits of clinics are now so widely accepted in India that the Bar Council, which officially accredits law schools, has recently made clinical education a mandatory prerequisite for accreditation. This will expand the educational benefits of clinics to a greater number of Indian students and is a strategy worth consideration in other countries.

Some Chinese students have stressed that exposure to practical skills has helped them to comprehend the concepts presented in law lectures on both substantive and procedural law. These students were referring to their experience at Wuhan University's Centre for the Protection of the Rights of the Socially Vulnerable, founded in 1992. It now accepts ten law students each year and provides experience in cases involving senior citizens, women, youth, and the disabled, as well as administrative lawsuits against government agencies and officials.

In Eastern Europe, clinics allow both teachers and students to see how the law really works—and does not work, says Wortham. She stresses that supplementing law lectures with practical education is extremely important in a region where legal education, and the law itself, has been largely theoretical. To encourage greater appreciation for the many possibilities of clinical legal education, a seminar was convened in Hungary in 1998 for twenty-five law school deans from throughout Central and Eastern Europe. The seminar was organized by the Budapest-based Constitutional and Legal Policy Institute, an affiliate of the Open Society Institute, which supports the development of clinics throughout that region.

Typically, universities open clinics to offer training to their own students, but this is not the only successful approach. Tver State University outside Moscow is developing a clinical program with input from Professor M. Rahman of the University of Dhaka, the former head of a Ford-supported legal aid clinic there. Tver State started a summer school open to fifty law students from across Russia. The summer school, which reaches law students who already work as volunteers for human rights centers throughout the country, uses a hypothetical human rights case as a teaching tool and introduces students to interactive teaching methods. Students have responded positively by introducing the topics and teaching methods to fellow students and faculty in their home universities.

Supplementing Legal Services

In addition to their educational benefits, university clinics can serve as both supplements and complements to other indigent legal services. Clinics in India and South Africa, to name only two countries, work in contexts where the combined forces of government legal aid, NGOs, and community-based paralegals still cannot meet the legal service needs of their societies. Clinics there use a financial means test to screen potential clients and provide free legal services, typically in targeted communities. Even though the unmet need in both countries is still far beyond the collective capacity of their university clinics, they nevertheless help to service particularly egregious cases and oppressed communities, often outside of city centers.

In India, clinical legal services are recognized as so potentially important that the judiciary now actively encourages their development, according to NLS's Nagaraj. The NLS clinic now operates from three venues, one attached to the court complex in Bangalore, one on campus, and a third in an outlying rural area. The official legal aid entity of the government also recognizes the value of clinics as service providers. While students and full-time teachers are not allowed to make court appearances in India, they work with clients and prepare cases that are then passed on as needed to private lawyers who are compensated by the government as members of its legal service panel. In addition to these direct client services, the NLS clinic trains NGO and community-based paralegals who then serve additional people and communities.

In South Africa, where there is no adequate state legal services program, such clinics are often the only options available to the poor. South Africa's university clinics now generally concentrate on "poverty law" but they also aided the struggle against apartheid by working on cases of police brutality, freedom of movement, freedom of residence, detention without trial, racial and ethnic discrimination, and other breaches of fundamental human rights. In some parts of the country, says Lebo Malepe, clinics are the only sources of formal assistance, particularly in the civil sphere. Malepe works with the Tshwaranang Legal Advocacy Centre to End Violence Against Women, the first specialist legal group in that regard. In other instances, South African clinics are providing backup legal services to a larger independent network of community-based paralegals, while referring more specialized cases to experienced public interest law NGOs, thereby complementing and magnifying the work of those groups.

When university clinics are the primary legal service providers, or where community legal needs are high, special care can be taken to manage tension between the two goals of providing adequate legal services and providing appropriate, structured clinical education. This point was emphasized by the late Professor M. Shanara Gilbert of the City University of New York Law School when she studied and advised seven South African university clinics as a consultant to the Foundation in 1993. This tension can arise from the pressure on instructors to supervise and teach students, as well as to manage a demanding caseload. It is increased by the students' need for diverse exposure to lawyering skills that may not always correspond to the clinic's pending cases. The inconsistency brought to a client's case due to student turnover makes this tension even more acute. Careful management is required, but there is no easy solution to this problem. Some schools have called upon assistance from adjunct instructors and private practitioners. In Eastern Europe, new clinics have begun to use returning clinic students as intermediate supervisors.

University clinics can also complement the work of existing human rights organizations. In Russia, for example, law faculties at universities in Tver, Kursk, and Krasnoyarsk teach and supervise students while the human rights organizations employ the students, either on a volunteer basis or for a small stipend. Although tensions can also arise between faculty and human rights organizations, which may have different primary objectives, donors can assist by encouraging fruitful cooperation in joint projects.

Generating Broader Social Impact

Some university clinics successfully expand the impact of their work by concentrating services on specific legal issues or population groups. Other clinics seek broad impact through class action suits, where possible. These strategies can complement, inspire, or enable the work of other organizations that focus on the status of women, the environment, the rights of HIV/AIDS patients, refugees, asylum seekers, or others. Wide jurisprudential impacts and public education can also flow from the work of clinics. Even cases that are lost can help influence the media and public opinion and increase understanding of human rights and the legal system. Clinics can enhance this by cooperating with other

social justice and nonlawyer NGOs. Likewise, the cases strategically selected and litigated by clinics can serve to better inform
judges about human rights standards and the magnitude of their
role in public interest law matters. In other instances, clinics can
reveal practical problems in a country's legal system, inspire policy review and reform over time, help improve the broader policymaking and lawmaking processes, and encourage greater citizen
participation.

The Palermo University law clinic in Argentina represents a
good example of such an approach. It pursues jurisprudential and
public education impacts through careful case selection and by
cooperating with the Argentine NGO Citizen Power, which conducts programs in civic education and citizen participation. The
synergy of the two groups has been productive. This strategy has
also been successfully used by others in the network of clinics
coordinated by Chile's Diego Portales University Law School.
This success has been in spite of obstacles such as judicial delays,
occasional judicial incompetence, and even corruption.
Cooperation with nonlawyer NGOs provides clinics with information about social issues and special population groups, which
helps them select the most representative and viable cases. NGOs
can encourage use of clinical services by educating their constituencies. For example, Citizen Power worked with other environmental and women's rights activists to prepare publications
and to teach about the various legal instruments available. NGOs
can also carry the impact of clinic cases further by disseminating
results to the broader public.

The clinic network in Argentina, Chile, and Peru has found
that even when litigation is ultimately lost, their cases do progress
through the courts. In the process, ensuing press coverage and
public education efforts can have important effects on public
opinion, judicial attitudes, and appreciation of human rights and
the roles and protections of law. This benefit is also found in the
work of university clinics in China. An example is the Beijing-
based Centre for Women's Law Studies and Legal Services
of Peking University (Peking University Women's Centre).
Observers and staff note that its cases cause both women and the
media to pay closer attention to the effects of law and the legal
system on women and inspire more women to utilize the system
by coming forward with legal grievances.

A greater challenge in clinical work is often the education of the judiciary itself. Some judges are sensitized to public interest issues by the arguments presented in particular clinical cases. Yet a report by the Diego Portales University clinic on public interest litigation explains that "making the judges familiar with the language of public interest law and persuading them of their key role in this matter seems to be the toughest challenge to confront." Some interviewed argue that increasing litigation on public interest matters, and systematizing it to affect judicial education, will help judges realize the magnitude of their role. Through permanent staff lawyers, assisted by students and educational objectives, clinics are often well placed to conduct the public interest litigation that pursues these broader social goals with the public and the judiciary. Nevertheless, cases should be carefully selected, researched, and developed in the interest of the client and for other public impacts. This is especially important because litigation of this type is often opposed by powerful and well-resourced interests that can easily afford the best and most extensive legal assistance.

The Peking University Women's Centre has developed the authority to challenge legal, practical, and policy obstacles to women's equality. This is true even though many of its cases have been unsuccessful. Its cases and publicity efforts may be helping to focus the attention of policymakers and officials on the ways in which law and the courts inadequately address, and even perpetuate, the problems facing women in China—conditions such as exploitation in employment, discrimination, and domestic violence.

The benefits of the Peking University Women's Centre differ in nature from the impacts sought by the Palermo University clinic. Some cases filed by the center test the routine application of women's rights laws. For example, one case was filed against a Beijing employer who refused to pay wages to a group of women for over two years. Other cases test the willingness and ability of Chinese courts to enforce judgments. In still other cases, the center draws attention to the way local corruption can exacerbate violations of women's rights. In addition to providing women with individual legal services, the center's work has led to increased government scrutiny of obstacles to women's rights.

In an unusual demonstration of a clinic's policy impact, the University of Natal-Durban's clinic in South Africa helped research and formulate new policies on community participation in development planning. The clinic's client was a provincial government, but it also played an important role in helping communities and citizens to access and understand the policymaking process and the opportunities for influencing it. Students and staff researched relevant national laws and policies, consulted local and regional authorities throughout the province, and interviewed community organizations. They also debated participatory mechanisms, recommended new administrative rules and procedures, drafted model legislation, and prepared policy recommendations that are currently being implemented.

Encouraging Public Interest Law

Another frequent motivation for creating university legal aid clinics is to introduce students to the possibilities of using the law for social justice purposes and to encourage and inspire such future work as lawyers. This creates a pipeline of young lawyers for public interest law and legal aid work. Again, the nature and degree of this benefit depends upon country and context. Students can be fully alerted to career options in these fields, where they exist, or compelled by the legal needs of their communities to think creatively about ways to serve the public interest while in private practice. Experts from all of the countries covered in this chapter conclude that this is a very real benefit of university clinics.

Professor Eleonora Zielinska, the first director of the University of Warsaw clinic, which opened in 1997, states, "Contact between law students and NGOs is important to creating future public interest lawyers. Hopefully public interest law firms will evolve from law clinic graduates." Zelinska has already observed a pattern of Polish law students volunteering extra time for the NGOs they encounter during their clinic assignments. Zielinska believes that this desire for public service is a direct result of a new consciousness brought about through the law clinic.

Nagaraj of India's NLS agrees. "In some students we see a total transformation of the personality," he says, "while in others we notice a sensitization and a desire to balance earnings with service." He also notes a relatively higher commitment to pro bono work in private practice by students who are graduates of the clinic. Peking University Women's Centre graduate intern Yang Xinxin feels that her experience at the center has had similar influences on her development. She writes, "China's legal education system might realize benefits by integrating a legal aid program into its law schools and using it as the basis for training future legal professionals with a strong sensitivity to public interests."

In the Philippines, graduates from several law schools have followed the pipeline into public interest law and legal services to the poor. University legal aid organizations there provide community legal services in a variety of forms and recruit students to work with legal services NGOs popularly known as "alternative law groups." Many of the lawyers now working for these NGOs had their first exposure to alternative law groups through their university legal aid organizations.

Obviously, many university legal aid clinic students will not go into public interest practice. But the clinic experience can still affect students' perspectives on their future roles as private legal professionals. In India, Nagaraj observes that clinics expose students to social justice needs at a formative stage in their careers. "While studying, the students are exposed to the real dynamics of law and legal disputes, bringing them closer to society, to down-to-earth realities, and teaching them not just through case reports. This ultimately improves the legal profession," he says. One clinic advisor in Bangladesh points out that a clinic can help put students in touch with some of that country's less obvious problems, because many law students are personally removed from those realities. In addition, as the professional influence of today's students increases over the years, they could become powerful voices for reform.

Enhancing Access to the Profession

In many countries an apprenticeship is required before a law graduate is certified for admission to the legal profession and law practice. Apprenticeships with experienced practicing lawyers are highly sought after and are often fewer than the number of law graduates. Consequently significant numbers of graduates are unable to enter the profession or, even worse, find themselves unemployed. Hiring for apprenticeships in some countries is also subject to a great deal of unjust patronage, social privilege, and other forms of discrimination. This problem has been experienced in Poland, South Africa, and elsewhere. It has blocked access to the profession for disadvantaged population groups such as women, ethnic and racial groups, candidates from poor backgrounds, and others. It robs the profession of a potentially enriching diversity.

By offering such apprenticeships, where allowed, under the supervision of a clinic's qualified legal staff, a clinic can serve to both improve access to and diversify the legal profession. Since 1993, clinics run by law faculties in South Africa have been permitted to offer apprenticeships for admission to law practice. By 1999, a combined total of approximately 250 additional lawyers were being admitted to practice each year through apprenticeships offered by law faculty and government-run clinics based at universities. The total number of available apprenticeship positions has been increased and new doors to the profession have been opened for women and nonwhite law graduates, thereby strengthening it through diversity. Clinics gain approval to host apprentices, just as any law firm would, if they meet certain criteria such as adequate supervision by qualified lawyers. The number of apprenticeships any clinic may offer depends upon the number of lawyers on staff. Apprenticeships also provide one additional opportunity to transmit skills, strategies, and values of public interest law. Beyond the benefits for the profession and the apprentice, the clinic can increase its legal work and gains assistant supervisors for its students.

Conclusion

As these examples suggest, university legal aid clinics are now part of the educational and legal landscape in most regions of the world. They have already made contributions to social justice and public service in the developing world, and there are compelling potential benefits that recommend their consideration in strategies for legal education and public interest law. There is, unfortunately, no general recipe for ensuring the success of a university legal aid clinic. However, there is a wealth of literature covering pedagogical and legal services approaches as well as management strategies for clinics.[1]

This closing section, therefore, will not address those topics nor summarize this chapter. Rather, its purpose is only to highlight a few brief suggestions for the consideration of those involved with clinics—suggestions derived from the successes, shortcomings, and observations of Foundation grantee partners in specific contexts.

- Try to observe the teaching and operations of other successful clinics. Such observations aided the development of university clinics in Bangladesh, South America, Eastern Europe, and elsewhere. Observe clinics that operate within similar legal, socioeconomic, and educational environments when possible, but don't ignore others that might nevertheless display innovative or instructive approaches. Also, the most prestigious clinics are not always the most instructive examples. Singling them out as models might unintentionally discourage fledgling efforts.

- Universities can aid success by recruiting clinic leadership from within the law faculty, wherever possible, by making clinic instructors equal partners with other law professors, and by developing successor leadership. This approach to staffing can help avoid common problems by integrating new clinics with university law faculties, thus facilitating access to the resources and talents of the university. Offering tenure track positions and teaching credits, and placing clinic instructors within the normal salary structure of the law faculty, also increases sustainability. Beginning early to develop a second tier of leadership can help alleviate the difficulties clinics have faced when founders or senior staff departed. Both university and Foundation staff cited the failure to do this as a deeply felt shortcoming in societies, such as South Africa, where social and democratic transitions caused the loss of key clinic leadership to new opportunities in government, private law practice, and the judiciary.

- Consider organizing community-based client consultations from satellite facilities (or outdoors) on a regular basis. This approach serves to increase community access. If possible, consider securing permanent offices within or near the law faculty for the best interaction with resources and colleagues there. Also foster a community presence to facilitate client access and other goals—such as exposure for students and a better understanding of the contexts of legal problems.

- Consider cooperating with community-based organizations and NGOs. Based on his experience in working in the Czech Republic, Professor Stefan Krieger of New York's Hofstra Law School clinic says that "people who experience the patterns of abuse and disadvantage that the clinic is meant to address" can also be essential to guiding a clinic toward social justice goals.

- National and regional associations of university clinics can be a boost for individual operation. It is inspirational, according to Zielinska of the University of Warsaw, for fledgling clinics to see themselves as part of a regional movement. Common problems then seem less insurmountable; common research can be undertaken and solutions fashioned. The network in Eastern Europe has generated regionwide momentum to achieve regulations allowing supervised student practice and appearance in court. Both seasoned and newer clinics in South Africa have benefited from the activities of their national association, such as training, fundraising, policy advocacy, information exchange, and more.

- Student practice rules that allow clinic students to make court appearances can bring important benefits—but don't let their absence be an obstacle to the creation of university clinics. In several countries, university legal aid clinics have operated for years without the benefit of such rules. Examples include India, where clinics are encouraged by the judiciary and will soon be mandatory for law school accreditation, and South Africa, where clinics emerged in the early 1970s and have evolved to offer general and specialized services.

• Consider pursuing regulations and permission to train legal apprentices who seek admission to the profession. Also strive to design the classroom component so that discussions of issues of diversity, discrimination, and human rights are integral components. Offering apprenticeships can help diversify the profession when such positions with other practitioners are subject to patronage or discrimination. Apprentices can also provide additional human resources for a clinic's other service objectives. Forthright education about a society's conditions, including topics such as discrimination, diversity and human rights, can also aid a clinic toward its broader social justice goals.

Note

1. See "Bibliographic Materials on Clinical Legal Education and Access to Justice," compiled by the Public Interest Law Initiative in Transitional Societies, New York: Columbia University Law School; "Guidelines for Clinical Legal Education," Report of the Association of American Law Schools–American Bar Association (AALS-ABA) Committee on Guidelines for Clinical Legal Education (1982); and Robert N. Dinerstein, "Report of the Committee on the Future of the In-House Clinic," *Journal of Legal Education* 42, no. 508 (1992): 561–574.

9

Public Interest Litigation: An International Perspective

HELEN HERSHKOFF & AUBREY MCCUTCHEON

This chapter provides an international perspective on public interest litigation by looking at the work of a sampling of Ford Foundation grantees that use public interest litigation in a number of ways to improve conditions for disadvantaged groups, such as the poor, women, and religious and ethnic minorities. Litigation can help to reform existing laws that hinder or prevent members of these groups from participating fully and fairly in society. It can enforce rights that existing laws guarantee, but are not followed in practice. Litigation can complement a broader political movement, or foster mobilization and encourage alliances that then produce political action. Furthermore, litigation can help change attitudes toward the law and create a culture in which government and private entities respect and enforce human rights values.

The Foundation first supported groups undertaking public interest litigation in the United States during the 1960s. In the following decades, the Foundation increased the range of its geographic commitment, and grantees now undertake litigation in many countries in Latin America, Asia, Africa, the Middle East, and Eastern Europe. These nongovernmental organizations address a broad range of social concerns—from job discrimination in China, to wrongful imprisonment in Peru, to violence against women in Poland. They use a variety of creative strategies and often work against great odds, nevertheless winning significant courtroom victories that seek to enforce human rights, to change entrenched practices and laws, and to encourage political consensus for social improvement.

An earlier chapter of this volume focuses on public interest litigation in the United States. This chapter turns attention to the equally important work of the Foundation's grantees in other parts of the world. The first part of the chapter provides an overview of public interest litigation, examining its goals, approaches, and structural adaptations in a global context. The second part highlights the specific litigation efforts of Ford grantees in Nigeria, India, and parts of the Middle East, Latin America, and Eastern Europe.

Public Interest Litigation: Goals, Approaches, and Adaptations

Over the last twenty years, the Foundation has supported groups conducting public interest litigation in a wide variety of political and social areas around the world. Organizations sometimes refer to their work as "social action litigation" or "social cause lawyering." By whatever name, these groups are seeking to use the courts to help produce systemic policy change in society on behalf of individuals who are members of groups that are underrepresented or disadvantaged—women, the poor, and ethnic and religious minorities.

Grantees litigate for multiple and reinforcing reasons and they select cases and clients with reform interests in mind. Their work builds on a model of group representation, where a single lawsuit can vindicate the rights of many individuals. They also make strategic use of individual cases that enable public interest lawyers to identify broader patterns of inequity; by representing a single client, grantees can enforce legal entitlements, declare new rights, change bureaucratic attitudes, and promote alliances in support of shared goals.

In using litigation as a vehicle for social change, public interest law NGOs face a uniquely complex set of incentives and challenges. Indeed, because domestic conditions vary considerably from country to country, one cannot generalize about litigation as a global strategy. In countries where the laws are themselves unjust, litigation can document the legal system's failures and inequities. Where legal procedures hinder or oppose legal rights, lawsuits can confront and eliminate those barriers. In transitional societies shifting from authoritarian rule to democratic governance, litigation can help new constitutional principles to take root, as well as increase public awareness of human rights and embolden those with legal claims to come forward. In communities where judges lack broad knowledge of legal alternatives, lawsuits can serve an educational function, teaching the courts and the public about basic rights and legal possibilities. Where national laws are repressive or insufficient, litigation based on international law can provide normative guidelines for domestic courts. Lawsuits do not always succeed in court, but they help to focus public attention and to shape public opinion in favor of reform.

Law affects society in many complicated ways; social and economic practices likewise affect legal possibilities. In the global transition toward human rights and rule-of-law values, litigation can be instrumental in achieving shared goals. Despite broad variations across countries in terms of legal, cultural, political, social, and economic conditions, one can nevertheless point to several key variables that seem to shape litigation and are in turn altered as litigation goes forward. These variables include the system of government and scope of existing laws, the independence of the judiciary and the operation of the court system, and public attitudes toward law.

Obviously, the nature of a country's governance structure—whether a military dictatorship, totalitarian, democratic, or a system in transition—shapes the role that courts can play in social reform and the kinds of problems that grantees can meaningfully address through litigation. South Africa, for example, where the Foundation has supported legal reform efforts since the 1970s, had a viable judicial system during the period of apartheid, but its judges were constrained by laws that were themselves unjust. Civil rights lawyers nevertheless successfully challenged discriminatory "pass" laws (as described in the South Africa case study). The Legal Resources Centre handled hundreds of individual cases to compel implementation of Supreme Court rulings that limited the reach of those laws.

The independence and operation of the court system also

affect the anticipated consequences of public interest litigation, creating opportunities as well as obstacles to reform. A number of factors seem to be important: whether a judicial system is insulated from political domination; whether the judge has formal power to review the legality of legislative action or to enforce judgments against the government and private entities; and whether the judiciary possesses professional capital in terms of resources, prestige, education, and credibility. In some countries, judges are not legally trained; elsewhere they may be corrupt, ideologically hostile, or politically subservient. In certain legal systems rulings in individual cases may build a body of legal precedent that can help other victims of injustice. In addition, court rules and procedures vary widely from country to country, affecting nearly every stage of the litigation process—from who is allowed to bring a lawsuit, to the kinds of evidence that the court will hear, to the types of questions that judges are authorized to decide. India's Supreme Court, for example, has exercised strong judicial leadership in establishing "epistolary" jurisdiction, allowing any person to write to the court to seek judicial help in resolving social problems. This procedure has generated a tremendous demand for legal services on behalf of disadvantaged groups.

Public attitudes toward the law also create challenges for public interest litigators. After living through years in which the courts were corrupt, inefficient, or complicit in oppressive practices, citizens may not trust the legal system and may be reluctant to assert claims for relief. Moreover, disadvantaged people may not regard their problems—often involving social and economic conditions—as ones that law can redress. Even where they perceive their injury in legal terms, they may fear that going to court is not safe and that they will be targeted for retribution. Ford grantees have used many different approaches in encouraging new forms of social trust.

Perhaps the most salient feature of public interest litigation worldwide is its synergistic relation with a wide range of other activities—many of which are described in other chapters in this volume—that grantees undertake to promote broader social, political, and economic change. As in the United States, the groups profiled in this chapter regard their work as part of a larger reform effort that may include community organizing, public education, research, media publicity, and other nonadversarial legal strategies. Public interest litigation thus depends on the work of a great many people, legal and lay, with a wide range of interests, expertise, and experience.

Public Interest Litigation: Selected Highlights of Grantee Work

From Nigeria to India, public interest lawyers have used litigation for various purposes: they have documented injustice and exposed the inequities of repressive regimes; they have repeatedly gone to court to help implement constitutional principles and laws, as well as to further legal reform through creative forms of lawyering; and they have struggled to integrate favorable international norms into their domestic legal systems and pursued vindication of rights in international tribunals. This section highlights several of these important efforts, focusing on cases involving law reform.

Exposing Repressive Regimes

NGOs often use litigation as a way to document and thus expose institutionalized injustices, even where the lawsuit as a formal matter is unlikely to succeed in court. By creating a record of official practices, grantees try to use well-targeted litigation to document official abuse or private violence; to crack the veneer of legality that some repressive government practices claim; and to lay the foundation for future action. In Chile, for example, the Vicariate of Solidarity repeatedly filed lawsuits during the years of military rule to seek the release of prisoners (called "habeas corpus" actions). They thus created a powerful record of abuses that over time acquired political importance. Although the Vicariate could count few courtroom victories, its massive documentation later played an important role in proving the extent of the government's rights violations. After changes in the political regime, the Vicariate's work in documenting prior repression contributed to the work of the National Commission on Truth and Reconciliation.

In Nigeria, groups have similarly used litigation to document and expose official injustices. In 1999, Nigeria held democratic elections that reinstated civilian rule after more than fifteen years. Since shortly after its independence in 1960, a series of military regimes had run the country without regard for constitutional requirements, sometimes with grave consequences for human rights. The government suspended a 1979 constitution, and never implemented a 1989 constitution. In addition, military authorities often used decrees to usurp judicial authority and to suspend human rights. (A 1994 study identified at least forty-one decrees that were in force that stripped the courts of power to decide disputes involving land use, newspaper publication, treason, civil disturbances, and trade matters.) Even when the courts issued rulings to stop repressive practices, the military regimes frequently did not obey them.

The Constitutional Rights Project (CRP) was established in 1990 with the aim of using research and litigation to promote basic rights and to strengthen the judiciary. The Foundation began supporting CRP the following year. Although Ford and CRP staff may not have expected the group's courtroom actions to produce significant legal victories under very difficult circumstances, they nevertheless believed that CRP's work could help build public awareness of rights abuses and sustain the momentum of those working for democracy. CRP and other law groups brought case after case charging the government with a wide range of abuses of power. In some cases, they were able to win release of prisoners illegally detained; in others, they were able to win limited victories for free speech. Much of their litigation, however, was hamstrung by interminable delays, judicial apathy, and corruption, and in many instances the courts threw out cases or otherwise denied relief. Even when the court ruled in favor of CRP's clients, the military authorities ignored the rulings.

CRP nevertheless succeeded in focusing a public spotlight on the injustices of the military regime. Newspapers that did not dare report a public demonstration would nevertheless cover a court case and give the reform effort much-needed publicity. For complicated reasons, litigation became a somewhat safe way to challenge government practices. Those undertaking direct human rights campaigns, by contrast, often faced jail, torture, and even death for their efforts. Despite "losing" many cases in court, CRP's litigation served as a vital tool for educating the public at home and for exposing official crimes to an international audience.

Implementing Laws

Public interest lawyers try to use court cases to win equal enforcement of existing laws and to enforce wide-ranging victories on behalf of large classes of people. Many courtroom victories, however, are accomplished piecemeal, with incremental successes matched by repeated failures over the course of many years. This building block approach depends on steady and persistent efforts to hold government and private interests accountable for complying with the law. Lawyers thus file many lawsuits to enforce laws that are on the books, but which, for various reasons, remain unenforced.

In Argentina, for example, groups mounted similar efforts to enforce rights that existed on the books on behalf of the physically disabled. In 1997, two NGOs—the Argentine Association of Civil Rights and Citizen Power—petitioned the courts to implement a law that requires buildings to be accessible to the disabled. One case was brought on behalf of an attorney with physical disabilities who could not enter the courthouse. Although the lawsuit produced results—the decision required all court buildings in Buenos Aires to have ramps and be accessible to wheelchair-bound individuals—the lawsuit did not require enforcement of the law elsewhere in the country.

Grantees also try to address the problems of unequal enforcement of the laws. Governments in some countries respect the legal rights of some groups, but deny those same rights to others. For example, Palestinian residents of the Occupied Territories face serious environmental health hazards from industries that have moved there to avoid Israel's enforcement of environmental codes. In 1992, LAW—the Palestinian Society for the Protection of Human Rights and the Environment—filed a lawsuit on behalf of residents of Tulkarem in the Occupied Territories to close a chemical factory that manufactured insecticides. The factory had relocated to the Occupied Territories after the residents of an

Israeli town won a court order closing it down for environmental violations. The order specifically barred the factory from operating in agricultural or residential areas, but the factory nevertheless ran unimpeded for several years in Tulkarem. LAW filed its case in military court, the presiding court in the Occupied Territories. LAW argued that the factory was operating in violation of Israeli environmental laws, producing evidence showing that factory outputs were damaging water, croplands, and the health of residents.

The military court granted LAW a partial victory. It allowed the factory to continue operating in Tulkarem, but it ordered the company to stop production of the more toxic chemicals and required the factory to protect workers with masks. The case also provided the impetus for a cohesive community education effort—including workshops, lectures, films, and publications—that continued to raise public awareness of environmental issues in the area. Finally, publicity about the lawsuit helped pressure government agencies to provide more evenhanded enforcement of environmental regulations in the Occupied Territories.

Encouraging Legal Change

Grantees also use litigation to try to reform laws and to secure official recognition of human rights. Some of these efforts aim at expanding the fabric of legal protection to include groups and interests that society has historically ignored or mistreated.

In India, for example, *dalits* (those formerly known by the derogatory term "untouchables") continue to suffer widespread discrimination despite laws that guarantee equal rights. India's constitution guarantees all persons a right to life. In addition, the Scheduled Castes and Scheduled Tribes (Prevention of Atrocities) Act aims at erasing the caste system and its discriminatory effects, providing for stringent penalties against those who practice "untouchability." Enforcement of and compliance with this law, however, remains uneven and inconsistent.

The Centre for Social Justice (CSJ) has worked to broaden and interpret these existing laws to remedy specific injustices against the dalits. For example, the village of Borsad received a water pipeline from the government, but residents tampered with the line and cut off water to dalits who lived in the village. CSJ, in partnership with the Navsarjan Trust, brought suit on behalf of the Borsad dalits, arguing that the state had a duty to ensure a supply of drinking water. CSJ's case was brought directly to the High Court of the State of Gujarat because it involved violation of a basic human right—the Indian Constitution's guarantee of a right to life—through the denial of drinking water. The lawsuit, one of a series of cases that CSJ has filed on behalf of dalits, also claimed violations of the Prevention of Atrocities Act. The Gujarat High Court ruled in favor of the dalits, and directed the state to repair the pipeline and to provide an interim water service while making the repairs. The litigation contributed to building a human rights foundation for future antidiscrimination efforts by public interest lawyers. The case also helped to promote development on behalf of groups being discriminated against, for it holds the state responsible for providing basic life resources and for ensuring fair delivery of necessary services.

Public interest law advocates in Israel have also filed dozens of lawsuits before the Supreme Court to strengthen and expand that country's legal protections for marginalized people. Through such litigation before the Supreme Court, the Association for Civil Rights in Israel (ACRI) has slowly helped develop human rights jurisprudence in Israel. Its landmark victories include cases involving gender equity, freedom of information, gay and lesbian rights, and freedom from discrimination.

In September 1999, ACRI and other groups won a historic victory on behalf of Palestinians when the Supreme Court outlawed use of physical force by Israeli security officers during interrogations. For years, human rights organizations had contended that Israeli security often abused Palestinians who were detained for questioning. Although public interest lawyers had brought dozens of cases, the court had avoided making a precedent-setting ruling. In May 1998, the Court agreed to address the legality of the interrogation methods, and it heard a series of petitions brought by ACRI and other public interest law groups. By now, each of the nine justices had heard many such cases in which ACRI had marshaled important facts during its years of litigation.

The Court's September ruling constituted a major legal step toward more equitable treatment of Palestinians and an affirmation of human rights principles more generally.

Using International Law

Public interest lawyers are also making innovative use of international human rights law where domestic venues or laws fall short. Grantees use two strategic approaches. They argue for the application of international laws in domestic courts and they take cases to international tribunals when domestic options have proved unsuccessful.

Grantees in Latin America, Eastern Europe, and Africa are working to implement international laws through domestic litigation. It will be years before the broad impact of such litigation is known. At present, its benefits may be best gauged not solely in terms of cases won and lost, but in its educational value, as judges learn about human rights standards and integrate international norms into domestic systems.

In Hungary, the Legal Defence Bureau for National and Ethnic Minorities (NEKI) repeatedly relies on international human rights law in domestic courts in order to cultivate an increased awareness of human rights norms. In as many cases as possible, NEKI cites international and European human rights law. It believes that this strategy, in conjunction with political changes in the country, will over time spawn a change in judicial attitudes and activity.

Similarly, several public interest law organizations in Nigeria are attempting to break new legal ground through lawsuits that seek to implement international law in domestic courts. The Shelter Rights Initiative and the Social and Economic Rights Action Center (SERAC) are two grantees focusing on poverty-related problems. They are asking domestic courts to develop enforceable remedies under the African Charter on Human and Peoples' Rights, and the United Nations International Covenant on Economic, Social and Cultural Rights. Problems of poverty are of special concern given decades of military rule, combined with mismanagement and corruption, that have left a deteriorating economic infrastructure and a nationwide housing crisis.

SERAC, founded in 1995, has filed cases in Nigerian courts on behalf of the former residents of Maroko, whose shantytown the government demolished in 1990, leaving three hundred thousand people without shelter. After protests from residents and advocates, the government promised to provide shelter at the housing colony of Ilasan. But housing at Ilasan was never completed. Eight years after the government demolished their homes, more than two hundred eighty-five thousand Maroko evictees remained without shelter, and as many as six hundred thousand people lived in Ilasan without water, electricity, roads, or a sewage system. SERAC's lawsuit charged the government with violating the Covenant on Economic, Social and Cultural Rights, which establishes rights to housing, education, food, health, and a safe environment. In one of the cases, although there was no final ruling as of this writing, SERAC had succeeded in persuading the court to hear a claim that the government, by evicting thousands of Maroko children from their homes and interrupting their studies, had violated their right to education under international human rights law.

Grantees also turn to international bodies to enforce international norms when domestic courts are unwilling to rule in favor of their claims. As lawyers repeatedly employ mechanisms for enforcing international law, domestic governments find it more difficult to avoid or ignore international decrees. Not least, actions based on international law help draw the attention of an international human rights community to ongoing abuses, and strengthen ties among regional NGOs working for human rights.

Groups working in Eastern and Central Europe, for example, have developed lawsuits that seek to enforce the European Convention on Human Rights. As more countries in postcommunist Europe have joined the Council of Europe, the Convention has become applicable in their domestic laws. As a first step, grantees try to vindicate the norms of the Convention in their national courts. When those efforts fail, lawyers and their clients take cases to the European Commission of Human Rights and the European Court of Human Rights in Strasbourg. An important example of this strategy is found in the regional work of the Budapest-based European Roma Rights Center, which successfully represented Anton Assenov, a Roma teenager who was beaten by Bulgarian police. In 1998, the European Court issued a land-mark ruling finding that the Bulgarian government violated Assenov's rights by subjecting him to torture and degrading treat-ment while he was in police custody, and also by failing to under-take an official investigation of the incident. The ruling extended the scope of international law by making the right to an investiga-tion part of the right to be free of official mistreatment.

Similarly, in Latin America, the Center for Justice and International Law (CEJIL), a regional organization founded in 1991 by a consortium of ten prominent NGOs from the Americas, has successfully used the American Convention on Human Rights and its enforcing institutions—the Inter-American Commission on Human Rights and the Inter-American Court—to redress human rights violations that have gone unenforced in domestic courts. (The commission holds hearings, facilitates negotiated set-tlements, issues recommendations, and can forward selected cases to the Inter-American Court, whose rulings are accepted as bind-ing by twenty-one of the thirty-four members of the Organization of American States.) Advocates here have had to deal with the legacy of military rule and civil wars, years in which governments carried out widespread violations of human rights with impunity. Moreover, even in the context of democratic regimes, a wide range of human rights violations exists. Some Latin American countries have since adopted broader constitutional protections for human rights, but their judicial systems remain lax or ineffec-tive in prosecuting offenders and enforcing penalties.

By 1999, CEJIL was handling more than one hundred fifty cases involving forced "disappearances," extrajudicial executions, violations of due process rights, limits on freedom of expression, and torture. Some cases have resulted in legal victories, but, not surprisingly, CEJIL often faces considerable difficulty in enforc-ing a favorable ruling from the Inter-American Commission or Court. Although domestic governments may officially acknowl-edge the Inter-American system's authority, very few have enforcement mechanisms built into their national laws. Without persistent monitoring and subsequent efforts by CEJIL and other NGOs to enforce decisions in domestic courts, most Inter-American Commission and Court decisions would probably go unheeded.

In particular, the Inter-American system has been critical to

CEJIL's efforts to improve conditions for indigenous peoples whose land and livelihoods face threats from encroaching miners, farmers, and loggers. For decades the Enxet-Lamenxay people of Paraguay, for example, suffered as their ancestral land, part of the last intact wilderness in South America, was parceled out to cattle ranchers. Despite a domestic court decree affirming their land rights, the Enxet were not even given access to the area except as laborers. CEJIL took their case to the Inter-American Commission, and in 1998 the Paraguayan government agreed to buy back more than twenty-one thousand acres from ranchers to help the Enxet move back to their lands, and to develop projects to improve their living conditions. The agreement, which calls for a return of lands to an indigenous people, sets a precedent for future cases on behalf of indigenous land rights.

Conclusion

Today's world is at an important crossroads as many societies advance from authoritarian regimes to democracies in which the values of human rights and the rule of law take root. The public interest litigation described in this chapter supports this broad movement, while seeking to assure that disadvantaged populations do not become worse off in the process of globalization and law-based reform. Public interest litigation serves as an important instrument for publicizing human rights abuses and for helping to provide protection to marginalized groups. Even if a lawsuit fails to change an unjust law, the act of going to court can influence or even change attitudes about the law and contribute to a climate for reform. Unorthodox arguments can serve to suggest innovative uses of the law; complaints can present a cumulative record that documents mistreatment. Grantees recognize that the relationship between litigation and social change is complex and incremental, and that litigation comprises only one of many important approaches for reform. As the other chapters in this volume show, building a system of justice demands sustained efforts on many fronts; the work requires a long-term perspective and a great deal of patience. In that struggle, public interest litigation is an incomplete strategy, but nevertheless an essential one.

Note

The authors gratefully acknowledge the contributions of Sara Bullard, Daria Caliguire, and Priscilla Hayner for conducting interviews and reviewing documents. The authors also thank Suhani Kamdar, a student at the New York University School of Law, for her helpful assistance.

10

Nonlawyers as Legal Resources for Their Communities

STEPHEN GOLUB

Ask most people in most countries what the key elements of their legal systems are and their answers may well feature attorneys, judges, prosecutors, police, courts, and prisons. In many low-income communities across the globe, though, nonlawyers are playing increasingly pivotal roles. They often are paralegals—persons with specialized training who provide legal assistance to disadvantaged groups, and who often are themselves members of those groups. Or they may be ordinary community residents who use the law to collectively or individually help themselves. This chapter is about several Ford Foundation grantee organizations and their community-based legal work with nonlawyers. While the Foundation also supports U.S. efforts in this area, this discussion is limited to the work of grantees in other countries. It sketches accomplishments, and highlights several insights arising from those efforts.

The paralegals discussed in this chapter include both NGO personnel and community-based volunteers. Both typically receive nonformal (i.e., non–law school) legal training from NGOs before undertaking paralegal work. Drawing on that training and on subsequent practical experience, they educate and help women, farmers, indigenous peoples, the urban poor, and other disadvantaged populations regarding legal issues. Though they may assist litigation, paralegals often strive to resolve problems without going to court—whether through administrative processes, alternative dispute resolution, or community action. Many aspects of their work involve what women's rights advocates Margaret Schuler and Sakuntala Kadirgamar-Rajasingham term "legal literacy"—"the process of acquiring critical awareness about rights and the law, the ability to assert rights, and the capacity to mobilize for change."[1]

By fortifying paralegals' knowledge of the law, grantees have enabled them to gather evidence, construct affidavits, conduct interviews, and use legal arguments to achieve their goals. In broad terms, these NGO efforts have increased disadvantaged people's access to justice by enhancing their capacity to use legal processes; strengthened implementation of laws by applying informed pressure on government bodies and private offenders; and heightened participatory development by bringing previously powerless voices into local decisionmaking processes. There are also indications that paralegal assistance helps enhance women's health, environmental protection, low-income groups' livelihoods, and law reform. On a most basic level, paralegals have raised communities' awareness of the rights due to them—a significant advance for the many societies in which legal ignorance abounds. Citizens have learned to think critically about the law and to raise concerns about inequitable aspects of many laws.

Paralegal activity, widespread legal awareness, and strategies such as community organizing can blend to help disadvantaged groups become more cohesive and active in addressing the legal problems and related issues that affect their members. In some cases, there have been shifts in the power imbalances that negatively affect such groups, enabling them to deal more effectively with abusive husbands, indifferent or repressive police, and exploitative landlords.

As paralegals enable disadvantaged populations to become more legally self-sufficient, they have also helped fill the huge legal aid voids that exist because most societies have relatively few lawyers and government programs addressing the legal needs of the poor. Their effectiveness is enhanced because they are in touch with community dynamics in ways that even the best-intentioned lawyers often cannot be. Not least, paralegals provide a cost-effective supplement to expensive legal talent. Paralegals are not complete substitutes, however, for attorneys or for broader community-wide education regarding the law. Legal services lawyers, paralegals, and community legal education generally work best where they work together. This chapter describes several styles and purposes of grassroots legal efforts: individual self-help, professional and volunteer paralegal work, community mobilization, and impacts beyond the community.

Individual Self-Help

At their most basic level, grassroots law-oriented efforts seek to enhance individuals' knowledge of the law through the dissemination of legal information. While this may not involve paralegal or community activism, it can help people help themselves in dealing with law-related problems.

In carrying out this work, grantees focus on legal issues most pertinent to their specific audiences. For example, a South African group, the University of Natal-Durban's Centre for Socio-Legal Studies, adapted the U.S.-based Street Law model, which employs role playing and other innovative devices to teach audiences about legal issues they encounter in daily life. Launched in the mid-1980s, its Street Law program helped school-age youths deal with the brutal facts of apartheid repression and resistance. Using law students to provide the training, the program touched on international human rights laws, which were certainly salient in a society whose legal system sought to legitimize racism. It also advised adolescents on everyday practical concerns, such as how to relate to police. Such advice included the fact that during demonstrations or under other circumstances, resisting or running from arrest could prove fatal, for it gave authorities the ostensible right to employ potentially lethal "justifiable force." Continuing to adapt to changing conditions, in recent years the program has focused on citizen rights and duties under the nation's new democracy and constitution. This Street Law model has in turn been adopted and adapted in many different countries today.

Building grassroots legal knowledge entails attention to the medium as well as to the message. The words of a Filipino lawyer about paralegal education apply equally acutely to broader non-formal legal education efforts: "I used to think we were doing paralegal training, but now I see that we were just delivering law lectures." For poorly educated audiences, such lectures are boring and delve into unnecessary, incomprehensible nuances. Many law-oriented NGOs and university-based programs around the world, such as Street Law, have therefore turned to games, quizzes, simulations, discussions, and other popular education methodologies.

Kenyan NGOs have demonstrated a flair for packaging legal information in understandable and usable forms. Given that many people are illiterate, some of their products take the form of radio dramas, interactive plays, and audiotapes. The Legal Resources Foundation employs all of these devices to address such issues as domestic violence and women's inheritance rights. Where it relates directly to target audiences (as opposed to working through media), it employs a "participatory principle" that emphasizes the active component in learning: "I hear, I forget; I see, I remember; I do, I know." An important element that is missing, however, from NGOs' nonformal legal education work in Kenya and elsewhere is testing and evaluation of its effectiveness. As noted in a generally positive Foundation-sponsored evaluation of the Kenyan organizations' efforts, "Little of the material appears to have been formally tested to elicit feedback about how the product is perceived by the target group."[2]

That observation suggests an important question. What are the most effective ways of disseminating legal information? Answers would vary according to contexts, target audiences, and overall strategies. Organizations such as Namibia's Legal Assistance Centre (LAC) are moving toward increasing use of radio and television, both because of the mass audiences they reach and because many in those audiences are illiterate. The interactive Kenyan approach is more targeted, and may better serve to identify community needs and potential paralegals. Appropriate testing of the various methods in specific contexts could help maximize effective use of inevitably limited donor funds and NGO energy. The many ways in which this can be done for targeted training, for example, include selectively assessing audiences' retention of information a year later (perhaps in preparation for further training if possible); comparing their legal knowledge with that of control groups that did not receive training; and undertaking qualitative inquiries into effect on attitudes and actions. Such research also would identify impacts that often go undocumented in legal information dissemination projects.

Professional Paralegals

Under many circumstances in many societies, people need more than legal awareness in order to assert their rights and get the law implemented. A report by the South African NGO Black Sash Trust sums up some of the challenges that citizens face in dealing with government agencies. It states, "Many of our clients are illiterate and intimidated by officialdom. They have little or no access to telephones. In spite of this they have usually tried many avenues to resolve their problems before coming to a Sash Advice Office."[3]

To address these problems, NGOs such as Black Sash and Namibia's LAC employ paralegals to render or arrange legal services for individuals. These paralegals sometimes are themselves members of the communities they serve. They receive special training regarding pertinent legal issues and procedures, help clients navigate judicial and bureaucratic systems, and sometimes deal with those systems on the clients' behalf. Both Black Sash and LAC base these personnel in field offices throughout their respective countries. Under apartheid, paralegals helped clients deal with race-based repression and discrimination. Today, a primary focus of their work is domestic violence. The steps and strategies they pursue depend on the individual circumstances and preferences of clients. Sometimes paralegals are able to obtain injunctions that evict and bar abusers from their houses. Alternatively, they may arrange interventions by the police and government social workers.

Other common issues addressed by these paralegals include unfair job dismissals, fathers' failure to pay maintenance for children, and government benefits for the aged, infirm, widowed, and orphaned. Black Sash helps clients access benefits withheld or delayed by corrupt or lethargic state bureaucracies. Sometimes it provides simple advice on forms, and sometimes it follows up

directly. Black Sash's Durban office, for example, has documented a forty-two-month-long saga of letters and telephone calls to
secure a government pension for an elderly client.

Where legal problems are severe, excessively complicated, or
otherwise require skills beyond those the paralegals possess,
Namibia's LAC and South Africa's Black Sash turn to attorneys
to conduct litigation and provide other legal backup. LAC has its
own large corps of lawyers, while Black Sash relies on other
NGOs such as South Africa's Legal Resources Centre. The paralegals' work does not end when they refer clients to attorneys,
however. In monetary damage suits sparked by police brutality,
for example, paralegals help gather evidence, identify witnesses,
and otherwise assist with the cases. They similarly may assist
attorneys when domestic violence victims seek the imprisonment
of abusive husbands. Here, though, there is the tragic constraint of
a wife's financial dependence on her spouse, which sometimes
precludes resorting to this option.

China's Qianxi County Rural Women's Legal Services
Centre, while a newer organization operating in a far different
context, employs paralegals in some similar ways. Paralegals dis-
pense advice, mediate disputes, staff educational outreach desks
at weekly rural markets, and occasionally refer cases to lawyers.
Out of both necessity and effectiveness, the center is operated by
the local branch of the state-sponsored All China Women's
Federation, and bases some of its paralegals at the local offices of
the Ministry of Justice. As an experimental effort with a limited
track record, the center's significance lies in its trying new and
potentially replicable approaches in a society whose legal system
is undergoing significant transition.

The paralegal experiences of Qianxi and other organizations
suggest that while nonformal legal education can raise disadvantaged populations' legal knowledge, many people need the direct
assistance paralegals can provide in order to assert their rights. To
varying degrees, these groups employ media, booklets, and other
outreach efforts to spread such awareness, but they do not consider these devices substitutes for paralegals' legal expertise.
Paralegals can serve as an important component of grassroots
efforts to help disadvantaged people secure government benefits,
participate in civic and political life, and use the justice system to

protect their rights. They can also effectively stretch the limited financial resources of legal services NGOs. But paralegals are not a complete substitute for lawyers. Lawyers are necessary to train the paralegals, to handle problems that require court work or in-depth legal expertise, and to follow up where legal implementation proves beyond the paralegals' grasp.

One could argue that paralegals unfairly condemn the poor to "second-class" legal services. But the real choice often is not between second-class help by paralegals and first-class help by lawyers, but between paralegals' assistance and no assistance at all. Even where lawyers are available, paralegals sometimes can be equally competent. In any event they are far more accessible and cost effective. With paralegals in place, lawyers can operate in a more selective manner. Finally, as illustrated later in this chapter, the community mobilization efforts by paralegals often reach beyond the typical purview and skills of most attorneys.

Volunteer Paralegals

In some countries, the level of community organization, the degree of formal education, and the nature of government operations are such that volunteer paralegals can carry out manifold functions. In some respects, their work resembles that of NGOs' professional paralegals, though it generally is less structured. But there also are distinct differences. Volunteer paralegals' work sometimes is buttressed by the fact that they belong to a community-based association. In turn, their activities strengthen the association. Finally, just as NGO paralegals are inexpensive substitutes for lawyers who cannot be everywhere handling every problem, community-based volunteers extend the reach of legal services even further into grassroots communities. For these and other reasons, NGOs such as Namibia's LAC and South Africa's Black Sash train volunteer paralegals, often using their own paralegal staffs to do so.

The partnership between a Philippine legal services NGO, Sentro ng Alternatibong Lingap Panlegal (Saligan), and a twelve-hundred-household association of coconut farmers illustrates how lawyers and volunteer paralegals can work together. Saligan, whose lawyers work on land reform and other development issues, trained several dozen of the association's members to provide basic legal information to their fellow farmers on both farm-related and other matters. Fifteen of the trainees ultimately became active in processes that enabled the association's members to achieve more secure and potentially profitable land tenure arrangements under the country's agrarian reform law.

The fifteen paralegals gathered data, interviewed farmers, prepared affidavits, processed land reform applications, and taught their communities about the law. They also countered landlord resistance in various ways. Where the landlords sought to evade the law by hiding ownership or revenue information, the paralegals tracked it down. Where the landlords brought in lawyers to fight agrarian reform at the quasi-judicial hearings of the relevant government agency, the paralegals represented the farmer applicants. And where landlords filed suit against farmers (alleging, for example, that the farmers had stolen crops) to frustrate the process, the paralegals helped Saligan attorneys prepare for trial in defense of the farmers. In the absence of the paralegals, most of the land reform applications would have withered due to bureaucratic delays or landlord resistance.

The experiences that Saligan and other Ford grantees have had with volunteer paralegals highlight several important aspects of paralegal development. First, specificity of training is important. Although knowledge of constitutional or international human rights precepts may be useful for some purposes, such as attitudinal change, the farmer paralegals make far more use of their knowledge of agrarian reform laws and regulations. Second, organization is equally crucial. The paralegals are effective partly because they belong to a cohesive community group that grants them legitimacy and countervailing political influence in dealing with landlords. The saying "knowledge is power" has some truth to it, but "organization is power" may carry even more weight.

Third, in-depth training for extended and repeated periods often is necessary. This need is frequently underestimated by lawyers. As the aforementioned review of Kenyan NGOs emphasizes, "It is ironic that it is often professionals who have received extensive education and training on a full-time basis over many years who have unrealistically high expectations of what can be achieved in a brief period of training."4 Finally, ongoing contact with lawyers, or at least with greater sources of expertise, is necessary. This is a form of "on-the-job" training. As new questions arise, the paralegals need easy contact with individuals who can answer them. In the coconut farmers' case, such individuals are Saligan attorneys and staff of another NGO that works with the farmers. The notion of "ongoing paralegal development" therefore may be more appropriate than "paralegal training."

The very elements that make for effective volunteer paralegals also raise questions about when and where their development should be a priority. Can their work be sustained if, for example, donor withdrawal of support to a legal services NGO ends the paralegals' access to lawyers and ongoing training? The issue here, though, may not be whether their work is sustainable but whether their impact is. Paralegal activity need not be a lifelong avocation if it has raised farmers' income or contributed to environmental protection. There is the strong possibility that volunteer paralegals continue to function to varying degrees even after donors and NGOs lose contact with them.

The fact that these elements may be necessary to maximize volunteer paralegals' effectiveness indicates that this strategy does not flourish under all circumstances. Not all communities or legal problems benefit from utilizing paralegals. On the other hand, they can often make a difference, even under trying conditions.

One matter about which there is apparent difference of opinion and experience among grantees concerns the degree to which formal education is useful or necessary for paralegals. On the one hand, Kenya's Legal Resources Foundation maintains that paralegals must be able to read and write. Certainly, Saligan-trained paralegals need to do so in order to carry out many of their tasks regarding land reform advocacy. Namibia's LAC too feels that these skills are very helpful. On the other hand, some Filipino NGO attorneys emphasize that often the best paralegals are not well educated, and that biases and assumptions sometimes need to be "unlearned" by individuals who start paralegal training with too much of a legal background. The experience of India's Center for Social Justice is that even illiterate individuals can prove very useful. And at least one of the most effective paralegals conducting mediation for Banchte Shekha, the Bangladeshi women's movement, has had only a few years of schooling. The question of formal education, then, at least partly hinges on the functions that given paralegals perform. Indeed, not all paralegal activities involve reading and writing, as illustrated below.

Alternative Dispute Resolution

So far, the chapter has focused on ways in which NGOs, community groups, and paralegals help citizens gain access to government services and legal processes. But there are key areas, most notably alternative dispute resolution efforts, in which NGOs are building substantial substitutes for the formal legal system. Noteworthy work in this vein can be found in Bangladesh. The Madaripur Legal Aid Association (MLAA), Ain O Salish Kendra, and other NGOs involve community residents in modified versions of the traditional dispute resolution procedure known as *shalish*. (See Chapter 4 in this volume, *From the Village to the University: Legal Activism in Bangladesh*, for a more complete description of shalish.)

MLAA serves the million-plus residents of the country's Madaripur District by recruiting community leaders to serve on mediation committees, by training them about the law, and by encouraging them to apply the law rather than their biases in mediating disputes. It also employs paid staff as mediation workers. Effectively paralegals, they respond to community residents' requests for assistance by organizing shalish sessions or by referring them to other MLAA staff for help. MLAA and other NGOs most commonly serve women who are victimized by domestic abuse, husbands' illegal demands for dowry (payments made to them by wives' families when arranged marriages are negotiated), and related problems. Farmers engaged in land disputes also turn to NGO-led mediation to try to resolve their problems, as do other low-income individuals.

A key feature of some NGO-initiated shalish is that it is complemented by the threat of litigation. Where egregious criminal conduct is alleged, NGO lawyers generally seek prosecution rather than mediation. And the possibility of a lawsuit creates incentives for a recalcitrant husband to submit to the process and abide by its results. What's more, by virtue of selecting and training the mediation committee members, the NGOs have some impact on these influential community members, who in turn influence the outcomes of disputes.

A drawback of both alternative and traditional justice systems in many societies is their tendency to be male dominated. Women may struggle harder to make their cases heard. Some NGOs nevertheless pursue mediation because courts may be prone to delays, expensive, corrupt, and confusing for clients. Moreover, courts themselves can be subject to the same gender biases. Research supported by The Asia Foundation on NGO mediation in Bangladesh suggests that women welcome such mediation. A multicountry U.S. Agency for International Development study also identifies positive effects both for women and other disadvantaged populations.[5] In some instances, combined family planning and legal services efforts are mutually reinforcing.[6] Observations of NGO-initiated shalish over time indicate that women gradually are participating more, and are having a greater say and impact in the sessions. This puts them ahead of where they otherwise would be.

The approach sketched above is not the only way in which NGOs have employed alternative dispute resolution. Years of difficult organizing, livelihood development, and consciousness raising have enabled Banchte Shekha, one of several Bangladeshi groups, to put its female members on more equal footing, and to involve them, along with paralegals, prominently in its shalish sessions. India's Centre for Social Justice eschews reliance on predominately male community leaders to settle domestic disputes, convinced that their biases outweigh their influence. It prefers to have its own staff conduct conciliation sessions, backed by the implicit threat of a lawsuit. In a somewhat similar vein, volunteer paralegals trained by the Philippines' Women's Legal Bureau (WLB) employ an array of devices to get husbands' written commitments to abstain from spousal abuse. These include the threat of taking the man to court, the registration of complaints at police stations, educating police regarding the law, persuading the police to be responsive, and enlisting male "allies" to convince husbands to change their conduct. In striving to obtain the cooperation of community leaders, WLB's approach differs from that of the Centre for Social Justice. Finally, under apartheid, the Centre for Socio-Legal Studies helped familiarize South African black communities with legal principles and practices, so they could more fairly administer informal neighborhood courts. These functioned as alternatives to the government's all-white, expensive, and inefficient judicial system.

Clearly, strategies for dealing with traditional community leaders vary according to context. To the extent that involving community leaders in alternative dispute resolution has proven effective, it has been necessary for NGOs to keep pressing for growing gender equity in the procedures, and to complement mediation with related efforts, such as litigation, in order to maximize their impact.

Community and Group Mobilization

Some groups, like Banchte Shekha in Bangladesh, employ paralegals and legal information dissemination for the more explicitly political strategy of mobilizing communities. More specifically, the law can be used by grassroots groups seeking to pressure state agents or private parties that are frustrating legal implementation.

The volunteer paralegals trained by a Chilean NGO, Corporation for Legal Training for Citizenship and Democracy (FORJA), engage in community organizing, advocacy, and democracy-building work. A particular problem that the paralegals' community associations helped identify in Melipilla, a town outside of Santiago, involved commercial concerns dredging sand from a river. This caused flooding in nearby neighborhoods. After receiving training from FORJA regarding relevant environmental and legal issues, the paralegals in turn briefed and involved community leaders in a series of actions designed to persuade local officials to address the problem. These steps included press releases, meeting with the authorities, organizing residents affected by the issue, and publishing a newsletter about it. When these steps did not prove satisfactory, the paralegals and FORJA's lawyers took the issue to court, where it was pending as of this writing.

Advocacy of this sort inevitably engenders some problems. Bar associations in Chile argue that paralegals usurp attorneys' roles in dispensing advice. However, these objections have dissipated somewhat as lawyers have become more familiar with paralegal work and realized that such work does not necessarily threaten the lawyers' incomes. Another problem is that aggressive tactics by FORJA and its allies can antagonize government officials. And residents in certain communities have met some mobilization efforts with passivity. This may be because they have not attached high priority to the problems involved or because they see little chance of achieving change. This weighs in favor of careful selection of issues, and against mobilization and advocacy for their own sake.

Of course, often it is not government but private parties that are violating others' rights. There are many situations where paralegal actions that deal directly with such parties are more efficient and effective or become necessary because there are no legal aid lawyers available to pursue matters through government channels.

These factors all figure in the approach taken by the Indian NGO Hengasara Hakkina Sangha (HHS). Otherwise known as the Karnataka Women's Legal Education Program, it mainly works through what are known as *sanghas* (collectives) to provide women with paralegal training. A sangha, typically composed of twenty to twenty-five community members, often is formed by a small local NGO in order to help it address livelihood, family planning, or credit needs. HHS conducts paralegal workshops for both selected sangha members and NGO personnel.

A fundamental feature of sangha training in India is the emphasis on attitudinal change. Given the deeply ingrained feelings of inferiority that the culture inculcates in both *dalits* (untouchables) and women, NGOs seek to broaden their perspectives. HHS does this, in part, by emphasizing gender considerations such as the value of women's reproductive and household work. The Centre for Social Justice tries to get at attitudinal change partly through use of wordless cartoon illustrations for its illiterate audiences. One sequence, for example, shows that people lived as equals before castes arose. This undermines the belief that caste divisions are natural or that they always have been a fact of life.

Armed with knowledge, organization, and more assertive attitudes, sangha members trained by HHS have banded together to
assert their rights regarding both domestic relations and submini-
mum agricultural wages. They do not claim complete success.
Their newfound knowledge and perspectives regarding dowry, for
example, have not diminished that illegal activity. But they say
they have negotiated higher farm wages for themselves in certain
communities, and have achieved a reduction in domestic violence
on a more widespread basis. The latter may be significant not just
in terms of upholding women's rights and restraining immediate
physical harm, but because of research indicating the more long-
term damage to health suffered by battered women and their children.[7]

The fact that the women are organized is crucial. A wife in
isolation who confronts a violent spouse may simply invite further beating. A group of women is more likely to effectively pressure or shame him, particularly if they threaten to get the police
involved. Similarly, a woman who seeks police help alone may be
laughed out of the station, or worse. A group is harder to dismiss,
especially if they seem to know something about the law. The
experience of the Centre for Social Justice also indicates that
sanghas, local NGOs, and local lawyers carry more weight if they
have connections with those outside the community who can
complain to higher government officials about local authorities'
failure to enforce the law.

A noteworthy aspect of the HHS training of the sanghas is
that legal issues are not the entry points. This would be too controversial and too likely to prompt opposition among men within
a community. Rather, HHS builds on the fact that sanghas already
are organized (which itself can be a sensitive process) around
family planning, livelihood, or credit needs. Once the women
come together around those issues, they can start to discuss what
may be more controversial matters.

The experience of Kenya's Legal Advice Centre dovetails
with that of HHS in some ways. Staffed by attorneys, community
organizers, and social scientists, it views law as one of many
potential vehicles for community mobilization. It first ascertains
the problems to which a given community attaches priority, which
may be landlord-tenant disputes, garbage disposal, children's

well-being, youths' sexual health, or a host of other concerns. To the extent that such problems lend themselves to legal strategies, the center pursues paralegal training, the threat or reality of litigation, and related approaches. Where community organizing, mediation by local administrative chiefs, and political mobilization seem more appropriate, the center takes those routes. And of course, it blends legal and extralegal strategies where possible. The point is that its use of law flows from an overall political strategy.

Impact Beyond the Community

To talk about community-based nonlawyers' roles outside their communities might seem like a contradiction in terms—by definition, they operate on a local level. As in many development fields, there is the challenge of whether and how even the best local initiatives can yield wider benefits. Nevertheless, there are at least two respects in which nonlawyers' legal work can contribute to impact beyond where they live or work. One is policy reform, through such devices as legislation, regulations, and Supreme Court rulings. The other is replication of community-level activities.

The contributions of paralegals and community residents to policy reform take several forms. In the Philippines, for example, many legal services NGOs known as "alternative law groups" operate on both policy and grassroots levels to address environmental, agrarian, gender, and other issues. They often work in advocacy coalitions that include leaders of national federations of community-based associations, to convert what paralegals and community residents experience on the ground into successful proposals for reforming the national government's policies. Several years ago, for example, Saligan and Tungo sa Kaunlaran ng Kanayunan at Repormang Panasakahan (Kaisahan) drew on paralegals' experience to help identify problems with and push successfully for regulatory changes in the country's land reform program. The resulting modifications effectively lowered the prices of the plots farmers buy from landlords, and increased the shares of crop proceeds for farmers who lease land. More recently, a 1998 study by the two grantees documented the land reform recommendations flowing from the work of farmer paralegals from across the country.

Namibia's LAC and South Africa's Black Sash similarly draw on community-level work to push for policy reforms. LAC's Gender Research Project has used cases identified by paralegals to inform its policy recommendations regarding such issues as divorce, maintenance, and rape. Black Sash's paralegals have worked with South Africa's Legal Resources Centre, for example, to identify trends meriting public interest litigation and to locate clients whose cases could form the core of such suits.

Finally, the NGO-initiated shalish described above is being replicated throughout much of Bangladesh. By virtue of its pioneering work with this process, the MLAA has played a particularly prominent role in this regard. It serves both as a model and as an organization that trains other Bangladeshi NGOs regarding its approach.

Conclusion

Though it is difficult to generalize from such a broad array of experiences, some consistent themes seem to emerge from the law-oriented work of paralegals and other nonlawyers. Both the methods and the messages used in training paralegals and other community residents are best pitched at their specific legal needs and aptitudes. Paralegal training works best when it is in-depth, extended, repeated, and complemented by ongoing contact with lawyers or other sources of expertise. All of these educational efforts also benefit from being integrated with other forms of legal activism, such as litigation and policy advocacy. Perhaps most fundamentally, law-related assistance programs should take account of nonlawyers and nonjudicial processes. As with Indian sanghas, this can involve building on community organizing, family planning, or livelihood projects.

Explicitly law-oriented programs do not constitute the only arena in which legal and extralegal strategies can be integrated fruitfully. Development programs that focus on related priorities, such as governance, similarly might explore how law-oriented

NGOs can make government service delivery more responsive and accountable, as they have for Filipino farmers, South African pensioners, and Namibian women. Similarly, projects that aim to benefit women's health, reduce poverty, encourage environmental protection, and promote other mainstream development concerns might integrate nonlawyers using legal approaches to achieve these ends. Such integration holds potential for productively expanding paralegal work, and for bridging the gap that some-times divides human rights advocacy from mainstream develop-ment programs.

Notes

1. Margaret Schuler and Sakuntala Kadirgamar-Rajasingham, "Introduction," in Schuler and Kadirgamar-Rajasingham, eds., *Legal Literacy: A Tool for Women's Empowerment* (New York: WIDBOOKS, 1992), p. 2.

2. Rob Watson, *Understanding Our Rights: Review of the Public Education Work of Human Rights NGOs in Kenya,* a report prepared for the Ford Foundation's Kenya office (London: November 1996), p. 17.

3. Black Sash Trust, Report for the Period 1 January to 30 June 1998, p. 2.

4. Watson, p. 17.

5. Scott Brown, Christine Cervenak, and David Fairman, *Alternative Dispute Resolution Practitioners Guide,* a report prepared by the Conflict Management Group for the U.S. Agency for International Development's Center for Democracy and Governance, as part of the center's Technical Publications Series (Washington, D.C.: March 1998).

6. Karen L. Casper and Sultana Kamal, *Evaluation Report: Community Legal Services Conducted by Family Planning NGOs,* a report prepared for The Asia Foundation's Bangladesh office (Dhaka: March 1995). Though the results should be viewed with caution, The Asia Foundation also commissioned a 1999 study that determined that most women who went through NGO-initiated shalish were satisfied with the results.

7. Lori L. Heise with Jacqueline Pitanguy and Adrienne Germain, *Violence Against Women: The Hidden Health Burden; World Bank Discussion Paper No. 255* (Washington, D.C.: The World Bank, 1994).

11

Laying the Groundwork: Uses of Law-Related Research

MICHAEL SHIFTER & PRISCILLA HAYNER

In many societies, the very notion of research on legal questions is not widely accepted. Yet, experience shows that it is important to go beyond merely learning and applying the law. Research focused on the social purposes of the law—and the institutions of the justice system that implement it—can yield positive results.

Research helps to identify problems in need of reform; it bears witness to injustices that are not yet socially recognized; it initiates and informs public discussion; it documents problems when resolutions are not yet possible; and it can lead to concrete proposals to improve conditions. Research can contribute directly to the development of proposals for change, as well as actual policy. It also can contribute indirectly to the transformation of attitudes and intellectual culture.

The value of such work is also exemplified by the growing role of research in the proceedings of international tribunals. Responding to ineffective national court systems, NGOs are increasingly seeking redress through the United Nations, inter-American, or European systems. In the evolving processes of globalization in the legal field, research will no doubt be an indispensable tool.

As shown in this chapter, research can be used for many different purposes. It draws from a variety of disciplines, reflecting diverse approaches and methodologies. These include standard legal and jurisprudential research, social science methods such as

315

opinion surveys, and investigative techniques involving fact-finding and monitoring. Despite their variation, all of the approaches share a commitment to accuracy, reflect professional standards, and are designed to enhance credibility and objectivity. While research is but one of many elements that may be used to shape public opinion and policy outcomes, the multiple efforts described in this chapter have generated fresh perspectives that have often improved policy options and enriched and broadened the public debate.

The law-related work of Ford Foundation grantees around the world encompasses many different forms of research, undertaken by many different individuals in a range of settings to address a variety of legal needs; the image of the university scholar does not capture the rich diversity of activity in this field. In no setting does research provide a stand-alone strategy. But in tandem with advocacy, litigation, and other legal and political strategies, research can be a powerful tool for social change.

This chapter describes ways in which Foundation-funded groups have used law-related research to support policy and law reform, provide the factual basis for litigation, and help grantees engage more effectively in public debate. This is not intended to be an exhaustive list of the uses of law-related research. Instead, it aims both to highlight several important roles of this type of work by using illustrative examples, and to encourage practitioners, policy advocates, and funding agencies to consider the benefits of such research.

Research to Support Policy and Law Reforms

Policy reforms do not emerge in a vacuum. Reform measures based on sound information and well-developed ideas have a better chance of succeeding. Whether reforms are pursued through constitutional, legislative, or judicial channels, they nonetheless often call for some research effort. The circumstances under which policy reform will be considered will determine the nature, timing, and scale of such research.

Among the clearest contributions of research is its potential to undergird the development of specific constitutional, legislative, or judicial reforms. In some cases, a donor might fund research when it is not in a position to support policy reform more directly (or where such opportunities are very limited), hoping to prompt debate and promote critical thinking even in a politically constrained environment. Such a long-term perspective has resulted in important contributions in a number of countries.

In apartheid South Africa, for example, university research centers served as institutional shelters that made it more difficult for the government to quash opposition. They also provided legal and intellectual aid to activists. For example, researchers at university-based institutes significantly aided the labor movement, which was for many years black South Africa's most organized and important domestic political force. In addition to their ongoing litigation efforts, a handful of centers undertook research, produced publications, and hosted conferences that brought together a wide range of people involved in industrial relations. The Centre for Applied Legal Studies (CALS) researched international standards and other countries' laws regarding such matters as unfair labor practices and industrial health and safety, and then helped integrate those standards into South African law. At a time of government backtracking, CALS legal analyses and advice to unions contributed to the 1990 repeal of antilabor legislation adopted two years earlier.

In China, policy research, formulation, and promotion on sensitive topics was well served by the model of the Institute of Law at the Chinese Academy of Social Sciences. The Academy, with its various institutes, is affiliated with the government, providing the academic researchers with consistent access to policymakers and the opportunity to continually vet and promote new ideas. This model also encouraged the researchers to focus on policy-related research instead of more academic projects.

Constitutional developments, like reforms involving specific policies, have benefited significantly from research endeavors. In 1989, five years before the democratic elections in South Africa, a prominent scholar-activist from that country, Albie Sachs, undertook research on constitutionalism with the assistance of a Ford grant to the Institute for Commonwealth Studies at the University of London. Many credit this and similar efforts with key elements to the Bill of Rights that was ultimately incorporated into the interim and permanent constitutions, adopted in 1994 and 1997 respectively. CALS and the Community Law Center and other units at the University of the Western Cape (UWC) also carried out research on constitutional issues, and provided advice to African National Congress (ANC) representatives who were negotiating constitutional, legal, and other issues shortly before the transition. (Certain of the UWC personnel, in fact, were in their private capacities members of those ANC negotiating teams.) Their inquiries ranged from community consultations to scrutiny of other countries' constitutions. This research, along with resulting publications and conferences, focused on a range of questions including local, regional, and national governance structures; models for reintegrating quasi-independent black homelands into South Africa; judicial authority; and women's and children's rights.

In Nigeria in the late 1990s, the Shelter Rights Initiative (SRI), an NGO that focuses on social and economic rights, completed studies on housing, health, and education that provided the basis for recommendations to the Nigerian government for policy change and constitutional reform. Specifically, SRI carried out a review of the Nigerian constitution and all laws and policies pertaining to housing, health, and education, and has evaluated them in terms of their compliance with international standards.

Judicial and criminal procedure reforms in Chile have also benefited from applied research. Shortly after the end of the dictatorship there in the early 1990s, the Diego Portales Law School undertook major studies on the Chilean judiciary. At that time, very little empirical knowledge had been developed on the country's judicial system, and in a political context in which it was still difficult to engage judges in a constructive dialogue on these issues. As a result of this early research into judicial reform a number of professors developed considerable expertise in this work. In the years since, Diego Portales Law School has made important contributions to the reform of the judicial system in Chile. Several professors have advised the Minister of Justice on a wide range of judicial reform issues. They have, for example, contributed to the drafting of legislation to create a public prosecutor's office, and to the reform of criminal proceedings— reforms that greatly strengthened human rights protections for the accused. Some of this direct policy work was supported by other funders, including directly by the Chilean Ministry of Justice for more recent work, but early Foundation support for basic research was important in building expertise and a pool of independent legal analysts.

Similarly, in the criminal justice field, research has helped to establish or clarify new rights for Chinese citizens. There are numerous areas in which Chinese government entities and a cross section of legal academics agree about the need and agenda for research, development, and implementation of new laws and related policies. Research undertaken by the Centre for Criminal Law and Justice based at the China University of Political Science and Law contributed to important changes in a 1996 Criminal Procedure Law that included restrictions on pretrial detention, rules on the cross-examination of witnesses, and advances toward a more adversarial system. The center has since gone on to monitor the new law's implementation, with a view toward identifying problems and designing solutions where possible. This monitoring is done through both a small criminal defense clinic, and by recruiting legislators and judges to serve on monitoring panels and tours.

When the Russian constitution and other laws came under serious review in the early 1990s, academic lawyers suddenly found themselves in demand. Legal scholars associated with the Human Rights Project Group were funded in 1992 to help formulate criminal justice laws, as well as legislation on the creation of a Parliamentary Ombudsman, freedom of movement, minority rights, and the right to privacy. The Center for the Study of Constitutionalism in Eastern Europe, through its Moscow office, built an archive and library on constitutional questions for the use of law and policy specialists, and published the first Russian academic journal focused on constitutional issues. And researchers with the International Committee for the Promotion of Legal Reform in Russia conducted an independent monitoring project on the implementation of a new procedure, jury trials, in nine regions of Russia.

In the area of administrative law reforms, the Chinese-based Administrative Law Research Group has made key contributions to such reforms that help ensure government accountability. In

1989, its work contributed to a milestone in China's legal development with the passage of a law that strengthened the power of courts to overturn administrative agency acts and established significant, though limited, rights of citizens to sue government agencies and officials. The Group's subsequent research and drafting work laid the basis for a 1994 law that clarified citizens' rights to receive compensation for improper government action, as well as the procedures for compensation claims.

In the United States, research has played a crucial role in immigration law and policy by raising questions about the practice of expedited removal—one of the most fundamental developments of that field in recent decades. Before the enactment of the expedited removal policy in 1996, every person seeking to enter the United States who was denied admission had the chance to demonstrate his or her admissibility in a formal administrative hearing. Under expedited removal, whenever an inspecting officer suspects a lack of proper documents, she or he can make a final determination of inadmissibility based on an informal interview. In 1997, the International Human Rights and Migration Project of the Markkula Center for Applied Ethics at Santa Clara University initiated a four-year study of the policy's implementation. The initial findings suggested that expedited removal procedures may vary depending on the port of entry or nationality of the individual; and that the process disproportionately penalizes women, the poor, and those who do not speak English. The study as of this writing served as the only independent source of uniform and substantial information on the effects of expedited removal. By raising important questions about the practice, the research helped keep the issue "alive" for policymakers.

Research to Provide a
Factual Basis for Litigation

Using a variety of methods, a myriad of groups document injustice and collect information that is eventually used for litigation. But experience has shown that public interest litigation can often be more effective when a legal case is buttressed by structured, objective research and high-quality analysis. In some instances, patterns of wrongdoing need to be convincingly demonstrated. In others, research has to document and substantiate the consequences of particular policies and practices to bolster a party's case in court. Devoid of a grounding in research, litigation is that much weaker and more difficult to pursue.

A U.S. experience underscores the importance of linking public interest litigation with policy research. In the late 1980s, the American Civil Liberties Union (ACLU) initiated an ambitious, multistate campaign to reform public education through the enforcement of state constitutional rights. The ACLU reached out to experts in school finance and related areas to build an empirical base showing that many public education systems were inadequate judged by even the most basic standards. In addition to direct testimony from parents, schoolchildren, teachers, and school staff, the ACLU gathered testimony from nationally recognized experts on school finance, educational psychology, and curriculum development in order to make its case. Focused research showed the disparities between rich and poor schools, and the adverse effects of low financing on educational outcomes.

Armed with this data, the ACLU went to court in a number of states challenging school funding practices. While the outcomes have varied, most courts have upheld the principle of educational equity and adequacy. In Maryland, the ACLU's court action precipitated a historic negotiated agreement requiring increased state funding for schools, and in Connecticut, the court's order triggered a statewide planning process on how best to improve school quality through regional integration. In related work, the litigation efforts of the NAACP Legal Defense and Educational Fund to maintain desegregation also rely heavily on social science research to demonstrate the positive effects of desegregation on black and white student achievement levels.

Funding of research activities is also a core element of the work undertaken to advance equality for the Palestinian Israeli community. The Galilee Society is developing a computerized databank system detailing health, environmental, and socioeconomic conditions of the Palestinian Israeli population. The data is used by the Society and other activists, not only to identify community needs and bolster advocacy initiatives, but also to support litigation addressing inequalities faced by Palestinian Israelis.

In a case brought in 1997 by Adalah, the Legal Center for Arab Minority Rights (a Ford grantee since 1998), the Galilee Society's data was used to help illustrate the need for more equitable health services in the "unrecognized" Arab Bedouin villages of the Negev desert. Statistics showed that the infant mortality rate in these villages was the highest in Israel, the immunization rate of children was the lowest, and more than half of the Arab Bedouin children living there suffered from anemia and poor nutrition. While Israel's Ministry of Health provided mother and child preventive health services to neighboring Jewish towns, it did not provide clinics in the unrecognized Bedouin villages. Adalah's court petition on behalf of 121 Arab Bedouin women and children demanded that the Ministry of Health establish health care clinics in the ten largest of those villages.

Adalah, which specializes in high-impact litigation around Arab rights issues, argued that the failure to provide health services violated both the National Health Insurance Law and the Basic Law: Human Dignity and Freedom, which protects the right to life. In October 1998, when the Israeli Supreme Court heard the case, the Ministry of Health agreed to establish six new clinics in the unrecognized villages in the Negev and the Court ordered a follow-up hearing to monitor compliance.

In Eastern Europe, several organizations have turned to basic research to confront discrimination against the Roma (also known as "gypsies," a term considered pejorative). The European Roma Rights Center (ERRC) uses research to identify instances of discrimination and to bolster litigation challenging discriminatory government practices. In the Czech town of Ostrava, for example, the ERRC found that schools commonly separated Roma children into "special" schools intended for the remedial or mentally handicapped. To challenge this practice, ERRC undertook intensive research, interviewing families and closely documenting patterns of unfair school placement. That data became part of both a published report on the problem as well as several lawsuits charging school authorities with racial segregation and violation of the children's rights to equal education opportunities.

Comparable efforts have also been undertaken in Brazil. The Nucleus for the Study of Ethnic Relations (NUER) is one of several groups that has developed antiracist legal strategies in Brazil and challenged the judicial system's indifference to racism. NUER has surveyed lands claimed by African Brazilian communities in order to prepare documents that others can use in bringing litigation on the land claims. This strategy represents, for Brazil, one of the first experiences of using academic expertise in promoting antidiscriminatory jurisprudence.

While research can be an important tool to strengthen litigation, there are also times when litigation itself is a source of documentation. This was true in Chile under the military government of Augusto Pinochet, when court petitions helped to document official abuses. Human rights lawyers took virtually every case of illegal arrest or disappearance to court with a petition for the person's release. These actions sometimes resulted in small gains, such as the recognition that a person was being held by the authorities, but seldom were successful in getting prisoners released from detention. Despite the rarity of success, rights advocates continued to bring cases to court, coordinated first by the Committee of Cooperation for Peace, and later, after the government ordered the Committee dissolved, by the Vicariate of Solidarity, which operated under the protection of the Catholic Church. In the course of this work, the Committee and the Vicariate amassed reams of testimony from victims and their families, and the judges appointed to each case undertook at least minimal investigation of their claims.

Although these cases were not originally undertaken for documentation purposes, the Vicariate's thousands of case files became a powerful source of information on the patterns and practices of disappearances and the changing nature of the repression over time. From these case files, the Vicariate produced monthly and annual reports that were distributed around the world and widely used by international human rights organizations in their campaign to end the military's abusive practices in Chile. Many researchers have since relied on these reports as historical documentation of the repression. In addition, after the Pinochet government lost power, copies of these case files were turned over to the presidentially appointed National Commission on Truth and Reconciliation. The documentation developed through litigation provided a critical source of information for their subsequent investigations, and allowed the Commission to make important advances in the short nine months that it had to complete its investigations and report.

Research to Enhance the Public Debate

Law-related work can often be more effective when it reaches beyond a narrow, legal realm. To be broadly understood and widely supported, such work needs to be made public. This objective can, of course, be accomplished without research. But good information and high-quality analysis can help nourish and stimulate a public discussion about a legal question. If done creatively, with attention to targeted sectors of the population, research activities can significantly enhance public debate and help build support for legal policy reforms. Without accurate and convincing information, positive options and ideas are less likely to get the attention they deserve.

In a number of countries, issues of racial discrimination and minority rights have generated considerable research attention in an effort to engage the public in searches for solutions. Three examples from different parts of the globe follow.

When court decisions and political rhetoric in the United States led to a groundswell of attacks on affirmative action policies, Americans for a Fair Chance (AFC), a consortium of six of the most prominent U.S. civil rights and women's rights groups, was formed specifically to broaden public understanding of antidiscrimination policies. Using solid data about the use and effect of affirmative action programs, AFC challenges negative misconceptions, argues that affirmative action should not be equated with preferences or quotas, and shows that on the whole such programs have been fairly implemented. Research used by AFC ranges from intensive studies done by academic centers, government agencies, and other sources, to its own commissioned research. In addition, AFC has used public opinion polls, focus groups, town meetings, and other tools to assess the public response to the issues it works on, and to develop a better understanding of how best to deliver its own messages. While affirmative action policies continue to face difficult challenges nationwide, AFC's work has enabled defenders of those policies to craft substantive, fact-based messages that highlight the benefits of affirmative action and raise the overall level of public debate on the issues.

In Israel, the Palestinian Israeli community has struggled against both official discrimination and widespread public bias. The current status and future needs of this minority have been given scant attention in the popular press, and low priority within research units of governmental agencies, universities, and independent think tanks. To counter the paucity of accurate, up-to-date research, Sikkuy, an Israeli NGO working to advance equal opportunity, has undertaken a three-year project to promote affirmative action for Palestinian Israelis. The project's advocacy, educational, and policy-related activities all rest on research to document and analyze the participation by Palestinian Israelis in various sectors, including workforce, governmental posts, and corporate boards. In 1997, a Sikkuy survey showed that of 103 state-owned companies in Israel, only three had any Palestinian Israelis on their boards of directors. In publicizing these survey results, Sikkuy was able to generate significant media attention and raise public awareness of bias against Palestinians. And in the fall of 1999, the new Israeli Minister of Justice announced he would draft a law to mandate Palestinian Israeli representation on the boards of state-owned businesses.

Another research project seeks to enhance public debate on racially discriminatory hiring practices in Brazil. Judges in Brazil have interpreted the law to mean that the intention to discriminate must be proven. So the University of São Paulo is conducting research on hiring practices. They use social science research methodologies (known as audits) that test whether discrimination regularly occurs despite stated intentions. Even if discriminatory practices documented by this research are not ultimately used as evidence in the courts, the findings may have an important influence on the general public's view of the prevalence of racial discrimination.

Conclusion

The illustrations above underscore the vital role that research can play in advancing positive legal changes that, in turn, improve the lives of the underrepresented or vulnerable in different societies. Research does not always yield immediate, tangible improvements; its impact can be, and often is, long term and indirect. But conducted properly, and under the right circumstances, it can be tremendously compelling—strengthening policy reform, litigation, and public education. The challenge is to determine how best to integrate research in conjunction with other strategies to raise the level of debate and decisionmaking.

12

Weathering the Storm: NGOs Adapting to Major Political Transitions

MICHAEL SHIFTER

All nongovernmental organizations working on questions related to the law undergo strains at various points in their histories. That is inevitable, and has to do largely with the sensitivity of law-related work in changing political contexts. The demands of political change have pressed especially hard on NGOs operating in societies where entire governments have been reconstituted—from military to civilian rule, for instance, or from communism to democracy. Such changes can affect nearly all aspects of a law-related group's work, from its basic mission to its day-by-day activities, and organizations must be adaptable in order to survive. Less dramatic, but just as significant, are the subtle but frequent shifts in political priorities and public attitudes that characterize life in an established democracy. NGOs in those settings, too, have learned that flexibility must be an integral part of their organizational development.

This chapter focuses on the political changes that particularly impact human rights or public interest law NGOs, including fundamental changes in government structures as well as subtler changes in political climate and context. It does not deal with a myriad of other forces of change that may cause NGOs to retool or refocus, such as demographic shifts; economic transitions; technological advances; and unanticipated environmental, health, or social crises. Neither does it deal with the ordinary pressures of organizational development, such as staff turnover, budgetary problems, internal discord, and programming failures—the inevitable growing pains of all NGOs.

The key question here is: How have some law-related groups responded and adapted to the important political changes that have played so prominent a role on the world stage in recent decades? By tracing the paths of several Ford-funded NGOs through transitions—transitions that were, in most of their experiences, unprecedented and fraught with obstacles—it is hoped that useful insights will emerge for other NGOs facing the challenges of change.

Along the way, this chapter also attempts to identify the programming tools and approaches donors might consider and take advantage of in order to work more effectively with organizations experiencing such changes. Clearly, groups are better able to respond to challenges when they have in place stable organizational structures, committed staff, and an established reputation in their communities, as well as the capacity to develop a long-range strategic vision and to train new leadership. Donors can play an important role in helping to encourage these attributes.

Of course, even with donor support, not all organizations survive their country's political upheavals, nor should they. Some close down when staff move on to expanding opportunities within the government sector. Others, finding their original mission no longer necessary, quietly disband. Still others try and fail to adapt to new circumstances. For the purposes of this discussion, attention will focus on those organizations that were able to make successful transitions in the wake of political change.

Dealing with Regime Shifts

Over the past several decades, the world has witnessed profound changes that have brought major shifts in political regimes: from apartheid in South Africa, communism in Eastern Europe, and military dictatorships in Latin America, to some form of democracy in each of these regions. With those transitions have come fundamental changes in legal frameworks, judicial operations, and the enforcement of laws. By necessity, and in most cases with eagerness, law-related NGOs in these transitional societies responded with immediate shifts in strategies and activities, as well as long-term changes in overall goals. The adaptations of the Foundation grantees discussed here are notable for their ultimate success, but those successes have not come without a degree of hardship.

The Center for Legal and Social Studies (CELS), Argentina's leading human rights group, is an illustrative example. Founded in 1979 when the country was under military rule, the group, while adhering to the highest professional standards, collected extensive information on the massive "disappearances" of thousands of Argentines. In 1983, the country ended its nightmare, and a civilian, constitutional government took over. Unlike other Latin American countries—indeed, countries in transition to democracy elsewhere as well—the new government put members of the former juntas on trial for having committed human rights violations.

CELS played a central role in this process, providing the courts and other authorities with necessary information to move forward—and sustaining public pressure in pursuit of full justice. At the same time, however, CELS leadership sought to devise a fresh agenda that would focus less on past violations committed for political motives, and more on current abuses of civil liberties such as police brutality and discrimination. Following the democratic transitions, CELS began to incorporate some of the aims and features of the American Civil Liberties Union (ACLU), and in 1986, CELS's executive director visited various ACLU offices in the United States.

It would be another decade before CELS was able to fully settle on its new agenda. It took the passage of time and considerable experimentation and deliberation for CELS to resume a coherent focus and effectiveness, and to define its new role. In this case, it required a generational change as well, since CELS, characteristic of Argentina's human rights movement as a whole, had been dominated by family members of the "disappeared," who were understandably less inclined to give up the group's original purposes. During the long transition, strategic visits to the ACLU by CELS staff, as well as the work of external consultants who reviewed and evaluated the organization, proved justified and helpful. These kept alive valuable ideas and gradually helped develop support within the organization for pursuing a fresh agenda. The weight of the past and the continuing unresolved questions of justice accounted for the delay.

For donors, the CELS experience points to the importance of patience, maintaining a long-term perspective, and sticking with a group that is going through a difficult period—especially when that group shows signs of promise for renewal. Long-term core or institutional support (covering staff salaries, rent, office expenses, and the like) proved central, even when CELS was struggling to focus its agenda. A decision to withdraw support at an earlier moment would have likely had serious, negative implications for the only human rights group of its kind that had gained substantial recognition not only in Argentina, but throughout the region. Even during its growing pains, CELS had continued to perform valuable work, including documenting cases of police violence and delivering legal services to disadvantaged communities.

In other contexts, comparable NGOs went through the transition process with less stress. The fall of the Berlin Wall and shift to democratic politics in Eastern Europe meant that human rights groups that had at one time operated within underground dissident movements evolved into full-fledged rights and advocacy organizations, with significant commitments to public interest law reform and legal services. Before then, lawyers in these societies were widely seen as serving as government officials; the notion that they could be part of a dynamic, nongovernmental sector at first seemed alien.

Yet, both the Czech Helsinki Committee and the Polish Helsinki Committee—the two leading human rights groups in their countries under communist rule—managed to shift their focus in the postcommunist years toward greater attention to such areas as policy advocacy, public education, and monitoring legislation. Their successful adaptation was helped by a set of planning grants from Ford in the early 1990s. These were designed to enable the groups to undertake a serious institutional review and restructuring while maintaining core activities. Subsequent support helped the groups carry out further long-term strategic planning; assured stability also facilitated greater experimentation. The programming instruments applied in these cases helped give the organizations the opportunity to retool and chart new courses.

Today, both groups have wide-ranging agendas that focus on strengthening human rights standards, in accordance with domestic and international law, in both the Czech Republic and Poland. The experience of the International Memorial Society (Memorial) in Russia demonstrates both the problems posed by transition and the critical importance of creative adaptability. Memorial was created at the end of the Soviet period to preserve the memory of those who had been politically repressed, as well as to safeguard the rights of survivors. However, in the new freer environment, it found itself taking on an ever-wider range of activities. In a postcommunist society, where efforts on behalf of human rights are few and public interest lawyers barely exist, this small group of committed, creative individuals, many of whom were nonlawyers with little previous organizational experience, became overloaded with old and new issues. The repressed were joined by refugees and by victims of ethnic violence and war. There were pressing needs for public education, legislative initiative, and legal defense. In Memorial's case, there were actually too many tasks being attempted simultaneously by too few, and the strain within the organization threatened its future.

The efforts of Memorial's leaders to clarify the organization's mission and improve its structure were critical. Continued Foundation support, accompanied by grants that brought consultants to work closely with the leaders, helped advance such efforts. Memorial's historians, lawyers, and activists managed to define their different tasks while creating a structure that allowed them to interact with each other and to work together creatively. Members became more aware of the need to seek out professional legal advice, to attract young lawyers to public interest work, and to cooperate with international agencies. Without giving up its original mission, the newer, more multifaceted Memorial has since become one of the leading organizations addressing a variety of human rights issues in today's Russia.

South Africa offers examples of organizations successfully undergoing transitions in some respects, while facing continuing and new challenges in others. During the apartheid era, the Centre for Applied Legal Studies (CALS) conducted research critical of the regime, pursued cases that took on racism and repression, and helped build the labor movement's legal capacities. When the transition to democracy began in 1990, CALS quickly became involved in efforts to draft the country's interim and permanent constitutions. During and after the transition, CALS increasingly focused many of its efforts on the social and economic rights issues that assumed new salience. Several other law-oriented NGOs and university-based institutes have gone through similar changes.

South Africa NGOs also face the ongoing challenge of integrating blacks into their professional staffs—a task some have carried out better than others. And with the onset of democratic rule in 1994, many donors shifted their support away from NGOs and toward government agencies. These challenges have been met in various ways. For example, internships and clinical legal education programs have enabled black law students to develop valuable legal contacts, gain experience, and advance in the profession. Flexible Foundation funding has helped NGOs pursue these activities and, more generally, to adjust to the obstacles and opportunities presented by transitions. In some cases, such as South Africa's Legal Resources Centre, and the Legal Assistance Centre in neighboring Namibia (which also underwent a transition from apartheid), endowment support has helped build grantees' long-term funding bases. Endowments were seen as especially appropriate instruments for these groups, in light of their critical, long-term role in protecting rights and fostering democratic practice.

These South African and Namibian organizations will likely continue to face the ongoing challenge of staking out legal positions that may not sit well with their governments or even with the general populations of their countries. Defending prisoners' rights or mounting environmental challenges to government-backed projects does not command the same support and energy as battling apartheid. The NGO adaptation here may differ between the two countries. Both organizations are sticking to their principles, but given that Namibian democratic roots run less deep, the Legal Assistance Centre may face greater challenges in balancing the need to work with the government while opposing certain policies.

As important as it can be for NGOs to adapt—and for donors to flexibly support them along the way—sometimes new organizations appropriately arise from transitions. These new groups may in turn adapt to the evolving post-transition environment. With the fall of the Marcos dictatorship in the Philippines in 1986, many young attorneys (as well as other progressive Filipinos) turned their attention to social, economic, and environmental concerns. These lawyers launched several "alternative law groups" (ALGs), legal services organizations that used the law to pursue the development priorities of grassroots organizations, making them more legally self-sufficient by building knowledge and skills, and by promoting community mobilization.

The very founding of ALGs represented a kind of adaptation to new circumstances. As law students under the dictatorship, many of the ALGs' leaders had worked with an earlier generation of human rights NGOs and lawyers. Working together, both generations continued to battle pervasive civil and political rights abuses under the new democracy. But with the overthrow of the dictatorship, enduring social and economic inequities assumed greater salience for many Filipinos. ALGs seized the chance to challenge these disparities, working with NGOs and with grassroots groups composed of women, the urban poor, low-income farmers, fishing communities, indigenous peoples, and other disadvantaged populations.

ALGs' evolution demonstrated ongoing adaptation to the revived democracy's own changes. The emerging social, economic, and environmental priorities of partner communities were more appropriately addressed through executive agencies and local authorities, particularly after the passage of the 1991 Local Government Code, rather than through the often conservative and corruption-plagued courts. As the Philippine NGO movement gained more experience and ALGs more knowledge and credibility, ALGs were increasingly able to lend their legal expertise to policy advocacy coalitions. As ALG attorneys and other NGO leaders went into government, particularly during the 1992–1998 administration of President Fidel Ramos, these coalitions were further able to leverage influence. The coalitions favorably affected important policy on a wide range of key social issues.

Donor approaches complemented and facilitated ALGs' efforts in at least three ways. First, rather than narrowly confining funding to specific activities, Ford and other funders provided institutional support that gave these NGOs the leeway to experiment, learn, and adapt to the evolving Philippine scene. Second, the donors were willing to risk and accept failure from some of the activities they funded. And third, they did not hold the grantees to rigid indicators of accomplishment. Instead, they expected the ALGs to produce results that eventually benefited their partner populations.

ALGs' efforts have been impressive in many respects. Much of what these NGOs have accomplished was unanticipated. The unexpected, favorable results included positive impacts on national policies, concrete benefits flowing from paralegal training, successful engagement with local issues, and the indirect but powerful influence arising from ALG personnel going into government. Had expectations been framed and enforced along the lines of what some ALGs originally anticipated—impact on appellate court decisions, for example—they would have been deemed "failures," and support might have counterproductively ended.

In these and other societies that have faced shifts in political regime, a number of programming techniques have been employed to help deal with the important, often difficult, challenges of organizational adaptation. Apart from the instruments already mentioned, one of the most fruitful approaches has been exchanges and visits among key figures from the human rights and legal services sectors of Argentina, Chile, Eastern Europe, and South Africa. Though clearly each situation posed unique issues and concerns, these transitional societies had enough in common to make such consultations (arranged at carefully selected moments) worthwhile and effective.

Dealing with Changes in Political Climate

The experiences of organizations that faced the challenge of regime shifts, and the programming ideas that came about in response to those challenges, are instructive. It may also be useful to consider other changes in political climate or context that are likely to affect law-related NGOs in the future.

In this sense, the story of a Peruvian organization, the Legal Defense Institute (IDL), is an especially interesting one. The group has had to adapt to a number of difficult challenges throughout the years. The first was the substantial increase in violence and the deterioration of overall security conditions during political strife of the late 1980s and early 1990s, and the Peruvian government's failure to provide order and perform elementary democratic functions. IDL began to shift its strategies: it continued to document abuses committed by the various parties in the conflict, but also sought to strengthen and enlarge the democratic sector through education and training programs.

In 1992, IDL, along with other Peruvian NGOs, had to deal with two particularly critical moments. The first was a "self-coup" by Peru's president that effectively closed the Congress and judiciary and suspended the constitution. The second was the capture of the leader of the main insurgent group, the Shining Path. Taken together, these key developments called for consideration of a different kind of human rights approach. As a result, IDL, sensibly moving to fill a void, devoted greater effort to questions of institutional reform, and began to play an important role in the democratic process.

IDL's ability to adapt is manifest in a variety of its activities, though perhaps especially so in its education work. Its efforts in this sector can be divided into two distinct stages. From 1986 to 1992, IDL's main focus was on emergency work and prevention of human rights abuses. Since 1992, IDL has concentrated more on education and training activities to help build the capacity of institutions. This furthers its chief objective of reconstructing the country's badly frayed social and democratic fabric. The two stages have been accompanied by a shift in strategy, moving from targeting particular geographic zones of the country to targeting particular sectors such as local authorities, peasant leaders, self-defense communities, and the thousands who were displaced by the violence and have now returned to their communities.

IDL's adaptability derives in some measure from its sound leadership and capacity to think strategically and in the long term. In addition, however, at critical moments IDL benefited from flexible donor assistance, including institutional support. This was essential to enable the group to respond to such dynamic, difficult conditions. Several external consultants also worked closely with IDL staff at key moments to help them think through strategies and decide how to maintain a focus on "traditional" human rights work while at the same time dealing with the special problems posed by the deterioration of government institutions.

Finally, it is instructive to look at several examples of how public interest law NGOs in the United States responded to recent, important changes in the country's political context. The 1980 election of President Ronald Reagan signaled a different political environment. It ushered in a president who appointed more conservative judges, which, in turn, significantly affected the work of public interest lawyers. As a result, many public interest law NGOs that had previously given almost sole priority to the courts concentrated more of their efforts on public education. Moreover, groups that had traditionally litigated turned greater attention to activities like community organizing and administrative advocacy. Within a less hospitable political context at the national level, groups also pursued new opportunities for important legal work at the state and local levels. For example, as the federal judicial appointees became more politically conservative and less willing to find in their favor, such NGOs began to use state constitutions rather than the federal constitution as their bases for legal action.

Changing political contexts and corresponding shifts in programming approaches sometimes call for a reevaluation of institutional identity. Many U.S. nongovernmental law-oriented groups, worried about functioning effectively in an often less than friendly environment, became increasingly concerned about their identity. Some responded by developing greater technological expertise and using new communications strategies to advance a clear message of reform. The National Association for the Advancement of Colored People Legal Defense and Educational Fund, for example, created a new communications department and enlisted professional media relations assistance to maximize exposure for its issues in a different political climate. The Women's Legal Defense Fund enhanced its public image and developed new and productive alliances after it changed its name to the National Partnership for Women and Families. The Foundation responded favorably to these important institutional changes with funding support.

An alternative model used in the immigrant rights field was to concentrate communications capacity within a membership organization that supports the work of the broader, pro-immigrant legal and advocacy communities. The National Immigration Forum (NIF) conducts proactive, ongoing media education that communicates to the American public generally why immigration is in the U.S. national interest. NIF catalyzes select, ad hoc advocacy alliances that form around specific policy goals, and develops and builds consensus around common media messages and communications strategies for the alliances. NIF also responds to and handles reporters' queries, and trains individuals to be effective public speakers on immigration and refugee policy matters.

Conclusion

Sustained commitments—from both donors and NGOs—are among the key qualities that account for successful adaptations to changing political circumstances. It matters whether donors demonstrate patience and stick with groups even when they are experiencing difficulties. Flexible, long-term support can, under the right circumstances, be very helpful. Planning grants, networking, convening, and training can, when strategically conceived and used, be effective in making such groups more productive.

Although the programming approaches to assist organizations in making transitions can be widely applied, it is also crucial to take into careful account the particularities of each situation. Strategies will vary in different contexts, at different moments. Though there is no solution or formula that is fully satisfactory and applies across the board, different experiences in different parts of the world strongly point to the importance of providing core support over a longer time period. Such a posture would allow solid NGOs to determine how best to adapt to multiple, external challenges, while pursuing their agendas and navigating their own courses as successfully as possible.

ACRONYMS/ABBREVIATIONS

ACLU	American Civil Liberties Union
ACRI	Association for Civil Rights in Israel
AFC	Americans for a Fair Chance
ALG	alternative law groups
ALRG	Administrative Law Research Group
AMA	American Medical Association
ANC	African National Congress
ASK	Ain O Salish Kendra
AULAI	Association of University Legal Aid Institutions
BELA	Bangladesh Environmental Lawyers Association
BLAST	Bangladesh Legal Aid and Services Trust
BMFI	Balay Mindanaw Foundation, Inc.
BNWLA	Bangladesh National Women Lawyers Association
BRU	Bus Riders Union
CALS	Centre for Applied Legal Studies
CBO	community-based organization
CASS	Chinese Academy of Social Sciences
CCP	Chinese Communist Party
CEJIL	Center for Justice and International Law
CELS	Center for Legal and Social Studies
CEPA	Centre for Environment and Public Advocacy

CLC	Community Law Centre
CLEEC	U.S.-China Committee for Legal Education Exchange
COLPI	Constitutional and Legislative Policy Institute
COPACHI	Committee of Cooperation for Peace
CRP	Constitutional Rights Project
CSJ	Centre for Social Justice
CUNY	City University of New York
DAR	Department of Agrarian Reform
DEMUS	Office for the Defense of the Rights of Women
DENR	Department of Environment and Natural Resources
DLAC	Developmental Legal Aid Center
ELAC	Environmental Legal Aid Center
ERA	Equal Rights Advocates
ERRC	European Roma Rights Center
FLAG	Free Legal Assistance Group
FORJA	Corporation for Legal Training for Citizenship and Democracy
FUNDEPUBLICO	Foundation for the Defense of the Public Interest
GLPLI	Global Law Programs Learning Initiative
GRP	Gender Research Project
HCLU	Hungarian Civil Liberties Union
HHS	Hengasara Hakkina Sangha
IDL	Legal Defense Institute
ILC	International Legal Center
Initiative	Public Interest Law Initiative in Transitional Societies
IPG	Institute of Politics and Governance
Kaisahan	Tungo sa Kaunlaran ng Kanayunan at Repormang Panasakahan

LAC	Legal Assistance Centre
LAW	Palestinian Society for the Protection of Human Rights and the Environment
LCAC	Legal and Constitutional Affairs Committee
LDF	NAACP Legal Defense and Educational Fund
LRC	Legal Resources Centre
MC	mediation committee
MLAA	Madaripur Legal Aid Association
MM	Metro Manila
MTA	Metropolitan Transportation Authority
Memorial	International Memorial Society
NAACP	National Association for the Advancement of Colored People
NARF	Native American Rights Fund
NEKI	Legal Defence Bureau for National and Ethnic Minorities
NGO	nongovernmental organization
NIF	National Immigration Forum
NIPILAR	National Institute for Public Interest Law and Research
NLS	National Law School (of India University)
NORAD	Norwegian Agency for Development Cooperation
NP	National Party
NUER	Nucleus for the Study of Ethnic Relations
NWLC	National Women's Law Center
OSI	Open Society Institute
Panlipi	Tanggapang Panligal ng Katutubong Pilipino
Peking Women's Centre	Centre for Women's Law Studies and Legal Services of Peking University
PIL	public interest law
PILI	Public Interest Law Initiative
PO	people's organization
PRC	People's Republic of China

Qianxi Women's Centre	Qianxi County Rural Women's Legal Services Centre
SADAF	South African Defense and Aid Fund
Saligan	Sentro ng Alternatibong Lingap Panlegal
SERAC	Social and Economic Rights Action Center
SPDA	Peruvian Society for Environmental Law
SRI	Shelter Rights Initiative
TAF	The Asia Foundation
TK	Tanggol Kalikasan
UCT	University of Cape Town
UNDP	United Nations Development Programme
UNICEF	United Nations Children's Fund
UPPVO	University of the Philippines Paralegal Volunteer Organization
USAID	United States Agency for International Development
UWC	University of the Western Cape
WLB	Women's Legal Bureau
Wuhan Centre	Centre for the Protection of the Rights of the Socially Vulnerable

ABOUT THE AUTHORS

Hugo Frühling is a lawyer and social scientist based in Santiago, Chile. A graduate of the University of Chile with an S.J.D. from Harvard Law School, Frühling has taught at Ottawa Law School and Harvard Law School, and served as an advisor to the Chilean Minister of the Interior. Frühling is currently a professor at the Political Science Institute of the University of Chile and a researcher at the Center for Development Studies in Santiago, where he coordinated a comparative project on Policing in Democratic Societies. He has published widely on human rights, nongovernmental organizations, judicial reform, and policies to confront crime.

Stephen Golub, GLPLI project director, is an attorney and consultant based in Kensington, California, near Berkeley. A graduate of Brown University and Harvard Law School, Golub teaches International Development Law and Policy at the Boalt Hall School of Law of the University of California at Berkeley. His published products pertain to evaluation, human rights, legal services, the rule of law, and related fields. Golub's research and consulting experience spans over two dozen countries and fifteen years.

Priscilla Hayner, an independent writer and consultant based in New York, recently completed a book comparing truth commissions worldwide. She was previously a program officer for international human rights and world security at the Joyce Mertz-Gilmore Foundation, and is currently a program consultant to the Ford Foundation. Hayner holds a master's in International Affairs from the School of International and Public Affairs at Columbia University.

Helen Hershkoff is an associate professor at the New York University School of Law. She formerly served as an associate legal director of the American Civil Liberties Union; as a staff attorney at The Legal Aid Society of New York; and as a litigation associate at Paul, Weiss, Rifkind, Wharton & Garrison. She received her A.B. from Radcliffe-Harvard College in 1973 and her J.D. from Harvard Law School in 1978. From 1973 to 1975, she studied as a Marshall Scholar at St. Anne's College, Oxford University, where she was awarded a B.A. in Modern History. She has written about welfare and education reform, and her current scholarship focuses on state courts in the United States.

David Hollander served until June 1999 as chair of the board of the Gay Men's Health Crisis, Inc., and was previously cochair of the board of Lambda Legal Defense and Educational Fund, Inc. Until 1993, Hollander worked as an entertainment lawyer in New York and was a managing partner in the firm of Morrison & Foerster. He also served as managing editor of *New Times Magazine* (1975–1977). Hollander received his A.B. from Harvard College in 1971 and his J.D. from Harvard Law School in 1974.

Mary McClymont is senior director of the Peace and Social Justice program of the Ford Foundation, where she oversees GLPLI. She formerly served as national director for Legalization, Migration and Refugee Services, U.S. Catholic Conference; senior staff counsel, the National Prison Project of the American Civil Liberties Union; and trial attorney, Civil Rights Division, U.S. Department of Justice. She has an LL.M. in International Legal Studies with a specialization in human rights law from the American University Washington College of Law, and a J.D. from Georgetown University Law Center.

Aubrey McCutcheon is a U.S.- and U.K.-trained lawyer and
social scientist presently working as an independent consultant
based in South Africa. He previously worked as a Ford
Foundation program officer and earlier as a congressional staff
director. McCutcheon has also served as staff or board member
for several NGOs, including a post as Executive Director of the
Washington Office on Africa. He graduated from Yale College
and Georgetown University Law Center, and later earned an
M.Sc. at the London School of Economics in Social Policy and
Development and an LL.M. in Law and Development at the
University of London's School of Oriental and African Studies.

Michael Shifter is currently senior fellow and program director
in democratic governance at the Inter-American Dialogue in
Washington, D.C. He is an adjunct professor of Latin American
Studies at Georgetown University. Prior to joining the Inter-
American Dialogue, Shifter directed the Latin American and
Caribbean program at the National Endowment for Democracy.
Before that, he served as program officer for the Ford
Foundation's human rights and governance work in the Andean
Region and Southern Cone of South America. He writes and lec-
tures widely on U.S.–Latin American relations.

INDEX